Ferries 2019

Europe's leading guide to the UK & Northern European ferry industry

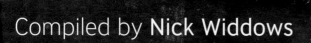

Compiled by **Nick Widdows**

Ferry
Publications

ISBN 978-1911268-208
Ferry Publications, PO Box 33, Ramsey, Isle of Man IM99 4LP
Email: ferrypubs@manx.net   Website: www.ferrypubs.co.uk

Europe's **leading** guide to the ferry industry

Contents...

© Ferry Publications 2018

ISBN: 978-1911268-208
Produced and designed by Lily Publications Ltd,
PO Box 33, Ramsey, Isle of Man, British Isles, IM99 4LP
Tel: +44 (0) 1624 898446   Fax: +44 (0) 1624 898449
www.ferrypubs.co.uk   E-Mail: info@lilypublications.co.uk

Europe's **leading** guide to the ferry industry

Introduction...

This is the thirty-first edition of this book, which first appeared in 1983 as the 24-page 'home published' *'Car Ferries from Great Britain and Ireland'*. The book aims to list every passenger/vehicle ferry in Great Britain and Ireland, ro-ro freight vessels which operate regular services between Great Britain and Ireland and to nearby Continental destinations and major passenger/vehicle ferries in other parts of Northern Europe. The coverage of Northern Europe is not fully comprehensive (to make it so would probably triple the size of the book) and does not include freight-only operations and vessels - although freight-only vessels have been included where the operators also run passenger services. Where operators use a mixture of ro-ro and container ships, I have only included the ro-ro ships. Exceptionally I have included the *Arx* of CLdN/Cobelfret Ferries and the *Elisabeth* of P&O as they operate to provide additional container capacity on ro-ro routes.

Each operator is listed alphabetically within sections - major operators, minor operators, freight-only operators, chain, cable and float ferries, passenger-only ferries, other North European passenger operators and vehicle/passenger vessels owned by companies not currently engaged in operating services. After details relating to each company's management, address, telephone numbers, email, website and services, there is a fleet list with technical data and then a potted history of each vessel with previous names and dates.

Nick Widdows

Whitstable, Kent

July 2018

European Seaway (Darren Holdaway)

Foreword...

I n his Foreword to 'Ferries 2018', Matthew Murtland noted that 'Brexit, Trump, emissions regulations, fluctuating oil prices, changeable exchange rates and an emboldened Russia' were external factors influencing the future of Northern European ferry routes. This list still remains pertinent, with several issues having achieved greater prominence or seem no nearer resolution some twelve months later. To these concerns could be added climate change, with hotter summer temperatures encouraging more 'staycations' and Northern European holidays. The ferry industry has long been one of the most adaptable of transport modes, adjusting to external challenges with flexibility, and changing route structure to match evolving patterns of traffic demand. It is adapting no differently to the present circumstances.

Brexit continues to cast the most substantial shadow across strategic direction for operators, with seemingly little progress made in clarifying the trading relationships and people-movement implications of the UK's decision to leave the European Union. Political prevarication is of little help when the consequences of decisions have potentially profound outcomes for transport geography and port operations, and the investment decisions required to meet these unknown and changing circumstances have a significant time-frame attached to them. High volume fast-transit ports like Dover operate on constrained sites with very limited ability to handle any enhanced requirements for customs and immigration checks. It remains unclear how the UK border will be policed to handle arriving passengers without adding to bureaucracy and delays, and there is already talk of converting the M20 to a lorry park to handle the seemingly inevitable delays on the short sea routes.

The issue of the Irish border remains a substantial stumbling block to progress, with operators already taking steps to future-proof the flow of freight traffic between Ireland and the rest of the European Union, through by-passing the present Landbridge arrangements. Two-thirds of Irish exporters shipping to the continent do so via Britain, and 57 per cent believe they could supply the EU directly through continental ports if transit time through the UK increased or costs rose. Brittany Ferries inaugurated a new twice-weekly link between Cork and Santander with the chartered *Connemara* in May 2018 - a decision hastened by Brexit - but Irish Ferries' ambitions to double the number of sailings and massively increase freight capacity between Dublin and Cherbourg have been delayed by the late delivery of *W B Yeats*. Meanwhile CLdN's new *Celine* and *Delphine* have boosted capacity on freight sailings between Zeebrugge, Rotterdam and Dublin.

The fall in the value of the GB pound relative to the Euro has yet to deter significant volumes of British travellers from heading overseas - P&O Ferries recorded their best July performance for four years in 2018 - and Britain has become an increasingly attractive destination for the Euro-based traveller. The potential return of duty-free shopping in the post-Brexit world would provide a significant boost to the finances of cross-channel operators, perhaps leading to consideration of operation across a wider range of routes, but this will requires investment in more Scandinavian-style retail facilities than the 'booze-cruise' environment endured by passengers in the past. This adaptation may be beyond some of the present fleet.

Political inertia is not confined to international relationships. Despite many previous promises, the Scottish government has so far failed to implement 'Road Equivalent Tariff' (RET) pricing on the Orkney and Shetland routes to bring them in line with their west coast cousins, leaving a significant disparity in fares between the two baskets of routes. Ironically there are concerns about available ship capacity being sufficient to meet demand when fares are reduced, but for now demand is constrained by price.

In a more pro-active government intervention, the Isle of Man government nationalised the 188 year-old Isle of Man Steam Packet Company in a remarkably short period of time from the initial proposal in Tynwald to conclusion of the £124.3m transaction during Spring 2018. The company had previously proposed a 25-year extension of the existing 'User Agreement' to support investment in new craft to replace *Ben-my-Chree* and *Manannan*, but this approach was rejected. Responsibility for

Côte des Dunes *(Darren Holdaway)*

Normandie *(Andrew Cooke)*

Red Jet 6 (Andrew Cooke)

St Cecilia (Brian Smith)

replacement vessels now lies in government hands, and these may be financed through the issue of public bonds. The Company has long been the scapegoat for the cost of living and the decline in tourist visitors to the island; it will be interesting to see how this changes now local politicians have control.

These developments will be watched with interest in the Channel Islands, were sea passenger carryings have declined to the lowest level for over fifty years and the future ownership of Condor is uncertain following the winding up of the controlling MacQuarie Fund. Peak season capacity to Guernsey and Jersey offered by the once-daily sailings of *Condor Liberation* and *Commodore Clipper* contrasts markedly with the levels of service enjoyed by the Isle of Man through the twice-daily operations of *Ben-my-Chree* and *Manannan*. The *Condor Liberation* remains the mainstay of winter capacity, but the craft has yet to achieve popularity with the travelling public.

Having put the services out to tender, the Norwegian Government awarded two of the three Kystrute contracts to incumbent Hurtigruten, who will offer seven of the eleven sailing-cycle departures, with Havila being awarded the remaining four. Hurtigruten intend to continue to operate a daily service, with more limited calls on the four 'commercial' sailings that replicate Havila departures. Although the two operators are required by the contract to cooperate on ticketing and service standards, there will be an interesting tension between them as the new contracts unfold. Havila Kystruten will build two new vessels in their Havyard facility, and have signed a preliminary contract with the Spanish yard Barrera for two more for delivery in 2021.

There remains plenty of optimism in the industry despite the political uncertainties, with the forward order book of vessels promising a succession of new arrivals. Stena Line's new Chinese-built E-flexer fleet seems destined to become a common sight on routes around Britain in the coming years. The first vessel will be operated by Stena Line on the Holyhead-Dublin route from 2020, displacing the *Stena Superfast X*, with the next two vessels earmarked for service between Birkenhead and Belfast from 2020 and 2021. With Brittany Ferries taking two further vessels in the series - to be named *Galicia* and *Salamanca* - for the UK-Spain routes from 2022 onwards to replace the *Baie de Seine* and *Cap Finistère*, and DFDS acquiring one to replace the *Calais Seaways* on the Dover-Calais route from 2021, the design is certainly living up to its billing as being adaptable to a wide range of market deployments. Two more larger E-flexers will be deployed in Northern Europe from 2022 and Stena has exercised an option for a further four vessels, making this a highly successful design concept and illustrating the emerging dominance of Chinese shipyards in the new build sector.

As profiled elsewhere in this volume, DFDS have two 230m 4,500lm 600 passenger capacity vessels on order from the Guangzhou yard in China for delivery in 2021; these represent the first new passenger vessels for the company since 1978. Brittany Ferries will introduce the *Honfleur* to the Portsmouth-Caen route in 2019, and Irish Ferries will take delivery of a new Dublin-Holyhead vessel in 2020. Fjord1 will meet their new Norwegian-domestic route obligations through the delivery of a fleet of twenty new vessels, with a further eight on order for other operators, marking a transformation of the local ferry scene by 2020. Color Line's 'hybrid' ferry is due to enter service in May 2019 and Finnlines have signed a letter of intent with Jinling for three 7,300lm vessels.

Viking Line's 2013-built *Viking Grace* acquired a Norsepower rotor sail at refit in 2018. This capitalises on differential air flows to help drive the vessel forward, as part of a package of measures to place the *Viking Grace* amongst the most ecologically-sound passenger vessels. The 24m high 4m wide cylindrical rotor towers above the vessel, giving her an unusual profile, but Viking Line are already planning to add two rotor sails to the design of their next new build for the Stockholm-Turku route, due in 2020. Unity Line have produced a concept ro-pax design with four rotor sails. Whilst the sails have yet to achieve ubiquity, is this the shape of ship design to come?

In recent years, the ferry industry has faced competition from the opening of tunnels and bridges, the rise of low-cost airlines, the loss of duty free sales, frequent industrial action particularly at French ports and the migrant crisis. There have been route casualties, but the industry has defied the sceptics and continues to invest in tonnage to meet the challenges of the future. Whatever the outcome of the Brexit negotiations, business will continue, and new fleets will reposition the industry as a greener mode of transport. Nimble adaptation to changing circumstances has served the ferry industry well in the past, and the foundations are now being laid for a resilient future.

Richard Kirkman, Editor, Ferry & Cruise Review

A SHORT HISTORY OF POLFERRIES
THE WANDERING COAST

Since its entry into the European Union in 2004, Poland has pushed its way to the heart of the continent, acting as a central power for the large bloc of formerly communist countries that joined the union in the same year. The nation has rapidly become a key player on the European stage, not only politically, but also culturally, perhaps seen most vividly in the lively diaspora that has sprung up across the British Isles in recent years as millions of Poles have headed westwards to take advantage of the freedoms that their new emergence into the international community has allowed.

The modern, vibrant nation that we now experience, characterised by its Polskie sklepy, the hovering presence of Donald Tusk in the Brexit negotiations and romantic weekends to Krakow, represents a remarkable triumph over the adversities that the nation has faced over the last few centuries, and no more so than during the nightmare of the Second World War and its subsequent collapse into the clutches of the Soviet Union.

The freedom and the subsequent salvation of Poland were forged in the shipyards of the Baltic coast. In the 1980s, the Solidarność (Solidarity) trade union was formed by Lech Walesa at the Lenin shipyard in Gdańsk, at the height of the communists' power. Despite early attempts to crush the trade union by the ruling authorities, its influence grew until the communist government was forced to begin negotiations which resulted in its own overthrow as the first revolution to hit Eastern Europe in August 1989.

This was not the first time that Polish history was made on the Baltic coast: almost exactly fifty years earlier and just a few miles away, the first shots of the Second World War were fired by the Nazi warship *Schleswig-Holstein* at the Polish garrison on the Westerplatte peninsular. The outbreak of hostilities here was focused on the Free City of Danzig, a geo-political anomaly that resulted from the cessation of the First World War and placed the formerly Prussian city of Danzig under the protectorate of the League of Nations and essentially under Polish jurisdiction. During the interwar years, Poland had precious little coast and the establishment of the Free City was in order to provide the nation with access to the sea. Following the war, Danzig became modern Gdańsk; Prussia was annihilated.

The Polish coast has long been an ephemeral phenomenon: on the emergence of the first conceivably "modern" Polish kingdom in the late middle ages, the only coast existed around what we now call the Bay of Gdańsk but subsequently stretched eastwards towards Riga, interrupted by the Kingdom of Prussia, existing as a sort of enclave centred on historic Königsberg (modern Kaliningrad). By the Napoleonic era, the remnant state of Poland had lost its coastline and the entire country subsequently disappeared off the map for a century until it re-emerged during the First World War. Following the Treaty of Versailles, the country was awarded a narrow 'corridor' of coast stretching from north of Danzig/Gdańsk to a little west of Wladysławowo and it was in this zone that the new port of Gdynia was constructed as the newly re-established nation's naval base. After this area was briefly, but terribly, subsumed into Nazi Germany, Poland was awarded its longest ever stretch of Baltic coastline from Frombork in the east to Świnoujście in the West. And it is as a result of these geo-political changes, that Polferries' and Unity Line's operations were established and developed over the last four decades.

KOLOBRZEG CALLING

The foundations of the modern Polferries date back to 31 January 1976 when the communist government took the decision to amalgamate the short-sea passenger operations of two existing state-owned companies: Polish Ocean Lines (POL) and Polish Steamship Company (PŻM). The new company – Polksa Żegluga Baltycka (Polish Baltic Shipping) – was to be headquartered in Kołobrzeg, mid-point on the Baltic coast between the western ports of Świnoujście and Szczecin and the eastern ports of Gdynia and Gdańsk. This was for overtly political reasons: to try and stimulate the economy in the middle region, which at the time (and, indeed, is still) isolated from the rest of the country. The new outfit acquired a number of different coastal vessels from both POL and PŻM that were involved in various coastal trades from ports around Kołobrzeg, but in

Wilanów *(Polferries)*

Lańcut *(Polferries)*

Nieborów *(Polferries)*

Rogalin *(Matthew Punter)*

particular, came four modern car ferries from POL as well as the ferry terminals at Świnoujście and Gdańsk. The four ferries had all been constructed for various Scandinavian operators during the 1960s but due to the dramatic growth in vehicle traffic across the northern continent during that decade, were soon replaced by second generation vessels. The *Gryf* was built in 1962 (of dubious parentage, being ordered by Viking Line but completed for Finnlines as *Hansa Express*) and passed to PŻM in 1967 and deployed on the Świnoujście – Ystad service before being transferred in 1970 to POL and moved to their Gdańsk – Helsinki/Nynäshamn services. The *Skandynawia* was built in 1964 as *Visby* for Rederi AB Gotland and sold in 1970 to POL, effectively to replace the *Gryf* at Świnoujście. The other pair was sisters, both constructed for Lion Ferry as the *Kronprins Carl Gustaf* in 1964 and the *Gustav Vasa* in 1965. They were early Knud E.Hansen iterations of the design which became familiar on the Irish Sea as B&I's *Munster*, *Leinster* and *Innisfallen* later in the same decade. The *Gustav Vasa* moved to POL in 1971 as the *Wawel* and was placed onto the charter market for a few years before opening a short-lived Świnoujście – Travemünde route which was soon diverted to Ystad. The *Kronprins Carl Gustaf*, after various changes of ownership during the complex and continuously fluctuating years of Scandinavian ferry operations in the late sixties, wound up at Lion Ferry before she, too, moved to POL as the *Wilanów* in 1975 for service between Świnoujście and Ystad replacing the *Skandynawia* which moved to join *Gryf* between Gdańsk and Helsinki.

The irony of all this of course, is that the little resort of Kołobrzeg completely missed out on all the comings and goings in the Polish ferry industry. Other than acting as the headquarters for the new operators, very little in the way of traffic passed through the town, although it would naturally have benefitted from some holiday-makers heading from Sweden or Denmark and transiting Świnoujście.

EXPANSION & MODERNISATION

Only a year or so after its foundation, Polferries embarked on a major expansion programme. The first acquisition was the *Aallotar* chartered from FÅA from October of 1977 for service between Gdańsk and Helsinki and purchased the following year and given the name *Rogalin*. Her sister, the *Regina*, was also chartered for most of 1978.

Polferries had also inherited a major ship order that had been made by POL, initially expected to comprise seven vessels. The first three of the class were under construction at the Stocznia yard at Szczecin and the lead ship, the *Pomerania* – the first sea-going car ferry constructed in Poland – entered service in July 1978 between Świnoujście and København. This was extended in the autumn to include a call at Felixstowe, very much in keeping with the zeitgeist of the 1970s with similarly unlikely services being started from the UK by a variety of experimental operators to Lisbon, Casablanca and other exotic destinations.

Sadly, if not unsurprisingly, the Felixstowe leg was to be short-lived as the *Pomerania* was moved to the Gdańsk route the following year and replaced by her sister *Silesia* with the third vessel in the class due in 1982 as the *Mazovia*. However, by the early 1980s, a currency crisis, caused by heavy borrowing of Western money, forced the Polish government to sell the ship to Turkey where she entered service as the *Ankara* in 1983. So taken were the Turks with their new acquisition, they secured a fourth in the class (the *Samsun*) and eventually constructed their own version – the *Iskenderun* – in the early 1990s.

The *Pomerania* and her sisters also formed the blueprint for a fascinating – and much ignored – class of similar ferries that were constructed at Szczecin for several Soviet operations. Seven of the series, all slightly different lengths and capacities, were constructed, taking the names of mostly long-forgotten Soviet dignitaries, and pressed into service for the Baltic, Estonian, Black Sea and Far East Shipping Companies.

RETRENCHMENT

By the early 1980s, the Polish economy was in full-blown crisis and the government was forced to explore every avenue it could to earn Western currency to service its debts. Additionally, it was clear that Polferries had overstretched itself significantly. The traffic was only one way with Poles forbidden from travelling to Scandinavia. The desire to earn foreign cash from tourists had to be offset against the opportunities to earn cash from selling or chartering the fleet.

The flagship *Pomerania* was chartered for the 1980 season to a new Swedish company that promptly went bankrupt and so she returned to Poland and opened a new Karlskrona – Gdynia route. The following year, both of the oldest units were sold: the *Gryf* heading to Fraglines and the *Skandynawia* to the Far East. In 1983 the *Rogalin* was chartered to an Icelandic company to link Reykjavik with Bremerhaven and although she returned to Poland between 1984 and 1986; the following year she began a longer stint with Swansea Cork Ferries. The *Silesia* also undertook intermittent charters to the Mediterranean during this time.

It wasn't all disposals, though: in late 1985, the company acquired the *Europafärjan Syd*, originally the second generation *Nils Holgersson*, renamed her the *Lancut* and placed her on the Świnoujście – København route. The final acquisition of the decade was the former *Prins Hamlet* which became the *Nieborów* from 1989, servicing across the network and effectively replacing the *Wawel*, which was sold.

The company also experimented with different routes: the Świnoujście centred operations saw routes into Malmö as well as between Ystad and Travemünde whilst Gdańsk also ran to Oxelösund in Sweden in lieu of Nynäshamn at times.

All this somewhat incomprehensible fleet deployment played out against a background of an increasingly unsustainable political and economic situation, with Solidarność at the heart of the push to overthrow the communists. When the end came, it came fast, with a new non-communist government installed during September 1989.

THE POST COMMUNIST ERA

As the nation, government and company slowly came to terms with the requirements of a free market economy, so changes were seen at Polferries. First to go was the somewhat pointless *Lancut* in 1994, followed by the *Wilanów* in 1997, despite having been significantly rebuilt in 1991. During the 1990s, the company acquired a ro-ro which became the *Parseta* (and was better known as P&O's *St Magnus*). The *Pomerania* also underwent a major reconstruction in 1997 to modernise her accommodation and increase her capacity.

By far the biggest post-communist era impact on the Polferries operation came in 1995 with the re-introduction of PŻM and POL passenger ferry services under the banner of Unity Line. That company ordered a major new vessel from Norway which entered service between Świnoujście and Ystad that year. Although the initial years saw some form of co-operation between the two companies, the rapid growth of Unity Line has seen significant competitive challenges for Polferries over the last two decades.

Polferries also invested in a fast ferry during 1997, taking one of the early generation Austal catamarans which was named *Boomerang* and operated between Świnoujście and Malmö. However, this service only survived until 2001 when the route was closed and the craft sold to Tallink. They also acquired a new freight ferry in the form of the *Kahleberg*.

The turn of the millennium saw a reduced, but stable fleet: the *Silesia* operated Gdańsk – Nynäshamn; the *Rogalin* Świnoujście – Ystad; the *Boomerang* to Malmö and the *Pomerania* to København with occasional jaunts to Rønne. But the creeping inefficiency and obsolescence of the fleet was still an issue. In 2003, the company invested in a "modern" cruise ferry in the form of the *Visby* which was renamed the *Scandinavia* (note the English spelling) and replaced the *Silesia* at Gdańsk which in turn moved to replace the *Rogalin* which was scrapped. Two years later, the *Alkmini A* (ex-*Fantasia*) was purchased, restructured as an overnight vessel and renamed the *Wawel* for Świnoujście – Ystad and the *Silesia* was disposed of. In 2007, the *Dieppe* was purchased from Transmanche Ferries and renamed *Baltivia* to join the *Scandinavia*. The *Pomerania* meanwhile, soldiered on, well after the Øresund bridge rendered her service to the Danish capital redundant, until the route was finally closed in 2010.

CRISIS AND PRIVATISATION

As the end of the noughties approached, Polferries was again facing financial difficulties and the Polish government decided to explore avenues for privatisation. The fleet was not modern and there was increasingly heavy competition from both Unity Line (which by now was a wholly

Pomerania *(Matthew Punter)*

Mazovia *(Matthew Punter)*

independent operator) as well as Stena Line whose route between Karlskrona and Gdynia was expanding rapidly.

Indeed, by late 2008 the situation was so dire that DFDS offered to step in and charter the *Wawel*, essentially making the Świnoujście – Ystad service a joint operation. The Danish company was able to add the service to its network – and provide much needed traffic for the route – whilst Polferries continued to crew, operate and market the vessel. It will of course be remembered that DFDS had previously operated its own Gdańsk – Trelleborg – København service during 2003 and 2004 using the *Duke of Scandinavia* (ex *Dana Anglia*).

Of course, DFDS's motives were not entirely altruistic; forming so close a relationship put them in pole position for the forthcoming privatisation. Several attempts were made from 2009 with DFDS, Finnlines and TT-Line all bidding for the operation. During this period, there were also ongoing rumours that TT-Line was considering establishing their own service into Świnoujście from their base at Trelleborg. This was earmarked to start in 2013, but with a deal to buy Polferries being apparently close, was put on hold.

By 2014, it was looking as though Finnlines was going to buy the company. The Finnish company proposed to sell their *Finnarrow* to Polferries and use the cash to buy the whole operation. With a Finnlines deal now on the horizon, TT-Line started its own route in January of that year using the *Nils Dacke* in a multi-purpose mode. The purchase of the *Finnarrow* by Polferries was secured in late 2014, financed by the sale of the *Scandinavia* to Ventouris. Shortly after, the Polish government decided that none of the foreign companies should purchase Polferries and a plan was announced in early 2015 to merge the operation with Unity Line.

A FRESH WAVE OF INVESTMENT

The first new Polferries' ship since the early 2000s was originally ordered in 1990 for Rederi AB Gotland as the first in what was planned to be a numerous class of new ro-pax vessels for the charter market. She was designed by Knud E. Hansen and in a highly unusual move, was ordered from a shipyard at Jakarta in Indonesia. However, the shipyard was inexperienced and lengthy delays beset the construction and it wasn't until 1997 that she was finally delivered as *Gotland*. She was initially chartered to several Baltic operators on a short-term basis during 1997 until at the end of the year when she was sold to Finnlines and renamed *Finnarrow* for service across their network. Between 2010 and 2013, she undertook a number of charters to Stena Line, operating from Gdynia, Killingholme and Holyhead. In 2013 she was sold to Grimaldi, renamed *Euroferrys Brindisi* and rebuilt, extending her deck nine superstructure aft over the vehicle deck in order to accommodate a large reclining seat area stretching across the ship as far as the funnel. She was deployed on their trans-Adriatic routes.

In late 2014, the Polferries deal was finalised and she was moved to first Szczecin and then Odense for further rebuilding work. This comprised the conversion of most of the reclining seating into a "Coffee Bar", dance floor and casino area and deck nine was further extended towards the stern to incorporate an additional sixty-nine cabins. Meanwhile, the deck 8 cafeteria was fully refurbished, also providing a central bar in addition to the port-side servery. Space for a small shop has also been carved out of the centre of this area, by making the cafeteria 'U-shaped', wrapping around the shop. Most strikingly, the vessel received an impressive new artwork across her bows, presumably inspired by similar devices that feature across the Norwegian Cruise Line fleet. The design was created by Mariusz Waras and features folk patterns from the Mazovia region of Poland.

On completion of the work, the new flagship was renamed *Mazovia* and pressed into service between Świnoujście and Ystad in July 2015, replacing the *Wawel* which moved to Gdańsk to release the *Scandinavia* for her new career in the Mediterranean.

In 2017, the company announced its intention to place an order for a new ro-pax vessel to be constructed at the MSR Gryfia Shipyard at Szczecin (which had recently been re-opened) for deployment between Świnoujście and Ystad. The new vessel's keel was laid on 23 June and she is due to enter service in time for the 2020 summer season. The ship will be 202 metres in length and offer capacity for 400 passengers with 3,000 lane metres of freight space. She will utilize

LNG, bunkering at both Świnoujście and Ystad, and will be equipped with diesel electric propulsion, including two stern-located Azipods. It is possible that a second vessel will also be ordered.

Not content with this, Polferries also turned to the second hand market the same year, acquiring a Bulgarian ro-pax vessel to augment the *Mazovia*'s operation and provide capacity headroom leading up to the introduction of the Szczecin newbuild. The vessel in question was originally built as the *Murillo* for Trasmediterránea in 2002, the fifth and final vessel in a class, the rest of which were ordered by Merchant Ferries of the UK. *Murillo* had extended passenger accommodation, enabling her to carry 550 passengers in addition to her lane meterage of nearly 2,200. She was sold out of the Trasmediterránea fleet in 2014, passing to Port Bulgaria West and renamed *Drujba* for service across the Black Sea from Burgas.

Prior to entry into service as *Cracovia*, she was comprehensively refitted at Szczecin and now offers a restaurant, a cafeteria and two bars in addition to reclining seating and cabins. Passenger capacity has increased to 650. She entered service – with another striking bow design, this time featuring a stylized humpback whale – in September 2017. In addition to taking the roster of the *Baltivia* (which was retained as a third ship on the route), she also inaugurated weekly crossings to Rønne.

Finally, in early 2018, Polferries announced the charter of the *Nova Star* to become the second vessel on the Gdańsk – Nynäshamn route. This ship was originally ordered from Singapore in 2009 for LD Lines for service between Portsmouth and Le Havre as the *Norman Leader*. However, lengthy construction delays and deadweight problems, led to her rejection by LD and, after languishing for some years in Singapore, she eventually entered the charter market. She initially sailed for Nova Star Cruises (for whom she was renamed *Nova Star*) between Portland, USA and Yarmouth, Canada between 2014 and 2015 but this operation was not a success. In 2016 she was chartered to Inter Shipping of Morocco for service between Tanger and Algeciras, and spent 2017 laid up at the latter port

For her new Baltic operation, Polferries brought the ship to Gdańsk, where she received a thorough refit and repaint, finally losing the vestiges of her LD Lines livery which she had worn since construction. She is expected to enter service, partnering the *Wawel*, in September.

CONCLUSION

The recent wave of investment for Polferries has demonstrated a significantly renewed confidence in its long-term future. The planned merger with Unity Line is no longer on the cards and both will· pursue independent operations. No longer under the shadow of privatization, and with a newbuild on the horizon, it appears that at long last the company is on a growth trajectory. The newly acquired trio of *Mazovia*, *Cracovia* and *Nova Star* in the last three years is paying dividends in terms of traffic.

Looking to the future, it is likely that two newbuilds will eventually emerge from Szczecin to operate the Świnoujście service but, despite the recent investment, it is not immediately obvious which ships will ultimately serve Gdańsk: *Wawel* is clearly due for replacement in the next few years but neither *Mazovia* nor *Cracovia* offer the onboard facilities and ambience to compete against Stena. Whether *Nova Star* can become a suitable long term fleet member depends on how she proves herself during her first season, but, on paper at least, she is the most suitable candidate for the future of the route.

The company still maintains an eclectic mix of second-hand vessels – albeit a different generation of such ships - and is still challenged by competitors on both its routes. But it has fought on, with valiance and determination and looks set to see out its fifth decade with renewed confidence.

Matthew Punter

UNITY LINE - A BALTIC SUCCESS STORY
BALTIC RENAISSANCE

One of the most fascinating aspects of the ferry industry over the last few decades has been the rapid growth in passenger and freight services to the former communist economies of Central and Eastern Europe. These were liberated from their shackles by the fall of the iron curtain and the break-up of the Soviet empire between 1989 and 1991. The most dramatic changes have emanated from Tallinn where a kaleidoscopic array of state-owned companies and private entrepreneurs eventually took form in the shape of Tallink, a giant of the cruise ferry industry. Elsewhere, Stena and DFDS have emerged as the leaders on services to Latvia and Lithuania which, due to their lengthy crossings and lack of major coastal cities to attract tourist traffic, have evolved into impressive ro-pax operations.

Further south, the Polish ferry network has become essentially a two-way race between Unity Line and Polferries, at least to the western part of the country, the region known as Pomerania. Partly due to its geographic proximity to the dominant economies of Western Europe and partly due to the relative openness of the Polish economy during the communist era, the region has long offered ferry connections to Scandinavia. However, on the liberation of the country in 1989, there was one organisation that was quick to seize the day, establishing one of the most modern and impressive operations out of the former communist nations. That company was Unity Line who, by 1995, had introduced the first purpose-built ro-pax ferry in the region, seven years before Tallink got their act together; DFDS and Stena have yet to build their own ships for their Eastern networks, although DFDS have two vessels on order for delivery in 2021.

The last two decades have seen Unity Line consistently develop into a large, modern ro-pax operation. Seldom a company to make the news, its quiet success has rarely made headlines. But the fact that it now dominates the key passage between Sweden and Poland is testament to the investment that has been made in the operation over the last twenty or so years.

BACK TO THE FUTURE

In 1976, the formation of Polferries was largely due to the decision of two of Poland's biggest state-owned shipping companies to withdraw from the short-sea passenger market. The state-owned Polish Ocean Lines (POL) and Polish Steamship Company (PŻM) placed their comparatively modern ferry operations into a new company which, as Polferries, became the sole provider of services in the region. Following the liberation of the economy in 1989, PŻM became interested once again in the opportunities for short sea shipping and entered negotiations with a number of other parties. These included both Euroafrica Shipping and Polferries itself. Euroafrica was a recent offshoot from POL which, despite having transferred its passenger operations to Polferries, had retained a freight service between Świnoujście and Ystad. This service had received two modern units in the mid-1970s: the *Mikołaj Kopernik* in 1974 and the *Jan Heweliusz* in 1977. The *Jan Heweliusz* suffered a never-ending series of mishaps, including two capsizings, the last of which tragically took 55 lives to the bottom of the Baltic Sea in 1993. A third freighter, the *Jan Śniedecki*, was commissioned in 1987.

The new organisation was fittingly called 'Unity Line', representing a desire to modernise by bringing together the talents of multiple Polish ship owners, with PŻM and Euroafrica taking a 50% stake each. The ambition for the future was impressive; it wasn't just a case of sprucing up the freight service, Unity Line wanted to modernise the sector through the creation of a truly modern ro-pax operation. To this effect, in May 1994, an order was placed for a major newbuild at a Norwegian shipyard. Unity Line opted for an existing design that had seen several iterations over the previous four years: Stena took the first two for its UK operations (*Stena Challenger* and *Stena Traveller*) with a passenger capacity of 500; Turkish Cargo Lines took two more freight-oriented vessels for its services (*Kaptan Burhanettin Isim* and *Kaptan Abidin Doran*) and Fjord Line had taken a fifth (*Bergen*) which was configured as an overnight ferry.

Kopernik *(Matthew Punter)*

Skania *(Matthew Punter)*

The new ship was named *Polonia*, with a more streamlined forward superstructure, radically different internal layout, significant cabin accommodation and total passenger capacity for 920. She entered service on 31st May 1995, joining a Unity Line operation that had already been established at the start of the year with Euroafrica's *Mikołaj Kopernik* and the *Jan Śniedecki*. The *Polonia* introduced a minimalist corporate branding in navy and turquoise with a double-"I" logo calling out the repetition of this letter in the words "Unity Line".

Although Polferries ceased formal involvement in the new operation before it started, the *Polonia* essentially operated a joint service with whatever vessel the existing operator was using at the time: *Nieborow*, *Rogalin* or *Silesia* during the early years of the service. Naturally, the mismatch between the two operations never reflected favourably on Polferries and the pooling arrangement had ended by the mid 2000s. It was undoubtedly a short-sighted decision of Polferries to not embrace the new service and it has continually played catch-up ever since. Indeed, plans were afoot during 2015 to merge the two companies but this was not pursued.

The route grew significantly during the late 1990s but, as is often the case with pooled operations, decision-making became sclerotic and so in 2004, it was decided that PŻM would buy out the shares of Euroafrica and the company would be a wholly-owned subsidiary. However, Euroafrica would continue to own the two freight ships which would be chartered to Unity Line - and have retained their Euroafrica funnel colours to this day.

GROWTH

The new ownership structure for Unity Line meant that it was immediately free to concentrate on growing the operation. The first investment took place in late 2004 when the *Kaptan Burhanettin Isim* was purchased by PŻM to join the Unity fleet as the *Gryf*. After running for much of the 2005 season between Świnoujście and Ystad, she was used to inaugurate a new freight-only service between Świnoujście and Trelleborg.

This route proved to be a success and in 2007 there was another major phase of investment. Firstly, the *Galileusz* – originally built for Tirrenia as the *Via Tirreno* – was introduced on the Trelleborg service and, proving that the ties with their former partners remained strong, this ship was purchased by Euroafrica and chartered to Unity Line. Later in the year, the closure of the SeaWind service between Stockholm and Turku provided a convenient windfall for Unity who acquired both of the redundant vessels. The *Sky Wind* came first, purchased by PŻM and renamed *Wolin* to provide passenger operation on the Trelleborg service. At the very end of 2007, Euroafrica purchased the *Star Wind*, renamed her *Kopernik* and in early 2008 introduced her on the Ystad service in lieu of the *Mikołaj Kopernik* which was disposed of.

The final phase of the investment programme occurred in mid-2008 when PŻM purchased the *Eurostar Roma* from Grimaldi Ferries. She had been constructed in 1995, the year Unity Line began, as the revolutionary *Superfast I*, transforming the Adriatic ferry market and driving significant change across the whole of the Mediterranean as local operators realised that fast, modern tonnage could indeed pay its way. In many respects the Attica Enterprises' Superfast operation acted more as a showroom for their tonnage on the second-hand market rather than as a genuine ferry operation in its own right. All but two of their initial twelve-strong fleet was quickly sold onto further owners, with the original twins not really settling down until each came to their third careers (*Superfast II* briefly served in Australia before being purchased by Corsica Ferries). Having moved to Grimaldi after nine seasons on the Adriatic, the ship arrived in Poland just thirteen years old, taking the name *Skania* and undergoing a major refit, including the extension of her aft passenger accommodation to provide an additional bar area. She was introduced onto the service between Świnoujście and Ystad in September 2008, partnering the *Polonia*. Offering daily departures in each direction at around 10am and 10pm, and finally with equally balanced "cruise ferries", Unity Line could finally claim to have among the best ferry operations in the Southern Baltic.

NED Concept Project *(Unity Line)*

During the late 2000s, Unity Line placed an order with the SSN shipyard at Szczecin for the construction of a pair of ro-paxes to be given the names *Piast* and *Patria*. However, the bankruptcy of SSN meant that this order was never fulfilled.

Despite this setback, Unity Line now offered a comprehensive offer between southern Sweden and western Poland: the *Polonia* and *Skania* on the "cruise" sailings and the *Kopernik* and *Jan Śniedecki* offering ro-pax support. The cruise ferries are referred to as "Passenger and Car Ferries" whilst the ro-paxes are "Car and Passenger Ferries", a mark of subtlety that must surely escape most people. Meanwhile, a three-ship roster comprising the *Wolin*, *Gryf* and *Galileusz* operate to Trelleborg, principally aimed at freight, but with passengers and their vehicles also conveyed.

TOWARDS THE 2020s

Unity Line is now the largest operator between Poland and Sweden, carrying 250,000 trucks and 340,000 passengers each year. Competition on the corridor is increasing with Polferries now operating daily crossings from both Świnoujście and Gdańsk whilst Stena's services from Gdynia have also expanded to include both Karlskrona and Nynäshamn. Unity Line has this year invested in new tonnage with the purchase of the *Puglia* by Euroafrica which has been renamed *Copernicus* and replaced the *Kopernik* on the Ystad service in August 2018.

The company is also exploring new tonnage for its services, publishing a design concept for a ro-pax, developed in conjunction with naval architects NED Project and Wärtsilä. The concept is designed with specific focus on the environmental credentials, with dual-fuel propulsion (LNG as main and marine diesel back-up) as well as four rotors providing additional power. The vessel would be 204 metres in length, the maximum that can currently be permitted in Ystad, with the design allowing for lengthening to 225 metres. Capacity would be 3,600 metres of freight and 521 passengers. A decision on the construction of the vessels is expected during summer 2018 and with the order expected to go to a Polish shipyard.

The next five years will provide an interesting opportunity to observe how this fascinating sector of the European ferry industry continues to grow and the increasingly important role that Unity Line will play in it.

Matthew Punter

Amorella *(Kalle Id)*

Rosella before the application of the current livery. *(Kalle Id)*

VIKING LINE TODAY AND TOMORROW

Viking Line, the northern Baltic Sea's second-largest ferry operator (after the Tallink Grupp), looks forward to both their 60th anniversary in 2019 and their next newbuilding due for delivery in 2020. In this article we take a look at Viking's operations today and the company's future plans.

TURKU-STOCKHOLM

The Turku-Stockholm route is today the company's premier service, operated by the flagship *Viking Grace* and the older *Amorella*. The route connects via the Åland Islands to allow tax-free goods to be sold onboard, with daytime crossings calling at the islands' capital Mariehamn, while during the night the ships call at the more remote Långnäs, handily located almost adjacent to the main shipping lane between Turku and Stockholm.

The need to call at Åland also offers unusual possibilities for ferry cruises. In addition to the pure transport function of passengers and freight, there are no less than three distinct cruise options available: a "picnic" day cruise, where passengers join the ship in the morning, change ships while they are simultaneously in Mariehamn during the day and return home in the evening; a 23-hour cruise with a night and day at sea (usually passengers choose the evening departure, but a morning option is also available); and a day in Stockholm/Turku cruise, where passengers do night crossings in both directions and spend a day in the destination.

The *Viking Grace*, which is on the evening departure from Turku, was completed by what was then STX Europe yard in Turku (today Meyer Turku) in 2013 as the world's first major ferry powered by liquidized natural gas (LNG). To further augment her environmentally friendly power system, a Flettner rotor was added to the ship in spring 2018. The *Viking Grace* is notably cruise-oriented, with cabin berths provided to her entire passenger complement of 2,800 (though deck passengers are also accepted), but also an impressive cargo carrier with 1,275 lane metres for freight and an additional 500 lane metres for private cars on a separate deck.

The *Viking Grace*'s running mate *Amorella* is, in contrast, of an older vintage, dating from 1988. She is also more oriented towards route passengers, with a passenger capacity of 2,450 but cabin berths for only 1,946. Her cargo capacity is 970 lane metres, but she too has an additional garage, albeit a smaller one than on the *Viking Grace*. The *Amorella*'s replacement, currently known only as Newbuilding 488A and slated for delivery in 2020 from the Xiamen Shipbuilding yard in China, will have the same length as the *Viking Grace* (218 metres) but will be wider, thus allowing for an extra lane of cargo to be carried, with a projected cargo capacity of 1,500 lane metres. The passenger capacity will be the same as on the *Viking Grace* at 2,800 and, like her future running mate, the ship will be powered by LNG and equipped with Flettner rotors.

The future of the *Amorella* once the new ship is delivered is uncertain, as Viking Line representatives have given conflicting information, stating both that the *Amorella* would join the Helsinki-Tallinn line and that she would be sold.

STOCKHOLM-MARIEHAMN

One of the reasons why Viking Line have been content to operate the Turku-Stockholm route with such a mismatched pair for the last five year is the existence of their Stockholm-Mariehamn cruise route, operated by the *Viking Cinderella*. Where the *Amorella* departs Stockholm at 20.00, the *Viking Cinderella* makes an earlier 18.00 departure (17.30 during the summer high season), makes a leisurely crossing to Mariehamn through the archipelago and returns to Stockholm at 15.00, making her schedule much more attractive to cruise guests than that of the *Amorella*. Furthermore, the 1989-built *Viking Cinderella* has more extensive and impressive public rooms, including a three-deck-high night club and a five-deck-high glass wall on her starboard side.

Mariella *(Kalle Id)*

As the new ship under construction for the Turku route looks to be becoming much more cruise-oriented than the *Amorella*, and the public spaces are to be designed with the Swedish passengers in mind, industry observers have pointed out that Viking Line might be planning to replace not just the *Amorella* but also the *Viking Cinderella* with the new ship, combining the two existing night-and-day cruise services from Stockholm into one. However, this "two birds with one stone" approach would have to take on the *Amorella*'s current schedule (optimised for cargo and the lucrative picnic cruises), which could mean losing some of the company's share on the short cruise market from Stockholm.

MARIEHAMN-KAPELLSKÄR

Viking's other Åland-Sweden route is quite a different animal; the 1980-vintage *Rosella* makes two to three return crossings a day (depending on day and season) from Mariehamn to Kapellskär (an outer harbour on the edge of the Stockholm archipelago), offering something of a lifeline service for Ålanders working or studying in Sweden – but this route, too, has a cruise aspect, as booking a return crossing as a lunch or dinner cruise is very popular. Despite her age, the *Rosella* has been lovingly maintained (and converted to be more of a day ferry, when originally she was designed for both day and night crossings), and looks set to continue on the route for some time.

HELSINKI-STOCKHOLM

Viking Line's offering on the capital cities service between Helsinki and Stockholm consists of the 1985-built *Mariella* and 1993-built *Gabriella* (ex-*Frans Suell* and *Silja Scandinavia*, acquired by Viking Line in 1997). The ships offer only night crossings, with departures from both ports late in the afternoon and arrival the following morning, with two-night cruises offered alongside route travel. On this route, Viking Line faces heavy competition from Silja Line's superb *Silja Serenade* and *Silja Symphony*, but both the *Mariella* and *Gabriella* have been given repeated refits during the past years to make them able to compete better – quite an amazing array of restaurants has been squeezed into the relatively modest dimensions of both ships, with Viking's duo rivalling the Silja twins in quantity of public rooms and the quality of the onboard product, if not in sheer size.

Since the early 1990s, the Helsinki-Stockholm route has taken the backseat when it comes to newbuildings, both for Viking and their competitors, and in light of the recent heavy refits this trend looks to be continuing. Reports also indicate that the profitability of the route is low, due to heavy competition not just between Viking and Silja but also Tallink's Stockholm-Tallinn and Stockholm-Riga routes for the Swedish market, which seems to render newbuildings for the route unfeasible in the near future.

HELSINKI-TALLINN

Viking's mainstay on the Helsinki-Tallinn line is the 2008-built *Viking XPRS* (pronounced "Viking Express") which, although a bespoke design in terms of passenger seas, shares the hull form with the *Côte des Dunes* and *Côte des Flandres* of DFDS, as well as her Helsinki-Tallinn competitor, the *Star* of Tallink. Operating two round trips from Helsinki per day (a day cruise plus an evening departure from Helsinki and an early morning one from Tallinn for the needs of freight), the *Viking XPRS* was the most popular ship on the route from her completion until 2017 and the arrival of Tallink's newbuilt *Megastar*.

2017 was a problematic year for Viking on the Helsinki-Tallinn line. The company chartered the Swedish-owned, 1998-built fast catamaran *Express* to sail alongside the *Viking XPRS* under the marketing name "Viking FSTR" for the extended summer season. While the *Express* did raise passenger numbers, the fuel-hungry fast ferry with minimal passenger facilities was ill-suited for Viking Line's business model of offering cheap tickets and making money from the onboard services. As a result, the financial result of the year was poor. The experiment was thus not repeated for the 2018 season, with the *Viking XPRS* sailing on the route alone for most of the year, but supplemented by the Helsinki-Stockholm ships making an additional return trip from Helsinki to Tallinn during the summer season, using the time they normally

Plate – Social Dining, one of three waiter-service restaurants onboard the Mariella. *(Kalle Id)*

Viking XPRS *(Kalle Id)*

Viking XPRS – Club X night club, added in a 2017 refit. *(Kalle Id)*

Viking Grace with the flettner rotor added 2018. *(Richard Kirkman)*

The interiors of Newbuilding 488A will be designed by Koncept Stockholm, a newcomer to ship interiors. (Viking Line/Koncept Stockholm)

spend moored in Helsinki during the day more profitably. This arrangement was premiered in 2014 and looks set as the pattern for several years to come.

The future of the Helsinki-Tallinn route is an interesting question. Although reportedly one of Viking's best money-makers (an assertion seemingly proven by the often overcrowded public rooms of the *Viking XPRS*), the company have not been eager to follow their main competitor Tallink in investing on new tonnage for the service. Viking may be forced to act in the near future, as Tallink in mid-2018 indicated they would be contracting a sister ship to the highly successful *Megastar* soon. Although no definitive order was placed at the time of writing, such a move by Tallink is likely to force Viking to act to preserve their market share, either contracting a new ship of their own, acquiring a suitable vessel second-hand, or transferring the *Amorella* to the Tallinn service once the new ship from China is delivered.

Kalle Id

An artist's impression of Newbuilding 488A. (Viking Line)

DFDS IN 2018
MASTERS OF THE EUROPEAN SEAS

DFDS achieved record results in 2017, posting an operating profit of DKK 1.7 billion in February 2018. The latter was mostly due to continuing positive increases in volumes on the company's core freight routes across the North Sea, whereas passenger volumes remained stable. Nonetheless, the past twelve months have been nothing but spectacular, DFDS having ordered no less than six newbuildings, securing a long-term charter for another one and purchasing one of Europe's most successful RoRo operators, the Turkish company UN RoRo. We hereby give an overview of the main developments at the Danish company since the last summer.

BALTIC SEA

DFDS' five routes on the Baltic Sea with regard to ship deployment and timetables remained more or less unchanged. While the Kiel – St. Petersburg route continues to be served by means of a slot charter agreement with Finnlines on the latter's *Finnsun*, *Finnmill* and *Finnpulp*, DFDS used a chartered vessel, the *Sailor* (ex *Finnsailor*) on its freight route between Paldiski and Hanko. The *Liverpool Seaways* continues to sail on the Paldiski – Kapellskär line, while the routes linking Lithuania with Sweden and Germany were served by two RoPax ferries each. Both are in the hands of Italian-built tonnage, the Karlshamn – Klaipėda route being operated by the Visentini-class *Optima Seaways* together with the Apuania-built *Athena Seaways* and the latter's sister vessels *Regina Seaways* and *Victoria Seaways* sailing on the route to Kiel. With DFDS anticipating further growth on its Baltic routes in the coming years, it announced on 12 February an order for two ropax ferries at the Chinese Guangzhou Shipyard International (GSI). The DKK 1.8 billion order includes an option on two further units. The ships will have a capacity of 4,500 lane meters and 690 passengers and are scheduled for a delivery in 2021. Meanwhile, the charter of the *Regina Seaways* from Grimaldi Holdings was extended to last until November 2019, but looks likely to be renewed next year to last until the first newbuilding is delivered. Also on its Baltic routes, DFDS deploys the *Patria Seaways* which carries out additional sailings between Karlshamn and Klaipėda at peak times. However, the ship has also spent a few weeks on charter, sailing between Travemünde, Rostock and Trelleborg for TT-Line between January and March 2018 to substitute for the *Peter Pan*. A more regular visitor to Klaipėda is the *Ark Futura* which maintains the Fredericia/Copenhagen (København) – Klaipeda route. All routes calling at Klaipeda moved to the new central Klaipeda ferry terminal in October 2017.

NORTH SEA AND WESTERN SCANDINAVIA

What was once an impressive network of overnight cruise ferry routes across the North Sea and in Western Scandinavia has been reduced to two services lately – the traditional Copenhagen (København) – Oslo line dating back to DFDS' founding days in 1866 and the Amsterdam (Ijmuiden) – Newcastle (North Shields) route, the latter being the last of DFDS' overnight services between continental Europe and Britain. In Copenhagen (København), the *Pearl Seaways* had received DFDS's new dark blue livery back in 2016, but partner vessel *Crown Seaways* finally followed after returning from her bi-annual docking in early 2018. The same goes for DFDS's Amsterdam stalwart *Princess Seaways*, while the *King Seaways* is not due to be repainted until autumn 2019. On its two North Sea cruise ferries, DFDS in spring 2018 implemented a new restaurant concept, introducing 'Explorer's Kitchen', 'North Sea Bistro' and the 'Coffee Crew Café'. Until as recently as June 2018, DFDS was reported to have had "advanced plans" for newbuildings to replace the *Princess Seaways* and *King Seaways* on the Amsterdam – Newcastle route, but these now seem to be put on hold.

Germany and Denmark had lost their direct passenger connections with England in 2005 and 2014 respectively, the Cuxhaven – Harwich and Esbjerg – Harwich routes being replaced by freight-only services from the same ports to Immingham. The Cuxhaven – Immingham route was served by the *Jutlandia Seaways* and the chartered *Stena Foreteller* in 2018 and the traditional link between Esbjerg and England by the *Ark Dania* and *Fionia Seaways*. On 21 December 2017, DFDS closed its own terminal in Esbjerg, moving to Østhavn where it now uses

Regina Seaways *(Kai Ortel)*

Regina Seaways *(Kai Ortel)*

Patria Seaways *(Kai Ortel)*

Magnolia Seaways *(Kai Ortel)*

DFDS's 'jumbo ferries' to be delivered in 2019. *(DFDS)*

a terminal operated by Bluewater Shipping.

With the two newbuildings from FSG in Germany deployed on for the Rotterdam (Vlaardingen) – Immingham route (see below), the ever-growing services between Göteborg and Immingham now look set to be reinforced by two ships ordered from the Chinese Jinling shipyard. The original order in October 2016 had been for two giant 6,700 lane metre vessels, but two more units were ordered on 16 June 2017. The launch of the lead ship took place on 16 July 2018. The ro-ro ferries are for delivery in 2019 and 2020 (two each year). For the time being, the Göteborg – Brevik – Gent route is served by the *Ark Germania, Begonia Seaways, Freesia Seaways* and *Primula Seaways* while the Göteborg – Brevik – Immingham route is operated by the *Petunia Seaways, Ficaria Seaways* and *Magnolia Seaways*. On 2 March 2018, the *Primula Seaways* was involved in a collision with the container ship *MSC Madrid* off Vlissingen. The DFDS ferry had to be taken to Fayard for repairs, her place being taken by the *Petunia Seaways*. The latter was replaced by the *Jutlandia Seaways* which in turn was substituted on the Cuxhaven – Immingham route by the short term-chartered *Neptune Dynamis*. Furthermore, DFDS announced on 22 March 2018 that it was now welcoming passengers on its Zeebrügge – Rosyth freight service (in addition to Göteborg - Gent). Ironically, the Belgium – Scotland vessel *Finlandia Seaways* was heavily damaged by fire on 16 April, leading to the closure of her route. At the time of writing, she remains under repair at Fayard.

On the shorter freight routes between Rotterdam (Vlaardingen) and England, the link to Immingham saw significant change in 2017/18 with the two newbuildings *Gardenia Seaways* and *Tulipa Seaways* being put in service on 27 July and 30 September respectively. The two 4,100 lane metre vessels are on long-term (5 years) charter from Siem Industries, owners of their German building yard FSG. The introduction of these two brand-new ships allowed for the charter of the smaller *Corona Seaways* and *Hafnia Seaways* to be ended. They were chartered to Transfennica as from January 2018. On the Rotterdam (Vlaardingen) – Immingham route, the *Gardenia Seaways* and *Tulipa Seaways* operate alongside a third vessel, the 2000-built *Anglia Seaways*. The shorter Rotterdam (Vlaardingen) – Felixstowe route is served by the three Fincantieri-built sister ships *Britannia Seaways, Selandia Seaways* and *Suecia Seaways*.

ENGLISH CHANNEL

DFDS's two main English Channel routes are Dover – Dunkerque (*Delft Seaways, Dover Seaways* and *Dunkerque Seaways*) and Dover – Calais (*Calais Seaways, Côte des Dunes* and *Côte des Flandres*). On 23 June 2017, DFDS declared a purchase option on the *Côte des Dunes* and *Côte des Flandres* which were acquired from Eurotunnel, having been on charter previously. On 24 April this year, DFDS announced it would long-term charter (ten years) a vessel from Stena RoRo upon its delivery. The ship from the Stena E-Flexer series will arrive in 2021 and replace the *Calais Seaways*, the oldest ferry in DFDS's English Channel fleet. A third Channel route, Newhaven – Dieppe, is being operated by DFDS on behalf of the French SMPAT, the public owner of the

A profile of the Stena 'E-Flexer' that will be customised for use on the DFDS Dover - Calais operation.
(DFDS)

route. The concession was renewed in November 2017, with the Danish company continuing to be in charge of its marketing and sales for another five years from January 2018. The service is operated by the French-flagged sister ships *Côte d'Albâtre* and *Seven Sisters*.

Another DFDS RoPax ferry, the *Sirena Seaways*, continues to sail on charter to Brittany Ferries on the Western Channel. Under the name of *Baie de Seine*, she had been chartered to the French operator for five years in March 2015 and will therefore not return to the DFDS fleet before March 2020.

MEDITERRANEAN

When DFDS formed a joint venture with French ferry operator LD Lines in late 2012, it inherited from the latter a RoRo freight service between Marseille and Tunis, extending its sphere of activities into the Mediterranean. The route continues to feature in the DFDS route map until the present day, being currently operated by the *Botnia Seaways*. However, DFDS took this to another level when on 12 April 2018 they announced the takeover of Turkish operator UN RoRo from private equity funds, a deal worth EUR 950 million. UN RoRo, founded in 1994, is a well-established shipping company which controls a major share of the trade flow between Turkey and the EU, most notably Italy and France. UN RoRo owns a modern fleet of twelve purpose-built RoRo vessels *(Cemil Bayülgen, Saffet Ulusoy, UN Marmara, UN Pendik, UN Trieste, UN Akdeniz, UN Karadeniz, Cüneyt Solakoglu, UN Istanbul, UND Atilim, UND Ege* and *UND Birlik)*, many of which are based on the same design as DFDS's own "flower class" ships. The Turkish operator also owns the port terminals in Pendik and Trieste; it also offers intermodal transport between Turkey and the EU. The four routes served by UN RoRo are Pendik – Ambarli – Trieste, Pendik – Bari – Trieste, Pendik – Toulon and Mersin – Trieste. A fifth one linking Patras with Pendik and Trieste was introduced in early July, shortly after DFDS got legal approval from the relevant authorities to complete the takeover on 8 June. At around the same time, DFDS extended its order from Jinling to include a fifth unit, with three vessels now assigned to DFDS' own routes and two to its new Turkish affiliate. A sixth vessel was firmly ordered when the Danish company presented its Q2 results on 16 August 2018.

DFDS has gone a remarkable way since its takeover of LISCO (2001), Lys Line (2005) and Norfolkline (2010) and forming a joint-venture with LD Lines (2013), expanding from its core market in the North Sea both eastward (to the Baltic Sea) and westward (to the English Channel and Irish Sea). With the takeover of UN RoRo, the Danish company has now turned into a truly pan-European operator, the only one beside the Italian Grimaldi Group. The 'Masters of the Northern seas' have become 'Masters of the European seas'. In its 2017 annual report, DFDS remarked that freight volumes, particularly un-accompanied units, are expected to grow on most routes in 2018 while passenger volumes are expected to be on level with 2017. Its cruise and ropax ferries in 2017 carried an overall 5.3 million passengers, and even with Brexit and other challenges on the horizon, there is no doubt that DFDS more than ever will form a substantial part of the European ferry industry in the years to come.

Kai Ortel

Crown Seaways *(Kai Ortel)*

Calais Seaways *(John Bryant)*

REVIEW 2017/18 -BRITAIN & IRELAND

The following is a review of passenger and freight ferry activities during 2017 and the first half of 2018. Some events occurring in the first half of 2017 will have also been mentioned in 'Ferries 2018'.

EAST COAST & THAMES

In April 2018 DFDS closed down the Rosyth - Zeebrugge fright service following a fire aboard the vessel used, the *Finlandia Seaways*. The route continued to lose money and this was seen as the 'final straw' - a sad end to the hopes when a passenger and freight service was launched with two 'Superfast' vessel in 2002. Only a few weeks before Finnlines had announced a new facility for conveyance of trailers between Rosyth and Bilbao using this service and their own route from Zeebrugge to Bilbao. In addition, DFDS had announced that passengers (up to a maximum of 12) could also be conveyed. In January 2018 the *Stena Foreteller* was chartered by DFDS and is used mainly on the Immingham - Cuxhaven service.

The first of two new Flensburg built freighters, the *Gardenia Seaways*, similar to the earlier flower class vessels, was delivered in July 2017 and entered service on the Rotterdam - Immingham route. The second, the *Tulipa Seaways*, was delivered in September. Both vessels are long term chartered to DFDS by the yard's owners with an option to purchase. Meanwhile work continued on the construction of four larger vessels at Jinling in China and the first one, the *Gothia Seaways*, was floated out in July. An option on a further two vessels was taken up.

The first of CLdN's two new 'jumbo' ro-ros - the largest short sea ro-ro's in the world - the *Celine* was delivered from the Hyundai Mipo yard in Ulsan, South Korea in October. Initially she was used on services from Rotterdam and Zeebrugge to Dublin with just two round trips to Purfleet but in March she started also operating between Zeebrugge and Killingholme and Zeebrugge and Dublin. Her sister vessel, the *Delphine*, was delivered in February and soon joined her on the same services The previous Zeebrugge - Killingholme regulars, the *Pauline* and *Yasmine*, were moved to the Rotterdam - Killingholme service.

During 2017 four 50,200t vessels were ordered from the same yard, of similar design to those ordered from the Uljanik Shipyard in Pula, Croatia in 2016.

The delivery of the *Celine* and *Delphine* enabled the charter of the *Cemil Bayulgen* and *Bore Sea* to be ended. The *Capucine* and *Severine* were re-delivered from Stena Line at the end of 2017. The *Capucine* was initially chartered to the Italian Defence Ministry and then to GNV in the Mediterranean and the *Severine* was initially placed on CLdN's Iberian service and in June the Capucine was chartered to Tirrenia of Italy to operate on a joint service with GNV between Genoa and Malta.

In spring 2017 both Hull - Zeebrugge passenger vessels, the *Pride of Bruges and Pride of York*, were sent to Gdansk for major refits to extend their lives for at least another five years. Because one of the Zeebrugge vessels covers on the Rotterdam route during the refit period, this meant an extended period when Zeebrugge passenger service operated on alternate days. The cover, in order to provide a daily freight service, in 2017 was the *Neptune Aegli* of Neptune Lines, a specialist car carrying company. The *Neptune Aegli* is a dual purpose car carrier or trailer ferry, with each of the two trailer decks having a hoistable mezzanine deck to create two car decks. In 2018 sister vessel, the *Neptune Dynamis* was chartered to cover for the routine dry docking of the *Pride of Rotterdam* and *Pride of York*. . In May 2017 the Dutch registered container ship *Elisabeth* was chartered to relieve pressure on the two passenger ships, operating between Hull and Zeebrugge.

In June 2018 the capacity on the Teesport - Zeebrugge service was boosted by replacing the *Mistral* with the *Estraden*, transferred from the Rotterdam service, and the Rotterdam service was taken over by the *Stena Carrier* (all P&O North Sea freight vessels are chartered). The boost in capacity on both routes was advertised as the best alternative for Scottish traffic no longer able to use the closed DFDS Rosyth - Zeebrugge route.

Gardenia Seaways *(John Bryant)*

Stena Forerunner *(Rob de Visser)*

Stena Britannica (John Bryant)

Pride of Kent (Darren Holdaway)

Mann Lines' new Visentini built freighter, the *ML Freyja*, was delivered in June 2017 but was then sub-chartered to SOL Continent Line, replacing the *Ark Forwarder* on the Zeebrugge - Gothenburg route. She moved to Mann Lines in January 2018 replacing the *Stena Foreteller*, which was chartered to DFDS.

Transfennica took on charter the *Bore Bank* in January 2017. An interesting vessel which was built at a conventional trailer ferry, converted to a car carrier and used by UECC and then, in late 2016, converted back. Sister vessel, similarly converted back, the *Bore Bay* joined the fleet in February 2018 but in April 2018 she was chartered to *Stena Line* to operate between, Gdynia and Nynäshamn. In January 2018 the company chartered the former DFDS vessels *Corona Seaways* and *Hafnia Seaway*. They were subsequently rebranded with Transfennica markings and renamed the *Corona Sea* and *Hafnia Sea* but retained their blue DFDS Hulls. These charters were to replace the *Misada* and *Misina*, which went to Stena Line and the *Miranda* which went to the Mediterranean. The company continued to operate one of their larger con-ro *Plyca* class vessels on the weekly service from Finland to Tilbury.

During 2017 Finnlines embarked on a process to lengthen its six Jinling built ships, boosting capacity by 1,000 lane metres. A 35m long midships section is being added to each vessel. The programme is expected to be completed in autumn 2018.

Stena Line made major changes to the services from Rotterdam to Killingholme and Harwich at the beginning of 2018. The charter of CLdN's *Capucine* and *Severine* on the Harwich route ended and they were replaced by the *Stena Forerunner* and *Stena Scotia*. On the Killingholme route the *Misana* and *Misida*, previously with Transfennica, took over to provide extra capacity. In September the *Stena Scotia* was transferred to the Irish Sea and was replaced by the *Mistral*, sub-chartered from P&O Ferries.

New vessels for the historic Woolwich Free Ferry, operated by Briggs Marine, replacing the three existing vessels which date from the 1960s will be delivered in late autumn 2018 and enter service in December. The *Ben Woollacott* and *Dame Vera Lynn* are being built at the Remontowa Shipyard in Gdansk with 210 lane meters of vehicle deck space. New berths are also being constructed to accommodate the vessels and the service will be suspended between October and December.

In June and July 2017, MBNA Thames Clippers to delivery of two further fast ferries, the *Mercury Clipper* and *Jupiter Clipper* from the Wight Shipyard at Cowes.

In May 2017 the Tilbury - Gravesend Ferry was taken over by Medway based JetStream Tours. The vessel used, the *Thames Swift*, is no stranger to the route having been operated by White Horse Fast Ferries as the *Martin Chuzzlewit* until the company went into liquidation in 2001.

EASTERN CHANNEL

Prospects of a ferry service returning to Ramsgate did not materialise during 2017 and the first half of 2018. Initially there were rumours that Polferries were interested in reviving the service to Ostend, possibly using the *Baltivia*, which had been operating supplementary services following the delivery of the *Cracovia* in 2017. There were reports that a UK company, Seaborne Freight, was planning to enter the market and the *Al Andalus Express*, the former Dover - Dunkerque train ferry *Nord Pas-de-Calais*, was quoted as a potential vessel. However to date nothing has happened. Ramsgate continues to pay host to a number of vessels importing Citroën and Peugeot cars when Sheerness runs out of capacity.

Dover had another quiet year during 2017 and 'Operation Stack' never had to be initiated. In June, DFDS Seaways purchased the *Côte des Dunes* and *Côte des Flandres*, which they had chartered from owners Eurotunnel since 2015. In December 2017 the *Pride of Kent* was caught by a freak gust of wind at Calais and, in crashing into the unused freight ro-ro berth at the other side of the harbour and grounding, seriously damaged one of her propellers and, more seriously, a propeller shaft. A new shaft had to be fabricated, then installed and tested and she did not finally re-enter service until May 2018. The implications of the UK's leaving the European Union in 2019 continued to exercise port and local authorities and there was talk of giant lorry parks, not just as a fall back in times of emergency, but as a permanent feature. Hopefully common sense will prevail and freight will continue to pass through the port, as now, without delays (other than intelligence led occasional checks to detect smuggling of goods and people) and unhindered transit will continue to the ultimate destination.

In April DFDS Seaways signed an agreement with Stena RoRo to charter a 42,000t 'e-flexer' on delivery from her Chinese builders in 2021. This vessel is likely to replace the *Calais Seaways* which will, by that time, be 30 years old. The original design will be modified during the build process to make her suitable for the 90 minute crossing. As the type name suggests, flexibility has been built into the basic layout.

Following a decision by the French courts in March 2016 that the agreement between DFDS Seaways and the local authorities to operate the Newhaven - Dieppe route was invalid and it should be put out to tender again, this duly took place. Not surprisingly, DFDS won and in November 2017 a new five year contact was awarded, starting in January 2018.

WESTERN CHANNEL AND SOLENT

In 2016 Brittany Ferries ordered a new vessel from FSG in Flensburg for delivery in 2019. However, the *Honfleur* as she will be called, will later be joined by two further vessels, this time 'e-flexer' vessels chartered from Stena RoRo, one arriving in 2021 and the second in 2022. These vessels, to be named *Galicia* and *Salamanca* respectively, are likely to replace the two chartered vessels, *Etretat* and *Baie de Seine* which operate the 'économie' services to France and Spain.

In July 2017 Wightlink opened their new double-deck car marshalling area at Portsmouth's Gunwharf Terminal, to enable the *St Clare* and the new vessel, *Victoria of Wight*, to employ simultaneous two deck loading and unloading. At Fishbourne a two deck linkspan was installed but, as there was rather more room, the marshalling area remained single deck. New terminal buildings were installed at both ports. The *Victoria of Wight* was expected to enter service in late summer 2018.

In February 2018 Red Funnel ordered a new vessel from Cammell Laird, Birkenhead. Unlike the 'Raptor' class, the vessel, to be called *Red Kestrel* will be a freight only vessel with a passenger capacity of 12. The order coincided with major terminal investments at Southampton and East Cowes. A new catamaran, *Red Jet 7*, an identical craft to the *Red Jet 6* and also built by Wight Shipyard at East Cowes, entered service in July 2018.

Isle of Wight Council's new Cowes Floating Bridge, called *Floating Bridge No 6*, arrived from Pembroke Dock in March 2017. The old vessel ceased to operate at the beginning of January 2017 and was towed away to a mooring at Gosport. As infrastructure modifications were necessary, it was not possible for the new vessel to enter service until May. In the interim a passenger only service was operated using a small launch. Problems with the new craft led to her being taken out of service for several weeks and these problems continued when she re-entered service in June. There were further periods out of service for the rest of the year and since modifications were made, she is now operating more reliably. However she is unable to run when low tide is lower than normal.

In April 2017, Blue Funnel Cruises took over the Southampton - Hythe passenger ferry from White Horse Ferries, trading on the route as Blue Funnel Ferries. This included the main vessel used, the *Great Expectations*, which was renamed *Hythe Scene*. The reserve vessel, the *Uriah Heap*, had been seriously damaged in a collision with Hythe Pier earlier in the year and was subsequently scrapped. Blue Funnel Ferries later added the *Jenny Blue* (formerly *Ossian of Staffa*) as the standby vessel and she entered service in May 2018.

IRISH SEA

In April 2018 Brittany Ferries chartered a second Visentini built vessel, the *Asterion*. She was renamed the *Connemara* and inaugurated a new twice weekly Cork - Santander service, with an additional weekly service from Cork to Roscoff. Unlike other Brittany Ferries vessels she

MN Pelican *(Darren Holdaway)*

Victoria of Wight *(Andrew Cooke)*

W.B. Yeats *(Irish Ferries)*

Stena E-Flexer class ships are due enter service on the Irish Sea by 2020/21 *(Stena Line)*

flies the Cypriot flag and employs a mainly East European crew, although French unions have been promised that if the new route is successful, the ship will be transferred to French registration.

Irish Ferries' new 54,975t ferry, the *W B Yeats*, was expected to be delivered in August 2018, rather later than planned due to a number of problems during the construction at Flensburg. She is due to operate between Dublin and Cherbourg in the summer and Dublin and Holyhead in the winter. A second, even larger vessel, has been ordered from the same yard to replace the *Epsilon* on the Dublin - Holyhead route. The, as yet un-named, vessel is due to enter service in 2020. The late delivery of the *W B Yeats* and mechanical problems with the *Ulysses* caused the company considerable problems during the peak summer period.

In April 2018 Irish Ferries replaced the Austal fast ferry *Jonathan Swift* with the larger *Dublin Swift*, which came from the same Australian yard. Formerly named the *Westpac Express*, she had been purchased by Irish Ferries in May 2016 but continued to be chartered to the US Government for military transport until November 2017. She was given the same name as the marketing name of the Dublin - Holyhead service which had been operated by the *Jonathan Swift*.

In May 2018 the Isle of Man Steam Packet Company was purchased by the Manx Government for £124 million. The purchase included the *Ben-my-Chree*, *Manannan* and terminal faculties at Douglas (the *Arrow* being on long-term charter from Seatruck Ferries).

In June 2018, Seatruck Ferries announced that the two of their vessels on charter to Stena Line - the *Stena Performer* and *Stena Precision* - would return to the company at the end of August resume their original names and replace two of their older vessels on the Heysham - Warrenpoint service.

It is assumed that Stena Line will move the *Stena Scotia* from the Rotterdam - Harwich service to join the *Stena Hibernia* on their Heysham - Belfast service but what vessels will operate the supplementary freight service on the Birkenhead - Belfast route is not known at the time of going to press. In June it was announced that the first of the new 'e-flexer' vessels, being built at Nanjing, China, would replace the chartered *Stena Superfast X* on the Holyhead - Dublin route in 2020 and the second and fourth of these vessels would take over the Birkenhead - Belfast service.

The prospect of the replacement of the two Cairnryan - Larne vessels, *Stena Superfast VII* and *Stena Superfast VIII*, by two of the new 'e-flexer' vessels diminished in December 2017 when the chartered vessels were purchased from Tallink by Stena.

IRELAND

Strangford Ferry's new vessel, the *Strangford II* was delivered from Cammell Laird of Birkenhead in December 2016. However, her entry into service was delayed as it was found that, at certain sates of the tide, her ramps could not be put down. After modifications, she entered service in February 2017. The *Strangford Ferry* was sold to Arranmore Island Ferry Services and painted in their red livery and renamed the *Strangford 1* but in June she was re-sold to Frazer Ferries, having operated on charter to them on the Lough Foyle service since May, the regular vessel being firstly under maintenance and then operating on the Carlingford Lough service.

In July 2017 Frazer Ferries launched a new service across Carlingford Lough from Greencastle to Greenore in July 2017 using the *Aisling Gabrielle* (formerly the *Foyle Venture*, previously used on the Foyle ferry). There was a fear that the Foyle service would not run in 2017 but in July it resumed, using the former German river ferry, *Berne-Farge*, renamed the *Frazer Mariner*.

The new Rathlin Island vehicle ferry, the *Spirit of Rathlin*, built by Arklow Marine Services, to replace the chartered *Canna* was completed in January 2017. However she was not able to enter service until June when necessary infrastructure works and modifications to the vessel's ramp hydraulics were completed.

SCOTLAND

The introduction of RET (Road Equivalent Tariff) prices on several Caledonian MacBrayne routes in summer 2016 created capacity problems, especially on the Oban - Craignure route and caused the regular Mallaig - Armadale vessel, the *Coruisk*, to be moved to that route to run along-side the *Isle of Mull*. In 2017 problems continued, although the larger *Loch Fyne* was moved from the Lochaline - Fishnish service, with some services operated by the *Lord of the Isles* between trips to Lochboisdale. In the spring of 2018, further problems were experienced following damage to the *Clansman* during her dry-docking, leading to a need for a replacement propeller shaft. This resulted in the cancellation of the Mallaig - Lochboisdale service for a period and a reduction of Mallaig - Armadale sailings.

In June 2017 it was announced that the new ferry for the Ardrossan - Brodick service, due for delivery in 2018, would be called the *Glen Sannox*, reviving the name of one of the earliest Clyde car ferries. Unfortunately, following her launch from the Port Glasgow yard on 21st November, progress has been very slow and the prospects of her entering service in time for the 2018 summer season soon disappeared. Indeed it now seems possible she will not enter service until 2019, raising the question of whether building this, and her as yet un-named sister vessel, was too big a project for this small yard.

In July 2017 Caledonian MacBrayne took over the service to the sparsely populated island of Kerrera, previously privately operated. They chartered the vessel *Gylen Lady* and the operator and his crew became CalMac employees. A new vessel called the *Carvoria* was ordered from a Shetland shipyard and entered service in September.

In 2018 Caledonian MacBrayne said farewell to the last of the 'Island Class' vessels which had pioneered ro-ro services to many of the smaller Scottish islands. The *Eigg*, with her unique raised wheelhouse, was sold to Clare Island Ferries and the *Raasay* and *Canna* (previously on charter to Rathlin Island Ferry) were sold to Mr Humphrey O'Leary of Clare Island.

Clydelink, operators of the Gourock - Kilcreggan ferry service, were, in May 2018, relieved of their contract awarded by Strathclyde Partnership for Transport after several years of unreliable service with a small, superannuated vessel. The previous operator, Clyde Marine, resumed operating, using the *Chieftain*, which had been purpose built for the route as the *Seabus* in 2007. However, as something of a kick in the teeth for users of the route, who had endured poor service since 2014, fares rose by 40%.

In April 2018, the three passenger ferries serving the Northern Isles, the *Hamnavoe*, *Hrossey* and *Hjaltland* were purchased outright by Caledonian Maritime Assets Ltd (CMAL) with loan funding from the Scottish Government; they had previously been leased from Royal Bank of Scotland. An 18 month extension to the Northern Isles Ferry Services contract was also agreed, allowing Serco NorthLink Ferries to continue to operate the services until 31st October 2019.

Orkney operators, Pentland Ferries, ordered a new 85m catamaran in March 2017 to replace the 10 year old *Pentalina* in 2018. The new vessel, 25m longer than the existing craft, is being built at the Strategic Marine Shipyard, Vũng Tàu, Vietnam.

Nick Widdows

A **guide** to using
this book

Sections Listing is in seven sections. **Section 1** - Services from Great Britain and Ireland to the Continent and between Great Britain and Ireland (including services to/from the Isle of Man and Channel Islands), **Section 2** - Domestic services within Great Britain and Ireland, **Section 3** - Freight-only services from Great Britain and Ireland and domestic routes, **Section 4** - Minor vehicle ferries in Great Britain and Ireland (chain and cable ferries etc), **Section 5** - Major passenger-only operators, **Section 6** - Major car ferry operators in Northern Europe, **Section 7** - Companies not operating regular services possessing vehicle ferries which may be chartered or sold to other operators.

Order The company order within each section is alphabetical. Note that the definite article and words meaning 'company' or 'shipping company' (eg. 'AG', 'Reederei') do not count. However, where this is part of a ship's name it does count. Sorting is by normal English convention eg. 'Å' is treated the same as 'A' and comes at the start, not as a separate character which comes at the end of the alphabet as is the Scandinavian convention. Where ships are numbered, order is by number whether the number is expressed in Arabic or Latin digits.

Listing of Ships When a ship owned by a company listed in this book is on charter to another company listed, then she is shown under the company which operates her. When a ship owned by a company listed in this book is on charter to another company not listed, then she is shown under the company which owns her.

IMO Number All ships of 100t or greater (except vessels solely engaged in fishing, ships without mechanical means of propulsion (eg. chain ferries), pleasure yachts, ships engaged on special service (eg. lightships), hopper barges, hydrofoils, air cushion vehicles, floating docks and structures classified in a similar manner, warships and troopships, wooden ships) are required to be registered by the International Maritime Organisation (IMO), an agency of the United Nations. The seven digit number (the final digit is a check digit) is retained by the ship throughout her life, however much the vessel is rebuilt. This number is now required to be displayed on the ship externally and on top so that it can be read from the air. The scheme is administered by Lloyd's Register-Fairplay, who maintain a database of all ships in excess of 100t (with some exceptions), not just those classified through them. Some vessels which do not qualify for an IMO number have a Lloyd's number in the same series.

Company Information This section gives general information regarding the status of the company. That is, nationality, whether it is public or private sector and whether it is part of a larger group.

Management The Managing Director and Marketing Director or Manager of each company are listed. Where these posts do not exist, other equivalent people are listed. Where only initials are given, that person is, as far as is known, male.

Address This is the address of the company's administrative headquarters. In the case of some international companies, British and overseas addresses are given.

Telephone and Fax Numbers are expressed as follows: + [number] (this is the international dialling code which is dialled in combination with the number dialled for international calls (00 in the UK, Ireland and most other European countries); it is not used for calling within the country), ([number]) (this is the number which precedes area codes when making long-distance domestic calls - it is not dialled when calling from another country or making local calls (not all countries have this)), [number] (this is the rest of the number including, where appropriate, the area dialling code). UK '08' numbers are sometimes not available from overseas and the full number must be dialled in all circumstances.

Internet Email addresses and **Website** URLs are given where these are available; the language(s) used is shown. The language listed first is that which appears on the home page when accessed from a UK based computer; the others follow in alphabetical order. In a few cases Email facility is only available through the Website. To avoid confusion, there is no other punctuation on the Internet line.

Routes operated After each route there are, in brackets, details of **1** normal journey time, **2** regular vessel(s) used on the route (number as in list of vessels) and **3** frequencies (where a number per day is given, this relates to return sailings). In the case of freight-only sailings which operate to a regular schedule, departure times are given where they have been supplied. Please note that times are subject to quite frequent change and cancellation.

Winter and Summer In this book, Winter generally means the period between October and Easter while Summer means Easter to October. The peak Summer period is generally June, July and August. In Scandinavia, the Summer peak ends in mid-August whilst in the UK it starts rather later and generally stretches into the first or second week of September. Dates vary according to operator.

Terms The following words mean *'shipping company'* in various languages: Redereja (Latvian), Rederi (Danish, Norwegian, Swedish), Rederij (Dutch), Reederei (German) and Zegluga (Polish). The following words mean *'limited company'*: AB - Aktiebolaget (Swedish) (Finnish companies who use both the Finnish and Swedish terms sometimes express it as Ab), AG - Aktiengesellschaft (German), AS - Aksjeselskap (Norwegian), A/S - Aktie Selskabet (Danish), BV - Besloten Vennootschap (Dutch), GmbH - Gesellschaft mit beschränkter Haftung (German), NV - Naamloze Vennootschap (Dutch), Oy - (Finnish), Oyj - (Finnish (plc)) and SA - Société Anonyme (French).

Spelling Unlike previous editions, the convention now used in respect of town and country names is that local names are used for towns and areas of countries (eg. Göteborg rather than Gothenburg) and English names for countries (eg. Germany rather than Deutschland). Many towns in Finland have both Finnish and Swedish names; we have used the Finnish name except in the case of Åland which is a Swedish-speaking area. In the case of Danish towns, the alternative use of 'å' or 'aa' follows local convention. The following towns, islands and territories, which have alternative English names, are expressed using their local names - the English name is shown following: Antwerpen/Anvers - Antwerp, Funen - Fyn, Génova - Genoa, Gent - Ghent, Gothenburg - Göteborg, Hoek van Holland - Hook of Holland, Jylland - Jutland, København -Copenhagen, Oostende - Ostend, Porto - Oporto, Sevilla - Seville, Sjælland - Sealand and Venezia - Venice.

Types of Ferry

These distinctions are necessarily general and many ships will have features of more than one category.

Car Ferry Until about 1970, most vehicle ferries were primarily designed for the conveyance of cars and their passengers and foot passengers. Little regard was paid to the conveyance of lorries and trailers, since this sort of traffic had not begun to develop. Few vessels of this type are still in service.

Multi-purpose Ferry From about 1970 onwards vehicle ferries began to make more provision for freight traffic, sharing the same ship with passengers and cars. Features usually include higher vehicle decks, often with retractable mezzanine decks, enabling two levels of cars or one level of freight and coaches, and separate facilities (including cabins on quite short crossings) for freight drivers.

Cruise Ferry In the 1980s the idea of travelling on a ferry, not just to get from A to B but for the pleasure of the travel experience, became more and more popular and ferries were built with increasingly luxurious and varied passenger accommodation. Such vessels also convey cars and freight but the emphasis is on passenger accommodation with a high level of berths (sometimes providing berths for all passengers).

Ro-pax Ferry A vessel designed primarily for the carriage of freight traffic but which also carries a limited number of ordinary passengers. Features generally include a moderate passenger capacity - up to about 500 passengers - and a partly open upper vehicle deck. Modern ro-pax vessels are becoming increasingly luxurious with facilities approaching those of a cruise ferry.

Ro-ro Ferry A vessel designed for the conveyance of road freight, unaccompanied trailers and containers on low trailers (known as 'Mafis' although often made by other manufacturers). Some such vessels have no passenger accommodation but the majority can accommodate up to 12 passengers - the maximum allowed without a passenger certificate. On routes where there is a low level of driver-accompanied traffic (mainly the longer ones), ordinary passengers, with or without cars, can sometimes be conveyed. On routes with a high level of driver-accompanied traffic, passenger capacity will sometimes be higher but facilities tend to be geared to the needs of freight drivers eg. lounge with video, high level of cabins on routes of three hours or more. Technically such vessels are passenger ferries (having a passenger certificate).

Con-ro Many ro-ro vessels are capable of having ISO (International Standards Organisation) containers crane-loaded on the upper 'weather' deck. In this book the term con-ro applies only to vessels whose upper deck can only take containers and has no vehicle access.

Fast Ferry Streamlined vessel of catamaran or monohull construction, speed in excess of 30 knots, water jet propulsion, generally aluminium-built but some have steel hulls, little or no freight capacity and no cabins.

Timescale Although the book goes to press in August 2018, I have sought to reflect the situation as it will exist in September 2018 with regard to the introduction of new ships or other known changes. Vessels due to enter service after September 2018 are shown as '**Under Construction**'. This term does not necessarily man that physical work has started but an order has been placed with a shipyard. The book is updated at all stages of the production process where this is feasible, although major changes once the text has been paginated are not possible; there is also a 'Late News' section on page 219 for changes which cannot be incorporated into the text.

List of vessels

NO (A)	GROSS TONNAGE (B)	SERVICE SPEED (KNOTS)	NUMBER OF PASSENGERS		VEHICLE ACCESS DECK (D)	IMO NUMBER
1 NAME	‡26433t 87 22.0k		150m 290P 650C 100L		BA2 UK	1234567
	NAME	YEAR BUILT	LENGTH OVERALL	VEHICLE (C) DECK CAPACITY	FLAG (E)	

(A) **>>** = fast ferry, ● = vessel laid up, F = freight-only vessel (max 12 passengers), F+ = freight-only vessel (with passenger certificate), p = passenger-only vessel.

(B) C = Cars, L = Lorries (**15m**), T = Trailers (**13.5m**), r = can also take rail wagons, - = No figure quoted.

(C) B = Bow, A = Aft, S = Side, Q = Quarterdeck, R = Slewing ramp, 2 = Two decks can be loaded at the same time, C = Vehicles must be crane-loaded aboard, t = turntable ferry.

(D) The following abbreviations are used:

AG = Antigua and Barbuda	DK = Denmark	IR = Republic of Ireland	PT = Portugal
AL = Åland Islands	EE = Estonia	LU = Luxembourg	PL = Poland
BB = Barbados	ES = Spain	LT = Lithuania	RU = Russia
BE = Belgium	FO = Faroes	LV = Latvia	SG = Singapore
BM = Bermuda	FI = Finland	MT = Malta	SE = Sweden
BS = Bahamas	FR = France	NL = Netherlands	TR = Turkey
CY = Cyprus	GI = Gibraltar	NO = Norway	UK = United Kingdom
DE = Germany	IM = Isle of Man	PA = Panama	
	IT = Italy		

In the notes ships are in CAPITAL LETTERS, shipping lines and other institutions are in *italics*.

Capacity In this book, capacities shown are the maxima. Sometimes vessels operate at less than their maximum passenger capacity due to reduced crewing or to operating on a route on which they are not permitted to operate above a certain level. Car and lorry/trailer capacities are the maximum for either type. The two figures are not directly comparable. Some parts of a vessel may allow cars on two levels to occupy the space that a trailer or lorry occupies on one level, some may not; some parts of a vessel with low headroom may only be accessible to cars. All figures have to be approximate.

Ownership The ownership of many vessels is very complicated. Some are actually owned by finance companies and banks, some by subsidiary companies of the shipping lines, some by subsidiary companies of a holding company of which the shipping company is also a subsidiary and some by companies which are jointly owned by the shipping company and other interests like a bank, set up specifically to own one ship or a group of ships. In all these cases the vessel is technically chartered to the shipping company. However, in this book, only those vessels chartered from one shipping company to another or from a ship-owning company unconnected with the shipping line are recorded as being on charter. Vessels are listed under the current operator rather than the owner. Charter is 'bareboat' (without crew) unless otherwise stated. If chartered with crew, vessels are 'time-chartered'.

Gross Tonnage This is a measure of enclosed capacity rather than weight, based on a formula of one gross ton = 100 cubic feet. Even small alterations can alter the gross tonnage. Under old measurement systems, the capacity of enclosed car decks was not included but, under the 1969 Convention, all vessels laid down after 1982 have been measured by a new system which includes enclosed vehicle decks as enclosed space, thereby considerably increasing the tonnage of vehicle ferries. Under this Convention, from 1st January 1995 all vessels were due to be re-measured under this system. Tonnages quoted here are, where possible, those given by the shipping companies themselves.

The following people are gratefully thanked for their assistance with this publication, many of them in ferry companies in the UK and abroad: Richard Kirkman, Kalle Id, Kai Ortel, Matthew Punter, Gary Andrews, John Bryant, Andrew Cooke, Matthew Davies, Ian Hall, Peter Therkildsen, Ian Smith (Camrose Media), and Gomer Press.

Whilst every effort has been made to ensure that the facts contained here are correct, neither the publishers nor the writer can accept any responsibility for errors contained herein. We would, however, appreciate comments from readers, which we will endeavour to reflect in the next edition which we plan to publish in summer 2019.

Move your business in the right direction

The port of Oostende in Belgium offers you a long established know-how in handling ro-ro freight. It's up-to-date infrastructure includes versatile berthing facilities and well situated parking areas. Major terminus of European highways, inland waterways, railroads and an international airport make Oostende a true global cargo hub.

Focus on renewable energy is a strategic policy for the future of the port of Oostende to become the prime green port of Belgium.

Port Oostende

AG Port Oostende
Slijkensesteenweg 2
8400 Oostende, Belgium
Website: www.portofoostende.be
E-mail: info@portofoostende.be
Tel: +32 (0)59 340 711
Fax: +32 (0)59 340 710

Cap Finistere *(Miles Cowsill)*

SECTION 1 - GB AND IRELAND - MAJOR PASSENGER OPERATORS
BRITTANY FERRIES

THE COMPANY *Brittany Ferries* is the trading name of *BAI SA*, a French private sector company and the operating arm of the *Brittany Ferries Group*. The UK operations are run by *BAI (UK) Ltd*, a UK private sector company, wholly owned by the *Brittany Ferries Group*.

MANAGEMENT CEO Christophe Mathieu, **Commercial Directors, Passengers** Simon Johnson (interim), Joëlle Croc, Florence Gourdon, **Commercial Director, Freight** Simon Wagstaff.

ADDRESS Millbay Docks, Plymouth, Devon PL1 3EW.

TELEPHONE Reservations *All Services* +44 (0)330 159 7000, **Freight - Administration & Enquiries** +44 (0)330 159 5000, **Reservations** +44 (0)330 159 5000.

INTERNET Passenger - Website www.brittanyferries.com *(English, French, Spanish, German)*, **Freight Website** www.brittanyferriesfreight.co.uk *(English)*,

ROUTES OPERATED Conventional Ferries *All year* Plymouth - Roscoff (6 hrs (day), 7 hrs - 9 hrs (night); *ARMORIQUE*, *PONT-AVEN*; up to 2 per day (Summer), 1 per day (Winter)), Poole - Cherbourg (4 hrs 15 mins; *BARFLEUR*; 1 per day), Portsmouth - St Malo (8 hrs 45 mins (day), 10 hrs 45 mins (night); *BRETAGNE*; (1 per day), Portsmouth - Caen (Ouistreham) (6 hrs (day), 6 hrs - 8 hrs (night); *NORMANDIE*, *MONT ST MICHEL*; 3 per day), Portsmouth - Le Havre (5 hrs 30 mins (day), 9 hrs (night); *BAIE DE SEINE*, *ETRETAT*; 1 per day), Portsmouth - Santander (Spain) (24 hrs; *BAIE DE SEINE*, *CAP FINISTERE*, *PONT-AVEN*; up to 3 per week, Portsmouth - Bilbao (Spain) (24/32 hrs; *BAIE DE SEINE*, *CAP FINISTERE*; up to 3 per week, *Summer only* Plymouth - Santander (Spain) (19 hrs 30 mins; *PONT-AVEN*; 1 per week (April - October)), Cork - Roscoff (14 hrs-16½ hrs; *CONNEMARA*, *PONT-AVEN*; up to 2 per week), Cork - Santander (28 hrs-32 hrs; *CONNEMARA*; 2 per week **Fast Ferries** *Summer only* Portsmouth – Cherbourg (3 hrs; *NORMANDIE EXPRESS*; up to 2 per day (April-September)). **Freight-only service** Poole - Bilbao (31 hrs; *MN PELICAN*; 2 per week).

Note: Sailings to France and Spain operated by the CONNEMARA, BAIE DE SEINE and ETRETAT are branded 'économie'.

1	ARMORIQUE	29468t	09	23.0k	167.0m	1500P	470C	65L	BA2	FR	9364980
2	BAIE DE SEINE	22382t	03	22.0k	199.4m	596P	316C	154T	A	FR	9212163
3	BARFLEUR	20133t	92	19.0k	158.0m	1212P	590C	112T	BA2	FR	9007130
4	BRETAGNE	24534t	89	19.5k	151.0m	1926P	580C	84T	BA	FR	8707329
5	CAP FINISTERE	32728t	01	28.0k	203.9m	1608P	1000C	140T	BA	FR	9198927
6	CONNEMARA	26500t	07	24.0k	186.5m	800P	170C	140L	BA	CY	9349760
7	ETRETAT	26500t	08	23.5k	186.5m	800P	185C	120L	A	FR	9420423
8F	MN PELICAN	12076t	99	20.0k	154.5m	12P	-	115T	A2	FR	9170999
9	MONT ST MICHEL	35592t	02	21.2k	173.0m	2200P	880C	166T	BA2	FR	9238337
10	NORMANDIE	27541t	92	20.5k	161.0m	2120P	600C	126T	BA2	FR	9006253
11»	NORMANDIE EXPRESS	6581t	00	40.0k	97.2m	900P	260C	-	A	FR	8814134
12	PONT-AVEN	41748t	04	26.0k	184.3m	2400P	650C	85L	BA	FR	9268708

ARMORIQUE Built by STX Europe, Helsinki, Finland for *Brittany Ferries* to operate between Plymouth and Roscoff.

BAIE DE SEINE Built as the GOLFO DEI DELFINI by Stocznia Szczecinska, Szczecin, Poland for *Lloyd Sardegna* of Italy for service between Italy and Sardinia. However, due to late delivery the order was cancelled. In 2002 purchased by *DFDS Seaways*, and, during Winter 2002/03, passenger accommodation was enlarged and refitted, increasing passenger capacity from 308 to 596. In June 2003, renamed the DANA SIRENA, she replaced unmodified sister vessel, the DANA GLORIA on the Esbjerg – Harwich service. In February 2013 she was

Pont-Aven *(Jack Parsons)*

Mont St Michel *(Miles Cowsill)*

51

renamed the SIRENA SEAWAYS. At the end of September 2014 the route ceased and she moved to the Paldiski (Estonia) - Kapellskär route, replacing the PATRIA SEAWAYS. In December she was replaced by the LIVERPOOL SEAWAYS and laid up. During the early part of 2015 she performed relief work in the Baltic. In April 2015 she was chartered to *Brittany Ferries* for five years and renamed the BAIE DE SEINE. She entered service in May 2015.

BARFLEUR Built as the BARFLEUR by Kvaerner Masa-Yards, Helsinki for the *Truckline* (freight division of *Brittany Ferries*) Poole - Cherbourg service to replace two passenger vessels and to inaugurate a year-round passenger service. In 1999 the *Truckline* branding was dropped for passenger services and she was repainted into full *Brittany Ferries* livery. In 2005 operated partly Cherbourg - Poole and partly Cherbourg - Portsmouth but in 2006 returned to operating mainly to Poole. In February 2010, she was laid up. The conventional car ferry service ended the following month. In February 2011 she resumed service on the Poole - Cherbourg route. In September 2011 she was withdrawn again. In April 2012 chartered to *DFDS Seaways* to operate between Dover and Calais and renamed the DEAL SEAWAYS. In November 2012 returned to *Brittany Ferries* and renamed the BARFLEUR. Resumed the Poole - Cherbourg service in March 2013, replacing the COTENTIN but offering a service for both freight and passengers.

BRETAGNE Built by Chantiers de l'Atlantique, St Nazaire for the Plymouth - Santander and Cork - Roscoff services (with two sailings per week between Plymouth and Roscoff). In 1993 she was transferred to the Portsmouth - St Malo service. In 2004 also operated between Portsmouth and Cherbourg. In 2005 operated between Plymouth and Roscoff. In 2006 returned to the Portsmouth - St Malo route.

CAP FINISTERE Built as the SUPERFAST V by Howaldtswerke Deutsche Werft AG, Kiel, Germany for *Attica Enterprises* (now *Attica Group*) for use by *Superfast Ferries* of Greece. Initially operated between Patras and Ancona and in January 2007 switched to the Patras - Igoumenitsa - Bari route. In 2008 the route became Patras - Igoumenitsa - Ancona. In 2010 sold to *Brittany Ferries*, renamed the CAP FINISTERE and in March placed on the Portsmouth - Santander service, also operating some sailings between Portsmouth and Cherbourg. In 2011 began operating also between Portsmouth and Bilbao and only operated between Portsmouth and Cherbourg during the winter period. Now operates on Portsmouth – Santander and Portsmouth – Bilbao routes only.

CONNEMARA Built by CN Visentini, Porto Viro, Italy. Whilst under construction, sold to *Stena RoRo* of Sweden and provisionally named the STENA AUSONIA. However, before delivery a charter was arranged with *Balearia* of Spain and she was delivered as the BORJA. Operated between Barcelona and Palma (Majorca). In February 2010 the charter ended and she was laid up at Rotterdam. In April 2010 chartered to *Ave Line* and renamed the BALTIC AMBER. In October 2010 chartered to *DFDS Seaways* to replace the fire-damaged LISCO GLORIA. In March 2011 chartered to *LD Lines* to operate between Marseilles and Rades (Tunisia). In April she was moved to the Saint Nazaire (Nantes) - Gijon route. In June 2011 renamed the NORMAN ASTURIAS. In October 2011 the charter was ended but resumed the following month. Also operated between Poole, Santander and Gijon. In September 214 chartered to *Intershipping*, Morocco and operated between Algeciras and Tangiers. In February 2016 chartered to *Anek Lines* of Greece, renamed the ASTERION and placed on the Patras - Igoumenitsa - Venezia route. In April 2018 chartered to *Brittany Ferries*, renamed the CONNEMARA and inaugurated a new twice weekly Cork - Santander service, with an additional service to Roscoff.

ETRETAT Built as the NORMAN VOYAGER by CN Visentini, Porto Viro, Italy for *Epic Shipping* of the UK and chartered to *LD Lines*. Operated between Le Havre and Portsmouth and Le Havre and Rosslare. In September 2009 sub-chartered to *Celtic Link Ferries*. Initially operated between Cherbourg and Portsmouth and Cherbourg and Rosslare but the Portsmouth service was abandoned in November 2009. In October 2011 returned to *LD Lines* and placed on the St Nazaire - Gijon route. In November moved to the Portsmouth - Le Havre service and, following the establishment of the joint *LD Lines/DFDS* venture, the charter was transferred to *DFDS Seaways*. In April 2012 sold to *Stena RoRo*; she continued to be chartered to *DFDS*. In March 2014 chartered to *Brittany Ferries* and placed on the new

For ***any***one wanting a better way to France or Spain

Cork
Plymouth
Poole Portsmouth
Cherbourg Le Havre
Caen
Roscoff St Malo
Santander Bilbao

Close to home yet a world away, France and Spain offer discoveries around every corner.

Sail with us and take your pick from the widest choice of routes to the finest holiday regions. On board you'll enjoy award winning levels of service and comfort whilst we save you the long drive through northern France.

Go online to find our latest ferry and holiday offers.

brittanyferries.com

Brittany Ferries

Baie de Seine *(Miles Punter)*

Barfleur *(Kevin Mitchell)*

'économie' services between Portsmouth and Le Havre and Portsmouth and Santander. Renamed the ETRETAT.

MN PELICAN Built as the TRANS BOTNIA for *SeaTrans ANS* of Norway. Hull constructed by Santierul Naval, Galatz, Romania and vessel completed by Fosen Mekaniske Verksteder, Frengen, Norway. Chartered to *Transfennica* for service between Finland and Western Europe. In June 2006 sold to *Maritime Nantaise* of France. In January 2007 renamed the MN PELICAN. Placed on long term charter to the *French MOD*. In 2015 placed on the charter market. In January 2016 time chartered to *Brittany Ferries*.

MONT ST MICHEL Built by Van der Giessen-de Noord, Krimpen aan den IJssel, Rotterdam for *Brittany Ferries*. Used on the Portsmouth - Caen route.

NORMANDIE Built by Kvaerner Masa-Yards, Turku, Finland for *Brittany Ferries*. Used on the Portsmouth - Caen route.

NORMANDIE EXPRESS Incat Evolution 10 catamaran built as the INCAT TASMANIA. In November 2000 chartered to *TranzRail* of New Zealand and renamed THE LYNX. Placed on the Wellington – Picton service. In July 2003 replaced by 1997-built Incat 86m craft INCAT 046, given the marketing name 'The Lynx' and laid up. In Spring 2005 chartered to *Brittany Ferries* to operate on their Cherbourg – Portsmouth and Caen – Portsmouth services and renamed the NORMANDIE EXPRESS. In 2007 purchased by *Brittany Ferries*. In 2015 operated to Cherbourg and Le Havre but in 2016 and 2017 only operated to Cherbourg.

PONT-AVEN Built by Jos L Meyer Werft, Papenburg, Germany for *Brittany Ferries* to operate on the Plymouth - Roscoff, Plymouth - Santander and Cork - Roscoff routes.

Under Construction

13	HONFLEUR	42400t	19	22.0k	187.4m	1680P	550C	150L	BA	FR	
14	GALICIA	42000t	21	22.0k	214.5m	1000P	300C	180L	BA2	FR	-
15	SALAMANCA	42000t	22	22.0k	214.5m	1000P	300C	180L	BA2	FR	-

HONFLEUR Under construction by Flensburger Schiffbau-Gesellschaft, Flensburg, Germany. To operate on the Portsmouth - Caen route, replacing the NORMANDIE. To be LNG powered.

GALICIA Under construction by AVIC International Maritime Holdings, Weihai, China for *Stena RoRo*. Designed to run on either methanol or LPG but before delivery she will be fitted with scrubbers to run on fuel oil. Upon delivery to be chartered to *Brittany Ferries* for five years and replace the BAIE DE SEINE.

SALAMANCA Under construction by AVIC International Maritime Holdings, Weihai, China for *Stena RoRo*. Designed to run on LPG. Upon delivery to be chartered to *Brittany Ferries* for five years and replace the CAP FINISTERE.

CONDOR FERRIES

THE COMPANY *Condor Ferries Ltd* is a Channel Islands' private sector company owned by the *Condor Group*, Guernsey which is owned by *Macquarie European Infrastructure*.

MANAGEMENT Chief Executive Officer Paul Luxon, **Executive Director – Commercial** Greg Yeoman, **Executive Director – Finance** Jason Clark, **Executive Director – Operations** Elwyn Dop, **Executive Director – Freight** Steve Champion-Smith, **Head of Sales and Marketing** Justin Amey, **Trade Sales Manager** Jonathan Godson.

ADDRESS Head Office New Jetty Offices, White Rock, St Peter Port, Guernsey GY1 2LL, **Sales and Marketing** Condor House, New Harbour Road South, Hamworthy, Poole BH15 4AJ.

TELEPHONE Administration *Guernsey* +44 (0)1481 728620, ***Poole*** +44 (0)1202 207207, **Passenger Reservations** +44 (0)345 609 1024, **Freight Reservations** +44 (0)1481 728620.

INTERNET Email *Passenger* contactcentre@condorferries.co.uk **Freight** freight@condorferries.co.uk **Website** www.condorferries.com *(English, French, German)*,

ROUTES OPERATED *Conventional Passenger Ferry* Portsmouth to Guernsey (from 7 hrs) and Jersey (from 9 hrs) (*COMMODORE CLIPPER*; daily except Sun). *Fast Ferries* Poole - Guernsey (from 2 hrs 40 mins) and Jersey (from 4 hrs) (*CONDOR LIBERATION*; 1 per day), Guernsey (2 hrs) and Jersey (1 hr 20 mins) to St Malo (*CONDOR RAPIDE*; 1 per day). *Freight Ferry* Portsmouth - Guernsey - Jersey (10 hrs 30 min; *COMMODORE GOODWILL*; 1 per day), Guernsey - Jersey - St Malo (13 hrs; *COMMODORE GOODWILL*; 1 per week).

1	COMMODORE CLIPPER	14000t	99	18.0k	129.1m	500P	100C	92T	A	BS	9201750
2F	COMMODORE GOODWILL	11166t	96	17.3k	126.4m	12P	-	92T	A	BS	9117985
3»	CONDOR LIBERATION	6307t	10	39.0k	102.0m	873P	245C	12L	A	BS	9551363
4»	CONDOR RAPIDE	5007t	97	40.5k	86.6m	870P	200C	-	A	BS	9161560

COMMODORE CLIPPER Ro-pax vessel built by Van der Giessen-de Noord, Krimpen aan den IJssel, Rotterdam for *Commodore Ferries* to operate between Portsmouth and the Channel Islands. She replaced the ISLAND COMMODORE, a freight-only vessel. Her passenger capacity is normally restricted to 300 between the Channel Islands and the UK but is increased to 500 between Jersey and Guernsey.

COMMODORE GOODWILL Built by Koninklijke Scheldegroep BV, Vlissingen, The Netherlands for *Commodore Ferries*.

CONDOR LIBERATION Austal 102-metre Trimaran built speculatively by Austal Ships Pty, Fremantle, Australia as AUSTAL HULL 270. Laid up. In August 2014 sold to *Condor Ferries*. During autumn and early winter 2014/15 she was modified by Austal Ships in their shipyard at Balamban, Cebu, Philippines and in March 2015 renamed the CONDOR LIBERATION and placed on the Poole - Channel Islands service.

CONDOR RAPIDE Incat 86m catamaran built at Hobart, Tasmania, Australia as the INCAT 045. Chartered to *Transport Tasmania* of Australia and operated between Melbourne (Victoria) and Devonport (Tasmania). In 1999 she was chartered to the *Royal Australian Navy*, renamed the HMAS JERVIS BAY and took part in moving Australian troops from Darwin to Dili (East Timor) as part of the United Nations operation. She operated over 75 trips between the two points carrying personnel and equipment for the United Nations Transitional Administration in East Timor (UNTAET). The charter ended in May 2001 and she was renamed the INCAT 045 and laid up. In Spring 2003 she was chartered to *Traghetti Isole Sarde (TRIS)* of Italy, renamed the WINNER and operated between Genoa and Palau (Sardinia). In Autumn 2003 the charter ended, she resumed the name INCAT 045 and was laid up at Portland, Dorset. In 2004 chartered to *SpeedFerries* and renamed the SPEED ONE. In May 2008 purchased by *SpeedFerries*. In November 2008 the services ceased and the company went into administration. She was laid up at Tilbury. In May she was sold at auction to *Epic Shipping* of the UK and renamed the SEA LEOPARD. In April 2010 sold to *Condor Ferries* and renamed the CONDOR RAPIDE. Entered service in May 2010.

DAVID MACBRAYNE GROUP

THE COMPANY *David MacBrayne Limited* is a Scottish registered company, wholly owned by the Scottish Ministers. Its ferry operations are conducted through two subsidiary companies - *Argyll Ferries Ltd* and *CalMac Ferries Ltd* (trading as *Caledonian MacBrayne*). The majority of *CalMac Ferries* vessels are owned by *Caledonian Maritime Assets Limited*, a separate company which is also owned by the Scottish Ministers.

ARGYLL FERRIES

MANAGEMENT Interim Managing Director ; Robbie Drummond, **Head of Stakeholder Communications** David Cannon.

ADDRESS Ferry Terminal, Gourock PA19 1QP.

TELEPHONE Administration +44 (0)1475 650100, **Customer services** 0800 066 5000.

FAX Administration +44 (0)1475 650336,

INTERNET Email info@argyllferries.co.uk **Website** www.argyllferries.co.uk *(English)*,

Condor Liberation *(Kevin Mitchell)*

Commodore Clipper *(John Bryant)*

Ferries 2019

ROUTE OPERATED All-year passenger-only ferry Gourock - Dunoon (20 mins; *ALI CAT*, *ARGYLL FLYER*, *CORUISK* of *Caledonian MacBrayne (winter only)*; 1 or 2 per hour.

1p	ALI CAT	74t	99	-	19.8m	250P	0C	0L	-	UK
2p	ARGYLL FLYER	300t	01	19.5k	29.9m	227P	0C	0L	-	UK	9231016

ALI CAT Catamaran built for *Solent & Wight Line Cruises* of Ryde, Isle of Wight. She operated a passenger service from Cowes to Hamble and Warsash and cruises from Cowes. At times chartered to *Wightlink* to cover for their fast catamarans. In 2002 chartered to *Red Funnel Ferries* who had contracted with *Caledonian MacBrayne* to operate passenger-only services between Gourock and Dunoon in the morning and evening peaks. In June 2011 purchased by and operated by *Argyll Ferries*.

ARGYLL FLYER Built as the QUEEN OF ARAN II by OCEA, Les Sables d'Olonne, France for *Inis Mór Ferries*. In 2007 sold to *Aran Island Ferries* and renamed the BANRION CHONAMARA. In June 2011 sold to *Argyll Ferries*, renamed the ARGYLL FLYER and replaced the car ferry SATURN on the Gourock - Dunoon service.

CALEDONIAN MACBRAYNE

MANAGEMENT Interim Managing Director Robbie Drummond, **Business Development Director** Karen McGregor, **Head of Stakeholder Communications** David Cannon.

ADDRESS Ferry Terminal, Gourock PA19 1QP.

TELEPHONE Administration +44 (0)1475 650100, **Vehicle Reservations** +44 (0)800 066 5000.

FAX Administration +44 (0)1475 650336, **Vehicle Reservations** +44 (0)1475 635235.

INTERNET Email enquiries@calmac.co.uk **Website** www.calmac.co.uk *(English)*,

ROUTES OPERATED All-year vehicle ferries (frequencies are for Summer – services are listed alphabetically by mainland port or larger island port where service is between two islands).

Ardmhor (Barra) - Eriskay (40 mins; *LOCH ALAINN*; up to 5 per day), Ardrossan - Brodick (Arran) (55 mins; *CALEDONIAN ISLES*, *ISLE OF ARRAN*; up to 6 per day), Colintraive - Rhubodach (Bute) (5 mins; *LOCH DUNVEGAN*; frequent service), Kennacraig - Port Askaig (Islay) (2 hrs 5 mins; *FINLAGGAN*, *HEBRIDEAN ISLES*; up to 4 per day), Kennacraig - Port Ellen (Islay) (2 hrs 20 mins; *FINLAGGAN*, *HEBRIDEAN ISLES*; service currently suspended due to harbour works), Largs - Cumbrae Slip (Cumbrae) (10 mins; *LOCH RIDDON*, *LOCH SHIRA*; every 30 or 15 mins), Leverburgh (Harris) - Berneray (1 hr 10 mins; *LOCH PORTAIN*; 3-4 per day), Lochaline - Fishnish (Mull) (15 mins; *LOCHINVAR*; up to 14 per day), Mallaig - Armadale (Skye) (23 mins; *LOCHNEVIS* (Winter) *LOCH FYNE*, *LORD OF THE ISLES* (Summer); up to 9 per day (2 in Winter)), Mallaig - Lochboisdale (South Uist) (3 hrs 30 mins; *LORD OF THE ISLES*; 1per day), Oban - Castlebay (Barra) (5 hrs); *ISLE OF LEWIS*; 1 per day), Oban - Coll - Tiree (2 hrs 45 min to Coll 3 hrs 50 min to Tiree via Coll; *CLANSMAN*; 1 per day), Oban - Colonsay (2 hrs 15 mins; *CLANSMAN*; 5 per week), Oban - Craignure (Mull) (45 mins; *CORUISK*, *ISLE OF MULL*; up to 7 per day), Oban - Lismore (50 mins; *LOCH STRIVEN*; up to 5 per day), Sconser (Skye) - Raasay (15 mins; *HALLAIG*; up to 11 per day), Tarbert (Loch Fyne) - Portavadie (25 mins; *ISLE OF CUMBRAE*; up to 12 per day), Tayinloan - Gigha (20 mins; *LOCH RANZA*; up to 10 per day), Tobermory (Mull) - Kilchoan (35 mins; *LOCH TARBERT*; up to 7 per day), Uig (Skye) - Lochmaddy (North Uist) (1 hr 45 mins; *HEBRIDES*; 1 or 2 per day), Uig (Skye) - Tarbert (Harris) (1 hr 40 mins; *HEBRIDES*; 1 or 2 per day), Ullapool - Stornoway (Lewis) (2 hrs 45 mins; *LOCH SEAFORTH*; up to 3 per day (one freight only)), Wemyss Bay - Rothesay (Bute) (35 mins; *ARGYLE*, *BUTE*; hourly).

All-year passenger and restricted vehicle ferries (frequencies are for Summer) Gallanach (near Oban) - Kerrera (5 mins; *CARVORIA*; up to 12 per day), Fionnphort (Mull) - Iona (5 mins; *LOCH BUIE*; frequent), Mallaig - Eigg - Muck - Rum - Canna - Mallaig (round trip 7 hrs (all islands); *LOCHNEVIS*; at least 1 sailing per day - most islands visited daily).

58

Note Although these services are operated by vehicle ferries special permission is required to take a vehicle and tourist cars are not normally conveyed.

Summer-only vehicle ferries Ardrossan - Campbeltown (2 hrs 30 mins; *ISLE OF ARRAN*; 3 per week), Claonaig - Lochranza (Arran) (30 mins; *CATRIONA*; up to 9 per day), Kennacraig - Port Askaig - Colonsay - Oban (3 hrs 35 mins; *HEBRIDEAN ISLES*; 1 per week).

Winter-only vehicle ferry **Tarbert (Loch Fyne) - Lochranza (Arran) (1 hr; *varies*; 1 per day),**

1	ARGYLE	2643t	07	14.0k	69.0m	450P	60C	-	BAS	UK	9365178
2	BUTE	2612t	05	14.0k	69.0m	450P	60C	-	AS	UK	9319741
3	CALEDONIAN ISLES	5221t	93	15.0k	94.3m	1000P	120C	10L	BA	UK	9051284
4	CARVORIA	9t	17	8.0k	-	12P	1C	-	B	UK	
5	CATRIONA	499t	16	9.0k	43.5m	150P	23C	2L	BA	UK	9759862
6	CLANSMAN	5499t	98	16.5k	99.0m	638P	90C	6L	BA	UK	9158953
7	CORUISK	1599t	03	14.0k	65.0m	250P	40C	-	BA	UK	9274836
8	FINLAGGAN	5626t	11	16.5k	89.9m	550P	88C	-	BA	UK	9482902
9	HALLAIG	499t	13	9.0k	43.5m	150P	23C	2L	BA	UK	9652832
10	HEBRIDEAN ISLES	3040t	85	15.0k	85.1m	494P	68C	10L	BAS	UK	8404812
11	HEBRIDES	5506t	00	16.5k	99.0m	612P	110C	6L	BA	UK	9211975
12	ISLE OF ARRAN	3296t	84	15.0k	85.0m	446P	68C	8L	BA	UK	8219554
13	ISLE OF CUMBRAE	201t	77	8.5k	37.7m	139P	18C	-	BA	UK	7521625
14	ISLE OF LEWIS	6753t	95	18.0k	101.2m	680P	123C	10L	BA	UK	9085974
15	ISLE OF MULL	4719t	88	15.0k	90.1m	962P	80C	20L	BA	UK	8608339
16	LOCH ALAINN	396t	98	10.0k	43.0m	150P	24C	-	BA	UK	9147722
17	LOCH BHRUSDA	246t	96	8.0k	35.4m	150P	18C	-	BA	UK	9129483
18	LOCH BUIE	295t	92	9.0k	35.5m	250P	9C	-	BA	UK	9031375
19	LOCH DUNVEGAN	549t	91	9.0k	54.2m	200P	36C	-	BA	UK	9006409
20	LOCH FYNE	549t	91	9.0k	54.2m	200P	36C	-	BA	UK	9006411
21	LOCH LINNHE	206t	86	9.0k	35.5m	199P	12C	-	BA	UK	8512308
22	LOCH PORTAIN	950t	03	10.5k	50.0m	200P	32C	-	BA	UK	9274824
23	LOCH RANZA	206t	87	9.0k	35.7m	199P	12C	-	BA	UK	8519887
24	LOCH RIDDON	206t	86	9.0k	35.5m	199P	12C	-	BA	UK	8519875
25	LOCH SEAFORTH	8478t	14	19.2k	116.0m	700P	143C	20L	BA	UK	9665437
26	LOCH SHIRA	1024t	07	13.0k	43.0m	250P	24C	-	BA	UK	9376919
27	LOCH STRIVEN	206t	86	9.0k	35.7m	199P	12C	-	BA	UK	8512293
28	LOCH TARBERT	211t	92	9.0k	34.5m	149P	18C	-	BA	UK	9039389
29	LOCHINVAR	523t	14	9.0k	43.5m	150P	23C	2L	BA	UK	9652844
30	LOCHNEVIS	941t	00	13.0k	49.1m	190P	14C	-	A	UK	9209063
31	LORD OF THE ISLES	3504t	89	16.0k	84.6m	506P	56C	16L	BAS	UK	8710869

Note In the following list, Gaelic names are shown in parenthesis.

ARGYLE *(EARRA-GHÀIDHEAL)*, BUTE *(EILEAN BHÒID)* Built by Stocznia Remontowa, Gdansk, Poland to operate on the Wemyss Bay - Rothesay route.

CALEDONIAN ISLES *(EILEANAN CHALEDONIA)* Built by Richards Shipyard, Lowestoft, UK for the Ardrossan - Brodick (Arran) service.

CARVORIA Built by Malakoff Limited, Lerwick, Shetland for *Caledonian Maritime Assets* and chartered to *Caledonian MacBrayne* to replace the chartered GYLEN LADY on the Gallanach - Kerrera service.

CATRIONA Built by Ferguson Marine Engineering, Port Glasgow. Near sister vessel of the HALLAIG and LOCHINVAR. Operates on the Claonaig - Lochranza service during the summer and other routes during the winter.

CLANSMAN *(FEAR-CINNIDH)* Built by Appledore Shipbuilders Ltd, Appledore, UK to replace the LORD OF THE ISLES on the Oban - Coll and Tiree and Oban - Castlebay and Lochboisdale services in the summer. She also serves as winter relief vessel on the Stornoway, Tarbert, Lochmaddy, Mull/Colonsay and Brodick routes.

CORUISK *(COIR' UISG')* Built by Appledore Shipbuilders Ltd, Appledore, UK to operate on the Mallaig - Armadale route during the summer. During the winter operates for *Argyle Ferries* in lieu of the ALI CAT during peak periods and when that vessel cannot sail due to adverse weather. In summer 2016 operated as second vessel on the Oban - Craignure service and this was repeated in 2017.

FINLAGGAN *(FIONN LAGAN)* Built by Stocznia Remontowa, Gdansk, Poland for the Kennacraig - Islay service.

HALLAIG *(HALLAIG)* Built by Ferguson Shipbuilders, Port Glasgow, UK to replace the LOCH STRIVEN on the Sconser - Raasay service. The vessel has both diesel and battery electric propulsion and can be 'plugged in' to a land supply on Raasay overnight.

HEBRIDEAN ISLES *(EILEANAN INNSE GALL)* Built by Cochrane Shipbuilders, Selby UK for the Uig - Tarbert/Lochmaddy service. She was used initially on the Ullapool - Stornoway and Oban - Craignure/Colonsay services pending installation of link-span facilities at Uig, Tarbert and Lochmaddy. She took up her regular role in May 1986. From May 1996 she no longer operated direct services in summer between Tarbert and Lochmaddy, this role being taken on by the new Harris - North Uist services of the LOCH BHRUSDA. In 2001 she was replaced by the HEBRIDES and transferred to the Islay service. In Autumn 2002 she operated between Scrabster and Stromness for *NorthLink Orkney and Shetland Ferries* before port modifications at Scrabster enabled the HAMNAVOE to enter service in Spring 2003. She then returned to the Islay service. She also relieved on the *NorthLink* Pentland Firth service between 2004 and 2007.

HEBRIDES *(INNSE GALL)* Built by Ferguson Shipbuilders Ltd, Port Glasgow, UK for the Uig - Tarbert and Uig - Lochmaddy services.

ISLE OF ARRAN *(EILEAN ARAINN)* Built by Ferguson Ailsa, Port Glasgow, UK for the Ardrossan - Brodick service. In 1993 transferred to the Kennacraig - Port Ellen/Port Askaig service, also undertaking the weekly Port Askaig - Colonsay - Oban summer service. From then until 1997/98 she also relieved on the Brodick, Coll/Tiree, Castlebay/Lochboisdale, Craignure and Tarbert/Lochmaddy routes in winter. In 2001 she was replaced by the HEBRIDEAN ISLES and became a reserve for the larger vessels. She has operated on the two-ship Islay service in summer since 2003; this service is now all-year-round. Following the delivery of the FINLAGGAN in May 2011 she became a spare vessel, and operates extra services between Ardrossan and Brodick and Ardrossan and Campbeltown during the peak summer period.

ISLE OF CUMBRAE *(EILEAN CHUMRAIGH)* Built by Ailsa Shipbuilding Ltd, Troon, UK for the Largs - Cumbrae Slip (Cumbrae) service. In 1986 she was replaced by the LOCH LINNHE and the LOCH STRIVEN and transferred to the Lochaline - Fishnish (Mull) service. She used to spend most of the winter as secondary vessel on the Kyle of Lochalsh - Kyleakin service; however, this ceased following the opening of the Skye Bridge in 1995. In 1997 she was transferred to the Colintraive - Rhubodach service. In Summer 1999 she was transferred to the Tarbert - Portavadie service. In May 2015 replaced by the new LOCHINVAR and laid up. In summer 2016 returned to the Tarbert - Portavadie service.

ISLE OF LEWIS *(EILEAN LEÒDHAIS)* Built by Ferguson Shipbuilders Ltd, Port Glasgow, UK for the Ullapool - Stornoway service. In February 2015 replaced by the new LOCH SEAFORTH. During peak summer period 2015 she operated an additional sailing between Ullapool and Stornoway. In summer 2016 operated between Oban and Castlebay.

ISLE OF MULL *(AN T-EILEAN MUILEACH)* Built by Appledore Ferguson, Port Glasgow, UK for the Oban - Craignure (Mull) service. She also operates some Oban - Colonsay sailings and until 1997/98 was the usual winter relief vessel on the Ullapool - Stornoway service. She has also deputised on the Oban - Castlebay/Lochboisdale and Oban - Coll/Tiree routes.

Isle of Mull *(Mark Nicolson)*

Loch Fyne *(Brian Maxted)*

Catriona *(Brain Maxted)*

Loch Riddon *(Brian Maxted)*

Clansman *(Mark Nicolson)*

Loch Seaforth *(George Holland)*

Isle of Lewis *(George Holland)*

Lord of the Isles *(Miles Cowsill)*

LOCH ALAINN *(LOCH ÀLAINN)* Built by Buckie Shipbuilders Ltd, Buckie, UK for the Lochaline - Fishnish service. Launched as the LOCH ALINE but renamed the LOCH ALAINN before entering service. After a brief period on the service for which she was built, she was transferred to the Colintraive - Rhubodach route. In 1998 she was transferred to the Largs - Cumbrae Slip service. In 2007 moved to the Ardmhor (Barra) - Eriskay service. She relieves the larger 'Loch' class vessels in the winter, with her own service covered by the LOCH BHRUSDA.

LOCH BHRUSDA *(LOCH BHRÙSTA)* Built by McTay Marine, Bromborough, Wirral, UK to inaugurate a new Otternish (North Uist) - Leverburgh (Harris) service. In 2001 the service became Berneray - Leverburgh. In 2003 she moved to the Eriskay - Barra service, previously operated by *Comhairle Nan Eilean Siar* vessels. In 2007 she became a spare vessel on the Clyde. In summer 2016 operated between Mallaig and Armadale. Note 'Bhrusda' is pronounced "Vroosta".

LOCH BUIE *(LOCH BUIDHE)* Built by J W Miller & Sons Ltd, St Monans, Fife, UK for the Fionnphort (Mull) - Iona service to replace the MORVERN (see *Arranmore Island Ferry Services*) and obviate the need for a relief vessel in the summer. Due to height restrictions, loading arrangements for vehicles taller than private cars are stern-only. Only islanders' cars and service vehicles (eg mail vans, police) are carried; no tourist vehicles are conveyed.

LOCH DUNVEGAN *(LOCH DÙNBHEAGAN)* Built by Ferguson Shipbuilders Ltd, Port Glasgow, UK for the Kyle of Lochalsh - Kyleakin service. On the opening of the Skye Bridge in October 1995 she was withdrawn from service and offered for sale. In Autumn 1997, she returned to service on the Lochaline - Fishnish route. In 1998 she was due to be transferred to the Colintraive - Rhubodach route but this was delayed because of problems in providing terminal facilities. She operated on the Clyde and between Mallaig and Armadale during the early summer and spent the rest of that summer laid up. In 1999 she was transferred to the Colintraive - Rhubodach route.

LOCH FYNE *(LOCH FINE)* Built by Ferguson Shipbuilders Ltd, Port Glasgow, UK for the Kyle of Lochalsh - Kyleakin service (see the LOCH DUNVEGAN). In Autumn 1997, she also served on the Lochaline - Fishnish route and was transferred to this route as regular vessel in 1998. In summer 2017 transferred to the Mallaig - Armadale route.

LOCH LINNHE *(AN LINNE DHUBH)* Built by Richard Dunston (Hessle) Ltd, Hessle, UK. Until 1997 she was used mainly on the Largs - Cumbrae Slip (Cumbrae) service and until Winter 1994/95 she was usually used on the Lochaline - Fishnish service during the winter. Since then she has relieved on various routes in winter. In Summer 1998 she operated mainly on the Tarbert - Portavadie route. In 1999 she was transferred to the Tobermory - Kilchoan service in summer.

LOCH PORTAIN *(LOCH PORTAIN)* Built by McTay Marine, Bromborough, Wirral, UK (hull constructed in Poland) to replace the LOCH BHRUSDA on the Berneray - Leverburgh service.

LOCH RANZA *(LOCH RAONASA)* Built by Richard Dunston (Hessle) Ltd, Hessle, UK for the Claonaig - Lochranza (Arran) seasonal service and used a relief vessel in the winter. In 1992 she was replaced by the LOCH TARBERT and transferred to the Tayinloan - Gigha service.

LOCH RIDDON *(LOCH RAODAIN)* Built by Richard Dunston (Hessle) Ltd, Hessle, UK. Until 1997 she was used almost exclusively on the Colintraive - Rhubodach service. In 1997, she was transferred to the Largs - Cumbrae Slip service. In January 2014 she became regular vessel on the Oban - Lismore service. However, after problems with using the slipways, she became the second vessel on the Largs - Cumbrae Slip service.

LOCH SEAFORTH *(LOCH SHIPHOIRT)* Built by Flensburger Schiffbau-Gesellschaft, Flensburg, Germany for the Stornoway - Ullapool service, replacing the ISLE OF LEWIS and freight vessel CLIPPER RANGER.

LOCH SHIRA *(LOCH SIORA)* Built by Ferguson Shipbuilders, Port Glasgow, UK for the Largs – Cumbrae Slip route.

LOCH STRIVEN *(LOCH SROIGHEANN)* Built by Richard Dunston (Hessle) Ltd, Hessle, UK. Used mainly on the Largs - Cumbrae Slip service until 1997. In Winter 1995/96 and 1996/97 she was used on the Tarbert - Portavadie and Claonaig - Lochranza routes. In 1997 she took over the Sconser - Raasay service. In winter 2014 replaced by the HALLAIG. In summer 2014 transferred to the Oban - Lismore route.

LOCH TARBERT *(LOCH AN TAIRBEIRT)* Built by J W Miller & Sons Ltd, St Monans, Fife, UK for the Claonaig - Lochranza service. She was the winter relief vessel on the Largs - Cumbrae Slip route between 1994/95 and 2007/08.

LOCHINVAR *(LOCH AN BARR)* As the HALLAIG. Initially operated on the Tarbert - Portavadie route. In summer 2016 transferred to Mallaig - Armadale and in summer 2017 to the Lochaline - Fishnish route.

LOCHNEVIS *(LOCH NIBHEIS)* Built by Ailsa Shipbuilding, Troon, UK to replace the LOCHMOR on the Mallaig - Small Isles service and the winter Mallaig - Armadale service. Although a vehicle ferry, cars are not normally carried to the Small Isles; the ro-ro facility is used for the carriage of agricultural machinery and livestock and it is possible to convey a vehicle on the ferry from which goods can be unloaded directly onto local transport rather than transhipping at Mallaig.

LORD OF THE ISLES *(RIGH NAN EILEAN)* Built by Appledore Ferguson, Port Glasgow, UK to replace the CLAYMORE on the Oban - Castlebay and Lochboisdale services and also the COLUMBA (1420t, 1964) on the Oban - Coll and Tiree service. She took over the Mallaig - Armadale and Mallaig - Outer Isles services in July 1998 but returned to her previous routes during the winter period. In Spring 2003 the Mallaig – Armadale service was taken over by the PIONEER standing in for the new CORUISK and she operated services from Oban to South Uist and Barra. In summer 2016 operated between Mallaig and Lochboisdale and also between Mallaig and Armadale.

Under Construction

32	GLEN SANNOX	5000t	19	16.5k	102.4m	1000P	127C	16L	BA	UK	9794513
33	NEWBUILDING	5000t	19	16.5k	102.4m	1000P	127C	16L	BA	UK	-

GLEN SANNOX *(GLEANN SHANNAIG)*, NEWBUILDING Under construction by Ferguson Marine Engineering, Port Glasgow for *Caledonian Maritime Assets* and to be chartered to *Caledonian MacBrayne*. The GLEN SANNOX will operate on he Ardrossan - Brodick service and the second vessel is likely to operate between Uig and Harris and North Uist.

DFDS SEAWAYS

THE COMPANY *DFDS Seaways* is a business unit within *DFDS A/S*, a Danish private sector company. Services from Dover, Newhaven and Marseilles are operated by *DFDS Seaways France* which was inaugurated in March 2013 following the establishment of a *DFDS Seaways/LD Lines* joint venture in November 2012. It is 82% owned by *DFDS* and 18% by *Louis Dreyfus Armateurs*. The Newhaven - Dieppe route is branded as *Transmanche Ferries*, operating under a franchise awarded by *Syndicat Mixte de L'Activité Transmanche* in Dieppe. In June 2018 DFDS acquired UN RoRo of

MANAGEMENT President and CEO DFDS A/S Niels Smedegaard, **Executive Vice President Shipping Division** Peder Gellert Pedersen, **Managing Director, DFDS Seaways PLC** Sean Potter, **Senior Vice President South** Kell Robdrup, **Head of English Channel Business Area** Kasper Moos, **Head of Passenger Business Area** Brian Thorsted Hansen.

ADDRESS (UK) DFDS A/S, Whitfield Court, White Cliffs Business Park Whitfield, Dover CT16 3PX.

TELEPHONE Administration +44 (0)1304 874001. **Passenger Reservations** *Dover-Calais* 0871 574 7223, +44 (0)208 127 8303, *Newcastle - Ijmuiden* 0871 522 9955, +44 330 333 0245, *Newhaven - Dieppe* 0844 576 8836, +33 232 144 729 **Freight Reservations** see website.

Carvoria *(Brian Maxted)*

Côte des Flandres *(Darren Holdaway)*

Ferries 2019

INTERNET Websites *Passenger* www.dfdsseaways.co.uk *(various)* **Freight** freight.dfdsseaways.com *(English)* **Corporate** www.dfds.com *(English)*,

ROUTES OPERATED *Passenger ferries* Newcastle (North Shields) - IJmuiden (near Amsterdam, The Netherlands) (15 hrs; *KING SEAWAYS, PRINCESS SEAWAYS*; daily). **ROUTES OPERATED** Dover - Dunkerque (2 hrs; *DELFT SEAWAYS, DOVER SEAWAYS, DUNKERQUE SEAWAYS*; 12 per day), Dover - Calais (1 hr 30 mins; *CALAIS SEAWAYS, CÔTE DES FLANDRES, CÔTE DES DUNES*; 15 per day), Newhaven - Dieppe (4 hrs; *CÔTE D'ALBÂTRE, SEVEN SISTERS*; up to 3 per day, *Freight ferries* Esbjerg - Immingham (18 hrs; *ARK DANIA*,; 6 per week), Cuxhaven - Immingham (19 hrs; *JUTLANDIA SEAWAYS, STENA FORETELLER*; 4/5 per week), Göteborg - Immingham (26 hrs (direct), *45 hrs (via Brevik (Fri)); *FICARIA SEAWAYS, FREESIA SEAWAYS, MAGNOLIA SEAWAYS*; 7 per week), Brevik - Immingham (25 hrs (direct), 42 hrs (via Göteborg); *FICARIA SEAWAYS, FREESIA SEAWAYS, MAGNOLIA SEAWAYS*; 2 per week), Göteborg - Brevik (Norway) - Gent (Belgium) (Göteborg 32 hrs, Brevik 32 hrs; *ARK GERMANIA, BEGONIA SEAWAYS, PETUNIA SEAWAYS, PRIMULA SEAWAYS*; 8 per week (1 per weeks via Brevik), Vlaardingen - Immingham (14 hrs; *ANGLIA SEAWAYS, GARDENIA SEAWAYS, TULIPA SEAWAYS*; 8 per week), Vlaardingen - Felixstowe (7 hrs; *BRITANNIA SEAWAYS, SELANDIA SEAWAYS, SUECIA SEAWAYS*; 3 per day). Note: vessels are often switched between routes.

1F	ANGLIA SEAWAYS	13073t	00	18.5k	142.5m	12P	-	114T	A	DK	9186649
2F	ARK DANIA	33313t	14	20.0k	195.2m	12P	-	206T	A	DK	9609964
3F	ARK GERMANIA	33313t	14	20.0k	195.2m	12P	-	206T	A	DK	9609952
4F	BEGONIA SEAWAYS	37722t	04	22.5k	230.0m	12P	-	340T	AS	DK	9262089
5F	BRITANNIA SEAWAYS	24196t	00	21.1k	197.5m	12P	-	200T	AS	DK	9153032
6	CALAIS SEAWAYS	28833t	91	21.0k	163.6m	1850P	600C	100L	BA2	FR	8908466
7	CÔTE D'ALBÂTRE	18425t	06	22.0k	112.0m	600P	300C	62L	BA	FR	9320128
8	CÔTE DES DUNES	33796t	01	25.0k	186.0m	1500P	700C	120L	BA2	FR	9232527
9	CÔTE DES FLANDRES	33940t	05	25.0k	186.0m	1500P	700C	120L	BA2	FR	9305843
10	DELFT SEAWAYS	35923t	06	25.5k	187.0m	780P	200C	120L	BA2	UK	9293088
11	DOVER SEAWAYS	35923t	06	25.8k	187.0m	780P	200C	120L	BA2	UK	9318345
12	DUNKERQUE SEAWAYS	35923t	05	25.8k	187.0m	780P	200C	120L	BA2	UK	9293076
13F	FICARIA SEAWAYS	37939t	04	22.5k	230.0m	12P	-	340T	AS	DK	9320568
14F	FINLANDIA SEAWAYS	11530t	00	20.0k	162.2m	12P	-	140T	A	LT	9198721
15F	FIONIA SEAWAYS	25609t	09	20.0k	184.8m	12P	-	250T	AS	UK	9395343
16F	FREESIA SEAWAYS	37722t	04	22.5k	230.0m	12P	-	340T	AS	DK	9274848
17F	GARDENIA SEAWAYS	32000t	17	21.0k	209.6m	12P	-	262T	A2	LT	9809095
18F	JUTLANDIA SEAWAYS	25609t	10	20.0k	184.8m	12P	-	250T	AS	UK	9395355
19	KING SEAWAYS	31788t	87	20.0k	161.6m	1400P	600C	104T	BA	DK	8502406
20F	MAGNOLIA SEAWAYS	32289t	03	22.5k	199.8m	12P	-	280T	AS	DK	9259496
21F	PETUNIA SEAWAYS	32289t	04	22.5k	199.8m	12P	-	280T	AS	DK	9259501
22F	PRIMULA SEAWAYS	37985t	04	22.5k	229.8m	12P	-	340T	AS	DK	9259513
23	PRINCESS SEAWAYS	31356t	86	18.5k	161.0m	1600P	600C	100T	BA	DK	8502391
24F	SELANDIA SEAWAYS	24196t	98	21.0k	197.5m	12P	-	206T	A	DK	9157284
25	SEVEN SISTERS	18425t	06	22.0k	112.0m	600P	300C	62L	BA	FR	9320130
26F	STENA FORETELLER	24688t	02	22.0k	195.3m	12P	-	210T	A2	SE	9214666
27F	SUECIA SEAWAYS	24196t	99	21.0k	197.5m	12P	-	206T	AS	DK	9153020
28F	TULIPA SEAWAYS	32000t	17	21.0k	209.6m	12P	-	262T	A2	LT	9809100

ANGLIA SEAWAYS Built as the MAERSK ANGLIA by Guangzhou Shipyard International, Guangzhou, China for *Norfolkline*. Entered service as the GUANGZHOU 7130011 (unofficially the 'China II') but renamed shortly afterwards. Operated on the Scheveningen (from 2007 Vlaardingen) - Felixstowe service. In June 2009 moved to the Heysham - Dublin route. In August 2010 renamed the ANGLIA SEAWAYS. In January 2011 service withdrawn. In February 2011 chartered to *Seatruck Ferries* to inaugurate their new Heysham - Dublin service. In January 2012 returned to *DFDS Seaways* and placed on the Vlaardingen - Immingham route as an extra vessel. In April 2012 moved to the Zeebrugge - Rosyth service but proved too slow. In May chartered to *Seatruck Ferries* to operate between Heysham and

Calais Seaways *(Darren Holdaway)*

Delft Seaways *(Brian Maxted)*

Côte d'Albâtre *(Richard Kirkman)*

Tulipa Seaways *(Rob de Visser)*

Belfast. In August, this service ceased and she was switched to the Heysham - Dublin route and in September to the Heysham - Warrenpoint route. In April 2014 returned to *DFDS Seaways* and placed on Kiel - St Petersburg service. In July 2014 transferred to the Travemünde - Klaipėda route and in September to the Vlaardingen - Immingham service, providing additional capacity. In March 2015 placed on the charter market. In May 2015 returned to the Rotterdam - Felixstowe route.

ARK DANIA, ARK GERMANIA Built by P+S Werften GmbH, Stralsund, Germany. They are used for the German/Danish joint ARK Project providing NATO transport but are also available for *DFDS* use and charter when not required. They have a crane for loading containers on the weather deck. In December 2012 the order for these vessels was cancelled due to late delivery. Following negotiations with the shipyard it was agreed that they would be completed under a new contract which was signed in February 2013. Both vessels were delivered to *DFDS* in April 2014, the ARK GERMANIA almost complete, the ARK DANIA still incomplete. The latter vessel was towed to the Fayard shipyard, Odense, to be completed. The ARK GERMANIA entered service a few days after delivery, the ARK DANIA in November 2014.

BEGONIA SEAWAYS Built as the TOR BEGONIA by Flensburger Schiffbau-Gesellschaft, Flensburg, Germany for *DFDS Tor Line*. Operates on the Göteborg - Immingham/Brevik route. In Summer 2009 lengthened by 30m by MWB Motorenwerke Bremerhaven AG, Germany. In July 2012 renamed the BEGONIA SEAWAYS.

BRITANNIA SEAWAYS Built as the TOR BRITANNIA by Fincantieri-Cantieri Navali Italiani SpA, Ancona, Italy for *DFDS Tor Line*. Operated on the Göteborg - Immingham route until 2004 when she was transferred to the Esbjerg - Immingham route. In January 2010 chartered to *Norfolkline* to operate between Vlaardingen and Felixstowe. In May 2011 renamed the BRITANNIA SEAWAYS.

CALAIS SEAWAYS Built as the PRINS FILIP by NV Boelwerf SA, Temse, Belgium for *Regie voor Maritiem Transport (RMT)* of Belgium for the Oostende - Dover service. Although completed in 1991, she did not enter service until May 1992. In 1994 the British port became Ramsgate. Withdrawn in 1997 and laid up for sale. In 1998 she was sold to *Stena RoRo* and renamed the STENA ROYAL. In November 1998 she was chartered to *P&O Ferries* to operate as a freight-only vessel on the Dover - Zeebrugge route. In Spring 1999 it was decided to charter the vessel on a long-term basis and she was repainted into *P&O Stena Line* (later *P&O Ferries*) colours and renamed the P&OSL AQUITAINE. In Autumn 1999 she was modified to make her suitable to operate between Dover and Calais and was transferred to that route, becoming a passenger vessel again. In 2002 renamed the PO AQUITAINE and in 2003 the PRIDE OF AQUITAINE. In September 2005 sold to *LD Lines* and renamed the NORMAN SPIRIT. In October, inaugurated a Le Havre - Portsmouth service, replacing that previously operated by *P&O Ferries*. In November 2009 moved to the Dover - Boulogne route. In March 2010 chartered to *TransEuropa Ferries*, placed on the Oostende - Ramsgate service (as part of a joint venture) and renamed the OOSTENDE SPIRIT. In May 2011 returned to the Portsmouth - Le Havre route and renamed the NORMAN SPIRIT. In November 2011 chartered to *DFDS Seaways* to add extra capacity to their Dover - Dunkerque route. In February 2012 transferred to the new Dover - Calais route, joint with *DFDS Seaways*. Ownership transferred to *DFDS Seaways* in late 2012. In March 2013 refurbished, repainted into *DFDS Seaways* colours and renamed the CALAIS SEAWAYS.

CÔTE D'ALBÂTRE Built by Astilleros Barreras SA, Vigo, Spain for *Transmanche Ferries* to operate between Newhaven and Dieppe. In February 2009 she was moved to the Boulogne - Dover and Dieppe - Dover routes for *LD Lines*. In September 2009 moved to the Le Havre - Portsmouth route. The vessel has had periods laid up when not required on the Newhaven – Dieppe route.

CÔTE DES DUNES Built as the SEAFRANCE RODIN by Aker Finnyards, Rauma, Finland for *SeaFrance*. Launched in November 2001. In November 2011 laid up. In June 2012 sold to *Eurotransmanche*. In July 2012 renamed the RODIN. In August 2012 chartered to *MyFerryLink* and resumed operation between Calais and Dover. In July 2015 chartered to *DFDS Seaways* and *MyFerryLink* operations ceased. After a prolonged occupation by former

MyFerryLink workers. *DFDS Seaways* took possession in early September and in November 2015 she was renamed the CÔTE DES DUNES. She re-entered service on the Dover - Calais route in February 2016. In June 2017 purchased by *DFDS Seaways*.

CÔTE DES FLANDRES Built as the SEAFRANCE BERLIOZ by Chantiers de l'Atlantique, St Nazaire for *SeaFrance*. Launched in March 2005. In November 2011 laid up. In June 2012 sold to *Eurotransmanche*, a *Groupe Eurotunnel* company. In July 2012 renamed the BERLIOZ. In August 2012 chartered to *MyFerryLink* and resumed operation between Calais and Dover. In July 2015 chartered to *DFDS Seaways* and *MyFerryLink* operations ceased. After a prolonged occupation by former *MyFerryLink* workers, *DFDS Seaways* took possession in early September and, in November 2015, she was renamed the CÔTE DES FLANDRES. She re-entered service on the Dover - Calais route in February 2016. In June 2017 purchased by *DFDS Seaways*.

DELFT SEAWAYS, DOVER SEAWAYS, DUNKERQUE SEAWAYS Built as the MAERSK DELFT, DOVER SEAWAYS and MAERSK DUNKERQUE by Samsung Heavy Industries, Koje (Geoje) Island, South Korea for *Norfolkline* to operate between Dover and Dunkerque. In July and August 2010 renamed the DELFT SEAWAYS, DOVER SEAWAYS and DUNKERQUE SEAWAYS.

FICARIA SEAWAYS Built as the TOR FICARIA by Flensburger Schiffbau-Gesellschaft, Flensburg, Germany for *DFDS Tor Line*. Operated on the Göteborg - Immingham/Brevik service. In Summer 2009 lengthened by 30m by MWB Motorenwerke Bremerhaven AG, Germany. In July 2011 renamed the FICARIA SEAWAYS. In March 2015 placed on the Vlaardingen - Immingham service.

FINLANDIA SEAWAYS Launched as the FINNMAID but renamed the FINNREEL before delivery. Built by Jinling Shipyard, Nanjing, China for the *Macoma Shipping Group* and chartered to *Finnlines*. In 2008 sold to *DFDS Lisco* and in January 2009 delivered, chartered to *DFDS Tor Line* and renamed the TOR FINLANDIA. Operated on the Immingham - Rotterdam route until January 2011 when she was transferred to the Rosyth - Zeebrugge route. In May 2012 moved to the Cuxhaven - Immingham service but returned in July. In December 2012 renamed the FINLANDIA SEAWAYS. In October 2013 moved to the Kiel - St Petersburg service. In April 2014 returned to the Rosyth - Zeebrugge route. This route closed in April 2018 following a serious engine room fire. She is currently under repair.

FIONIA SEAWAYS Built as the TOR FIONIA by Jinling Shipyard, Nanjing, China for *Macoma Shipping Ltd* of the UK. Launched as the JINGLING 3. She was time-chartered to *DFDS Tor Line* for ten years (with an option on a further three). Delivered in May 2009 and initially replaced the TOR BEGONIA, TOR FICARIA and TOR FREESIA while they were being lengthened. In October 2011 renamed the FIONIA SEAWAYS. In March 2015 placed on the Göteborg - Immingham service.

FREESIA SEAWAYS Built as the TOR FREESIA by Flensburger Schiffbau-Gesellschaft, Flensburg, Germany for *DFDS Tor Line*. Operates on the Göteborg - Immingham/Brevik service. In Summer 2009 lengthened by 30m by MWB Motorenwerke Bremerhaven AG, Germany. In August 2012 renamed the FREESIA SEAWAYS.

GARDENIA SEAWAYS, TULIPA SEAWAYS Built by Flensburger Schiffbau-Gesellschaft, Flensburg, Germany for the Siem Industries Inc (owners of FSG). They are bareboat chartered to *DFDS Seaways* for five years with an option to purchase at the end of the charter period. Operate between Vlaardingen and Immingham.

JUTLANDIA SEAWAYS Built as the TOR JUTLANDIA by Jinling Shipyard, Nanjing, China for *Macoma Shipping Ltd* of the UK and time-chartered to *DFDS Tor Line* for ten years. In July 2011 renamed the JUTLANDIA SEAWAYS.

KING SEAWAYS Built as the NILS HOLGERSSON by Schichau Seebeckwerft AG, Bremerhaven, Germany for *Rederi AB Swedcarrier* of Sweden for their service between Trelleborg and Travemünde, joint with *TT-Line* of Germany (trading as *TT-Line*). In 1992 purchased by *Brittany Ferries* for entry into service in Spring 1993. After a major rebuild, she was renamed the VAL DE LOIRE and introduced onto the Plymouth - Roscoff, Plymouth - Santander and Cork - Roscoff routes. In 2004 transferred to the Portsmouth - St Malo and Portsmouth -

Cherbourg services. In 2005 operated mainly Portsmouth - St Malo. In 2006 sold to *DFDS*, renamed the KING OF SCANDINAVIA and placed on the Newcastle – IJmuiden route. In January 2011 renamed the KING SEAWAYS.

MAGNOLIA SEAWAYS Built as the TOR MAGNOLIA by Flensburger Schiffbau-Gesellschaft, Flensburg, Germany for *DFDS Tor Line*. In July 2011 renamed the MAGNOLIA SEAWAYS.

PETUNIA SEAWAYS Built as the TOR PETUNIA by Flensburger Schiffbau-Gesellschaft, Flensburg, Germany for *DFDS Tor Line*. In July 2011 renamed the PETUNIA SEAWAYS.

PRIMULA SEAWAYS Built as the TOR PRIMULA by Flensburger Schiffbau-Gesellschaft, Flensburg, Germany for *DFDS Tor Line*. In July 2010 renamed the PRIMULA SEAWAYS. In July 2016 lengthened by 30m by MWB Motorenwerke Bremerhaven AG, Germany.

PRINCESS SEAWAYS Built by Schichau Seebeckwerft AG, Bremerhaven, Germany as the PETER PAN for *TT-Line* for the service between Travemünde and Trelleborg. In 1992 sold to *TT Line* of Australia (no connection) for use on their service between Port Melbourne (Victoria) and Devonport (Tasmania) and renamed the SPIRIT OF TASMANIA. In 2002 sold to *Nordsjøferger K/S* of Norway and renamed the SPIR. After modification work she was, in 2003, renamed the FJORD NORWAY and chartered to *Fjord Line*. Placed on the Bergen - Egersund - Hanstholm route. In 2005 placed on the Bergen - Stavanger - Newcastle route, but operated once a week to Hanstholm. In October 2006 sold to *DFDS* and renamed the PRINCESS OF NORWAY, remaining on the Newcastle - Norway service but no longer serving Hanstholm. In May 2007 moved to the Newcastle - IJmuiden route. In February 2011 renamed the PRINCESS SEAWAYS.

SELANDIA SEAWAYS Built as the TOR SELANDIA by Fincantieri-Cantieri Navali Italiani SpA, Ancona, Italy for *DFDS Tor Line*. Operated on the Göteborg - Immingham route until 2004 when she was moved to the Göteborg – Gent route. In 2005 she moved to the Göteborg – Harwich route. In July the UK terminal moved to Tilbury. In August 2010 renamed the SELANDIA SEAWAYS. Currently operates on the Rotterdam - Felixstowe route.

SEVEN SISTERS Built by Astilleros Barreras SA, Vigo, Spain for *Transmanche Ferries* to operate between Newhaven and Dieppe. In recent years generally held as a reserve vessel. In March 2014 transferred to the *DFDS Seaways* Portsmouth - Le Havre service. She continues to carry *Transmanche Ferries* branding. In 2015 returned to the Newhaven - Dieppe service as second vessel, continuing to operate for *DFDS Seaways*. The vessel has had periods laid up when not required on the Newhaven – Dieppe route.

STENA FORETELLER Built as the STENA FORETELLER by Dalian Shipyard Co Ltd, Dalian, China for *Stena RoRo*. Initially chartered by *Cetam* of France to operate between Marseilles and Tunis and renamed the CETAM MASSILIA. In November 2003 the charter ended and she resumed her original name. A number of short-term commercial and military charters followed until June 2006 when she was chartered to *StoraEnso* paper group to operate between Göteborg and Finnish ports. In September 2009 she was chartered to *Rederi AB Transatlantic* who took over responsibility to operate all *StoraEnso's* Baltic services. In February 2012 she was chartered to *Transfennica*. In January 2015 chartered to *Mann Lines*. In December 2017 chartered to *DFDS Seaways*.

SUECIA SEAWAYS Built as the TOR SUECIA by Fincantieri-Cantieri Navali Italiani SpA, Ancona, Italy for *DFDS Tor Line*. Operated on the Göteborg - Immingham route until 2004 when she was transferred to the Esbjerg - Immingham route. Later transferred to the Danish flag. In March 2010 chartered to *Norfolkline* to operate between Vlaardingen and Felixstowe and continued on the route when it was taken over by *DFDS*. In June 2011 renamed the SUECIA SEAWAYS.

Under Construction

29F	GOTHIA SEAWAYS	58000t	19	21.0k	237.4m	12P	-	480T	A2	DK-	9816838
30F	NEWBUILDING 2	58000t	19	21.0k	237.4m	12P	-	480T	A2	-	-
31F	NEWBUILDING 3	58000t	20	21.0k	237.4m	12P	-	480T	A2	-	-
32F	NEWBUILDING 4	58000t	20	21.0k	237.4m	12P	-	480T	A2	-	-

Dover Seaways *(George Holland)*

Begonia Seaways *(Peter Therkildsen)*

33F	NEWBUILDING 5	58000t	20	21.0k	237.4m	12P	-	480T	A2	-	-	-
34	STENA NEWBUILDING 5	42000t	21	22.0k	214.5m	1000P	300C	180L	BA2	-	-	-

GOTHIA SEAWAYS, NEWBUILDING 2, NEWBUILDING 3, NEWBUILDING 4, NEWBUILDING 5 Under construction by Jinling Shipyard, Nanjing, China.

STENA NEWBUILDING 5 Under construction by AVIC International Maritime Holdings, Weihai, China for *Stena RoRo*. Designed to run on either methanol or LPG but before delivery she will be fitted with scrubbers to run on fuel oil. Upon delivery to be chartered to *DFDS Seaways* for ten years. Note: called here STENA NEWBUILDING 5 because she is to be the last of five vessels under construction for *Stena RoRo*, three being listed under *Stena Line*. Passenger capacity may be changed.

IRISH FERRIES

THE COMPANY *Irish Ferries* is a Republic of Ireland private sector company, part of the *Irish Continental Group*. It was originally mainly owned by the state-owned *Irish Shipping* and partly by *Lion Ferry AB* of Sweden. *Lion Ferry* participation ceased in 1977 and the company was sold into the private sector in 1987. Formerly state-owned *B&I Line* was taken over in 1991 and from 1995 all operations were marketed as *Irish Ferries*.

MANAGEMENT Irish Continental Group Chief Executive Office Eamonn Rothwell, **Irish Ferries Limited Managing Director** Andrew Sheen.

ADDRESS PO Box 19, Ferryport, Alexandra Road, Dublin 1, D01 W2F5, Republic of Ireland.

TELEPHONE Administration +353 (0)1 607 5700, **Reservations *Ireland*** +353 (0)818300 400, ***Rosslare Harbour*** +353 (0)53 913 3158, ***Holyhead*** +44 (0)8717 300200, ***Pembroke Dock*** +44 (0)8717 300500, ***National*** 44 (0)8717 300400, *24 hour information* +353 (0)818300 400 (Ireland) or 44 (0)8717 300400 (UK).

FAX Administration & Reservations *Dublin* +353 (0)1 607 5660, ***Rosslare*** +353 (0)53 913 3544.

INTERNET Email info@irishferries.com **Website** www.irishferries.com *(English, French, German, Italian)*

ROUTES OPERATED Conventional Ferries Dublin - Holyhead (3 hrs 15 mins; *EPSILON*, *ULYSSES*, *W. B. YEATS*; 2-4 per day), Rosslare - Pembroke Dock (4 hrs; *ISLE OF INISHMORE*; 4 per day), Dublin - Cherbourg (17-19 hrs; *EPSILON*, *W. B. YEATS*; up to 4 per week), Rosslare - Cherbourg (France) (17 hrs 30 mins; *OSCAR WILDE*; average of 3 per week), Rosslare - Roscoff (France) (16 hrs; *OSCAR WILDE*; 1 or 2 per week (seasonal)). **Fast Ferry** Dublin - Holyhead (1 hr 49 min; *DUBLIN SWIFT*; 2 per day).

1»	DUBLIN SWIFT	8403t	01	35.0k	101.0m	900P	182C	-	BA	CY	9243227
2	EPSILON	26375t	11	24.0k	177.5m	500P	500C	190T	A	IT	9539054
3	ISLE OF INISHMORE	34031t	97	21.3k	182.5m	2200P	802C	152T	BA2	CY	9142605
4	OSCAR WILDE	31914t	87	22.0k	166.3m	1458P	580C	90T	BA	BS	8506311
5	ULYSSES	50938t	01	22.0k	209.0m	1875P	1342C	241L	BA2	CY	9214991
6	W. B. YEATS	54975t	18	22.5k	194.8m-	1850P	1216C	165L	BA2	CY	9809679

DUBLIN SWIFT Austal Auto-Express 101 catamaran built by Austal Ships Pty, Fremantle, Australia as the WESTPAC EXPRESS. Chartered through a number of third party companies to the *US Marine Corps* as a support vessel. In 2015 returned to *Austal Ships*. In May 2016 sold to the *Irish Continental Group*. Chartered to *Sealift Inc* of the USA and continued to be operated for the *US Marine Corps*. In November 2017 charter ended; laid up in Belfast. In March 2018 renamed the DUBLIN SWIFT and in April replaced the JONATHAN SWIFT on the Holyhead - Dublin route.

EPSILON Built as the CARTOUR EPSILON by CN Visentini, Porto Viro, Italy. Chartered to *Caronte & Tourist SPA* of Italy. In November 2013 chartered to *Irish Ferries*. In February 2014 renamed the EPSILON.

Ulysses *(George Holland)*

Dublin Swift *(George Holland)*

ISLE OF INISHMORE Built by Van der Giessen-de Noord, Krimpen aan den IJssel, Rotterdam for *Irish Ferries* to operate on the Holyhead - Dublin service. In 2001 replaced by the ULYSSES and moved to the Rosslare - Pembroke Dock route. She also relieves on the Dublin – Holyhead route when the ULYSSES receives her annual overhaul.

OSCAR WILDE Built as the KRONPRINS HARALD by Oy Wärtsilä AB, Turku, Finland for *Jahre Line* of Norway for the Oslo - Kiel service. In 1991 ownership was transferred to *Color Line*. In early 2007 sold to *Irish Ferries* for delivery in September 2007. Chartered back to *Color Line* until that date. When delivered, renamed the OSCAR WILDE and in November placed on the Rosslare - Roscoff/Cherbourg routes.

ULYSSES Built by Aker Finnyards, Rauma, Finland for *Irish Ferries* for the Dublin - Holyhead service.

W. B. YEATS Built by Flensburger Schiffbau-Gesellschaft, Flensburg, Germany. Operates between Dublin and Cherbourg in the summer and Dublin and Holyhead in the winter. Originally planned to enter service spring 2018, now expected to enter service in September.

Under Construction

7	NEWBUILDING	67300t	20	22.8k	226.0m	1800P	1526C	330L	BA2	CY	9847530

NEWBUILDING Under construction by Flensburger Schiffbau-Gesellschaft, Flensburg, Germany. This vessel is to effectively to replace the EPSILON service on the Dublin - Holyhead route.

ISLE OF MAN STEAM PACKET COMPANY

THE COMPANY The *Isle of Man Steam Packet Company Limited* is an Isle of Man-registered company owned by the Isle of Man Government.

MANAGEMENT Chief Executive Officer Mark Woodward.

ADDRESS Imperial Buildings, Douglas, Isle of Man IM1 2BY.

TELEPHONE Administration +44 (0)1624 645645, **Reservations** +44 (0)1624 661661

FAX Administration +44 (0)1624 645627.

INTERNET Email iom.reservations@steam-packet.com **Website** www.steam-packet.com *(English),*

ROUTES OPERATED Conventional Ferries All year Douglas (Isle of Man) - Heysham (3 hrs 30 mins; *BEN-MY-CHREE*; up to 2 per day), November-March Douglas - Liverpool (Birkenhead) (4 hrs 15 mins; *BEN-MY-CHREE*; 2 per week). Fast Ferries March-October Douglas - Liverpool (2 hrs 40 mins; *MANANNAN*; up to 2 per day), Douglas - Belfast (2 hrs 55 mins; *MANANNAN*; up to 2 per week), Douglas - Dublin (2 hrs 55 mins; *MANANNAN*; up to 2 per week), Douglas - Heysham (2 hrs; *MANANNAN*; occasional), Freight Ferry Douglas - Heysham (3 hrs 30 mins; *ARROW*; as required).

1F	ARROW	7606t	98	15.0k	122.3m	12P	-	84T	A	IM	9119414
2	BEN-MY-CHREE	12747t	98	18.0k	124.9m	630P	275C	90T	A	IM	9170705
3»	MANANNAN	5743t	98	43.0k	96.0m	865P	200C	-	A	IM	9176072

ARROW Built as the VARBOLA by Astilleros de Huelva SA, Huelva, Spain for the *Estonian Shipping Company*. On completion, chartered to *Dart Line* and placed on the Dartford - Vlissingen route. In 1999 she was renamed the DART 6. At the end of August 1999, the charter was terminated and she was renamed the VARBOLA. She undertook a number of short-term charters, including *Merchant Ferries*. In 2000 long-term chartered to *Merchant Ferries* to operate between Heysham and Dublin. In 2003 the charter ended and she was chartered to *Dart Line* to replace the DART 9; she was placed initially on the Dartford - Vlissingen route but later transferred to the Dartford - Dunkerque route. Later sub-chartered to *NorseMerchant Ferries* and placed on the Heysham – Dublin route. In 2004 the charter transferred to *NorseMerchant Ferries*. In 2005 sold to *Elmira Shipping* of Greece and renamed the RR ARROW. In October 2007 sold to *Seatruck Ferries* but the charter to

Leading the way.

Irish Ferries are proud to maintain the highest customer and maritime standards. We operate the finest fleet on the Irish Sea, including our new ship which is due to launch in the summer of 2018. Optimum schedules, and the best value fares for drivers, passengers and freight customers alike, make Irish Ferries Ireland's leading ferry company.

Norfolkline continued. Renamed the ARROW. In June 2009 returned to *Seatruck Ferries*. In April 2014 long term chartered to *IOMSP*. When not required she is sub-chartered to other operators.

BEN-MY-CHREE Built by Van der Giessen-de Noord, Krimpen aan den IJssel, Rotterdam for the *IOMSP Co* and operates between Douglas and Heysham. Additional passenger accommodation was added at her spring 2004 refit. In 2005 her passenger certificate was increased from 500 to 630. She operates some sailings between Douglas and Liverpool (Birkenhead) in the winter.

MANANNAN Incat 96m catamaran built at Hobart, Tasmania. Initially chartered to *Transport Tasmania* of Australia and operated between Port Melbourne (Victoria) and Georgetown (Tasmania). In 1999 chartered to *Fast Cat Ferries* of New Zealand and operated between Wellington (North Island) and Picton (South Island) under the marketing name 'Top Cat'. In 2000 she was laid up. In 2001 she was chartered to the *US Navy* and renamed the USS JOINT VENTURE (HSV-X1). In 2008 the charter was terminated and she was renamed the INCAT 050. Later purchased by *IOMSP*. Following conversion back to civilian use she was renamed the MANANNAN and entered service in May 2009.

NORTHLINK FERRIES

THE COMPANY *NorthLink Ferries* is a UK based company, wholly owned *Serco Group plc.* The service is operated on behalf of Scottish Ministers.

MANAGEMENT Managing Director Stuart Garrett, **Customer Service Director** Peter Hutchinson.

ADDRESS Ferry Terminal, Ferry Road, Stromness, Orkney KW16 3BH.

TELEPHONE Customer Services 0845 6000 449, (International +44 (0)1856 885500), **Freight Reservations** 0845 6060 449.

FAX +44 (0)1856 851795.

INTERNET Email info@northlinkferries.co.uk **Website** www.northlinkferries.co.uk *(English),*

ROUTES OPERATED *Passenger Ferries* Scrabster - Stromness (Orkney) (1 hr 30 min; **HAMNAVOE**; up to 3 per day), Aberdeen - Lerwick (Shetland) (direct) (12 hrs; **HJALTLAND**, **HROSSEY**; 3 northbound/4 southbound per week), Aberdeen - Kirkwall, Hatston New Pier (Orkney) (5 hrs 45 mins) - Lerwick (14 hrs; **HJALTLAND**, **HROSSEY**; 4 northbound/3 southbound per week). *Freight Ferries* Aberdeen - Kirkwall (Orkney) (12 hrs; **HELLIAR**, **HILDASAY**; 4 per week), Aberdeen - Lerwick (Shetland) (**HELLIAR**, **HILDASAY**; 4 per week).

1	HAMNAVOE	8780t	02	19.3k	112.0m	600P	95C	20L	BA	UK	9246061
2F	HELLIAR	7800t	98	17.0k	122.3m	12P	-	86T	A	IM	9119397
3F	HILDASAY	7606t	99	17.0k	122.3m	12P	-	84T	A	IM	9119426
4	HJALTLAND	11720t	02	24.0k	125.0m	600P	150C	30L	BA	UK	9244958
5	HROSSEY	11720t	02	24.0k	125.0m	600P	150C	30L	BA	UK	9244960

HAMNAVOE Built by Aker Finnyards, Rauma, Finland for *NorthLink Orkney and Shetland Ferries Ltd* to operate on the Scrabster - Stromness route. Did not enter service until Spring 2003 due to late completion of work at Scrabster to accommodate the ship. *Caledonian MacBrayne's* HEBRIDEAN ISLES covered between October 2002 and Spring 2003. Initially owned by the *Royal Bank of Scotland*, she was acquired by *Caledonian Maritime Assets Ltd* (owned by *Transport Scotland*) in May 2018.

HELLIAR Built as the LEHOLA by Astilleros de Huelva SA, Huelva, Spain for the *Estonian Shipping Company*. Initially used on *ESCO* Baltic services. In 1998 chartered to *Czar Peter Line* to operate between Moerdijk (The Netherlands) and Kronstadt (Russia). In 1999 chartered to *Delom* of France to operate between Marseilles and Sete and Tunis. In 2000 she returned to *ESCO*, operating between Kiel and Tallinn. In 2003 chartered to *Scandlines AG* and transferred to subsidiary *Scandlines Estonia AS*. Operated Rostock - Helsinki – Muuga

Ben-My-Chree *(George Holland)*

Hamnavoe *(Miles Cowsill)*

Hildasay *(George Holland)*

Hoy Head *(Miles Cowsill)*

initially and later Rostock – Helsinki. Service finished at the end of 2004 and in 2005 she was chartered to *P&O Ferries* to operate between Hull and Rotterdam and Hull and Zeebrugge. In 2005 sold to *Elmira Shipping* of Greece. Later renamed the RR TRIUMPH. In 2006 transferred to *P&O Irish Sea* to operate between Liverpool and Dublin. In 2007 chartered to *Balearia* of Spain and operated from Barcelona. In December 2007 purchased by *Seatruck Ferries* and renamed the TRIUMPH. In Spring 2008 she was sub-chartered to *Condor Ferries* to cover for the refit period of the COMMODORE GOODWILL. In June 2008 placed on the Liverpool - Dublin route and in July renamed the CLIPPER RACER. In February 2009 replaced by the new CLIPPER PACE. In April 2009 again chartered to *Balearia*. In January 2011 chartered to *NorthLink Ferries* and renamed the HELLIAR. In June 2017 sold to *CF Clip Helliar LLC*; the charter continued.

HILDASAY Built as the LEILI by Astilleros de Huelva SA, Huelva, Spain for the *Estonian Shipping Company*. Used on Baltic services. In 2002 chartered to *Crowley Maritime* of the USA and renamed the PORT EVERGLADES EXPRESS. In 2004 resumed the name LEILI and chartered to *NorseMerchant Ferries* to operate between Birkenhead and Dublin. In July 2005 moved to the Heysham - Belfast route and at the same time sold to *Elmira Shipping* of Greece and renamed the RR SHIELD. In 2007 sold to *Attica Group* of Greece and renamed the SHIELD. In January 2008 sold to *Seatruck Ferries* but continued to be chartered to *Norfolkline*. In June 2009 returned to *Seatruck Ferries*. In January 2009 chartered to *NorthLink Orkney and Shetland Ferries* and renamed the HILDASAY. In June 2017 sold to *CF Clip Hildasay LLC*; the charter continued.

HJALTLAND, HROSSEY Built by Aker Finnyards, Rauma, Finland for *NorthLink Orkney and Shetland Ferries* to operate on the Aberdeen - Kirkwall - Lerwick route when services started in 2002. Initially owned by the *Royal Bank of Scotland*, they were acquired by *Caledonian Maritime Assets Ltd* (owned by *Transport Scotland*) in May 2018.

ORKNEY FERRIES

THE COMPANY Orkney Ferries Ltd (previously the *Orkney Islands Shipping Company*) is a British company, owned by *Orkney Islands Council*.

MANAGEMENT Ferry Services Manager Andrew Blake.

ADDRESS Shore Street, Kirkwall, Orkney KW15 1LG.

TELEPHONE Administration +44 (0)1856 872044, **Reservations** +44 (0)1856 872044.

FAX Administration & Reservations +44 (0)1856 872921.

INTERNET Email info@orkneyferries.co.uk **Website** www.orkneyferries.co.uk *(English)*,

ROUTES OPERATED Kirkwall (Mainland) to Eday (1 hr 15 mins), Rapness (Westray) (1 hr 25 mins), Sanday (1 hr 25 mins), Stronsay (1 hr 35 mins), Papa Westray (1 hr 50 mins), North Ronaldsay (2 hrs 30 mins) ('North Isles service') (timings are direct from Kirkwall - sailings via other islands take longer; **EARL SIGURD, EARL THORFINN, VARAGEN**; 1/2 per day except Papa Westray which is twice weekly and North Ronaldsay which is weekly), Pierowall (Westray) - Papa Westray (25 mins; **GOLDEN MARIANA**; up to six per day (Summer service - passenger-only)), Kirkwall - Shapinsay (25 mins; **SHAPINSAY**; 6 per day), Houton (Mainland) to Lyness (Hoy) (35 mins; **HOY HEAD**; 5 per day), and Flotta (35 mins; **HOY HEAD**; 4 per day) ('South Isles service') (timings are direct from Houton - sailings via other islands take longer), Tingwall (Mainland) to Rousay (20 mins; **EYNHALLOW**; 6 per day), Egilsay (30 mins; **EYNHALLOW**; 5 per day) and Wyre (20 mins; **EYNHALLOW**; 5 per day) (timings are direct from Tingwall - sailings via other islands take longer), Stromness (Mainland) to Moaness (Hoy) (25 mins; **GRAEMSAY**; 2/3 per day) and Graemsay (25 mins; **GRAEMSAY**; 2/3 per day) (passenger/cargo service - cars not normally conveyed).

1	EARL SIGURD	771t	90	12.5k	45.0m	190P	26C	-	BA	UK	8902711
2	EARL THORFINN	771t	90	12.5k	45.0m	190P	26C	-	BA	UK	8902723
3	EYNHALLOW	104t	87	10.5k	28.8m	95P	11C	-	BA	UK	8960880
4p	GOLDEN MARIANA	33t	73	9.5k	15.2m	40P	0C	-	-	UK	

5	GRAEMSAY	90t	96	10.0k	20.6m	73P	2C	-	C	UK	
6	HOY HEAD	358t	94	11.0k	53.5m	125P	24C	3L	BA	UK	9081722
7	SHAPINSAY	199t	89	10.0k	32.6m	91P	16C	-	BA	UK	8814184
8	THORSVOE	385t	91	10.6k	35.0m	122P	16C	-	BA	UK	9014743
9	VARAGEN	928t	88	14.5k	49.9m	144P	33C	5L	BA	UK	8818154

EARL SIGURD, EARL THORFINN Built by McTay Marine, Bromborough, Wirral, UK to inaugurate ro-ro working on the 'North Isles service'.

EYNHALLOW Built by David Abels Boat Builders, Bristol, UK to inaugurate ro-ro services from Tingwall (Mainland) to Rousay, Egilsay and Wyre. In 1991 she was lengthened by 5 metres, to increase car capacity.

GOLDEN MARIANA Built by Bideford Shipyard Ltd, Bideford, UK for *A J G England* of Padstow as a dual-purpose passenger and fishing vessel. In 1975 sold to *M MacKenzie* of Ullapool, then to *Pentland Ferries*, *Wide Firth Ferry* in 1982, and *Orkney Islands Council* in 1986. Passenger-only vessel. Generally operates summer-only feeder service between Pierowall (Westray) and Papa Westray.

GRAEMSAY Built by Ailsa Shipbuilding, Troon UK to operate between Stromness (Mainland), Moaness (Hoy) and Graemsay. Designed to offer an all-year-round service to these islands, primarily for passengers and cargo. Between October 2009 and January 2010 lengthened by 4.4 metres.

HOY HEAD Built by Appledore Shipbuilders Ltd, Appledore, UK to replace the THORSVOE on the 'South Isles service'. During winter 2012/13 extended by 14 metres at Cammell Laird Shiprepairers & Shipbuilders, Birkenhead, England.

SHAPINSAY Built by Yorkshire Drydock Ltd, Hull, UK for the service from Kirkwall (Mainland) to Shapinsay. In April 2011 lengthened by 6 metres at the Macduff Shipyards, Macduff, Scotland to increase car capacity from 12 to 16 and re-engined.

THORSVOE Built by Campbeltown Shipyard, Campbeltown, UK for the 'South Isles service'. In 1994 replaced by the new HOY HEAD and became the main reserve vessel for the fleet.

VARAGEN Built by Cochrane Shipbuilders, Selby, UK for *Orkney Ferries*, a private company established to start a new route between Gills Bay (Caithness, Scotland) and Burwick (South Ronaldsay, Orkney). However, due to problems with the terminals it was not possible to maintain regular services. In 1991, the company was taken over by *Orkney Islands Shipping Company* and the VARAGEN became part of their fleet, sharing the 'North Isles service' with the EARL SIGURD and the EARL THORFINN and replacing the freight vessel ISLANDER (494t, 1969).

P&O FERRIES

THE COMPANY *P&O Ferries Holdings Ltd* is a private sector company, a subsidiary of *Dubai World*, owned by the Government of Dubai. In Autumn 2002 *P&O North Sea Ferries*, P&O Irish Sea, *P&O Portsmouth* and *P&O Stena Line* (*Stena Line* involvement having ceased) were merged into a single operation.

MANAGEMENT Chief Executive Officer Janette Bell, **Fleet Director** John Garner, **Finance Directo**r Karl Howarth, **Human Resources Director** Lesley Cotton, **Company Secretary** Susan Kitchin.

ADDRESSES *Head Office and Dover Services* Channel House, Channel View Road, Dover, Kent CT17 9TJ, **Hull** King George Dock, Hedon Road, Hull HU9 5QA, **Larne** P&O Irish Sea, Larne Harbour, Larne, Co Antrim BT40 1AW **Rotterdam** Beneluxhaven, Rotterdam (Europoort), Postbus 1123, 3180 Rozenburg, Netherlands, **Zeebrugge** Leopold II Dam 13, Havendam, 8380 Zeebrugge, Belgium.

TELEPHONE Administration *UK* +44 (0)1304 863000, **Passenger Reservations *UK*** 08716 64 64 64, *France* +33 (0)825 12 01 56, *Belgium* +32 (0)70 70 77 71, *The Netherlands* +31 (0)20 20 08333, *Spain* +34 (0)902 02 04 61, *Luxembourg* +34 (0)20

P&O FERRIES

YOUR TRIP. YOUR SHIP.

WE'LL HELP YOU ON YOUR WAY, YOUR WAY

With 30,000 sailings across nine routes, we help nine million of you (plus two million freight units) get to wherever it is you're headed.

And whether you choose to sit down, relax and grab forty winks or enjoy a cuppa, a bite to eat and the view — how you enjoy your trip is up to you.

Visit **poferries.com** to find out more and book today.

poferries.com   poferriesfreight.com

Dover/Calais   Hull/Rotterdam   Hull/Zeebrugge
Teesport/Rotterdam   Teesport/Zeebrugge   Tilbury/Zeebrugge
Larne/Cairnryan   Larne/Troon   Dublin/Liverpool

Pride of Bruges *(Rob de Visser)*

Pride of Canterbury *(Darren Holdaway)*

80 82 94. **Freight Reservations UK** 0870 6000 868, **Republic of Ireland** +353 (0)1 855 0522.

FAX Passenger Reservations UK East and South Coast +44 (0)1304 863464, **West Coast** 44 (0)02828 872195, **The Netherlands** +31 (0)118 1225 5215, **Belgium** +32 (0)50 54 71 12, **Freight Reservations Cairnryan** +44 (0)1581 200282, **Larne** +44 (0)28 2827 2477..

INTERNET Email customer.services@poferries.com **Website** www.poferries.com *(English, French, Dutch, German)* www.poirishsea.com *(English)* www.poferriesfreight.com *(English, French, German),*

ROUTES OPERATED Passenger Dover - Calais (1 hr 30 mins; *PRIDE OF BURGUNDY, PRIDE OF CANTERBURY, PRIDE OF KENT, SPIRIT OF BRITAIN, SPIRIT OF FRANCE;* up to 25 per day), Hull - Zeebrugge (Belgium) (from 12 hrs 30 mins; *PRIDE OF BRUGES, PRIDE OF YORK;* 1 per day), Hull - Rotterdam (Beneluxhaven, Europoort) (The Netherlands) (from 10 hrs; *PRIDE OF HULL, PRIDE OF ROTTERDAM;* 1 per day), Cairnryan - Larne (1 hr 45 min; *EUROPEAN CAUSEWAY, EUROPEAN HIGHLANDER;* 7 per day), Liverpool - Dublin (8 hrs; *EUROPEAN ENDEAVOUR, NORBANK, NORBAY;* up to 3 per day (some sailings are freight only). **Freight-only** Dover - Calais (1 hr 30 mins; *EUROPEAN SEAWAY;* 2/3 per day (plus services on passenger ferries)), Tilbury - Zeebrugge (8 hrs; *NORSKY, NORSTREAM;* 10 per week), Middlesbrough (Teesport) - Rotterdam (Beneluxhaven, Europoort) (16 hrs; *ESTRADEN;* 3 per week), Middlesbrough (Teesport) - Zeebrugge (15 hrs 30 mins; *BORE SONG, STENA CARRIER;* 6 per week), **Container service** Hull - Zeebrugge (Belgium) (from 12 hrs 30 mins; *ELISABETH;* 3 per week),

1F	BORE SONG	25586t	11	18.5k	195.0m	12P	-	210T	A2	FI	9443566
2F	ELISABETH	5067t	00	-	118.3m	0P		648teu	C	NL	9219862
3F	ESTRADEN	18205t	99	19.0k	162.7m	12P	130C	170T	A	FI	9181077
4	EUROPEAN CAUSEWAY	20646t	00	22.7k	159.5m	410P	315C	84T	BA2	BS	9208394
5	EUROPEAN ENDEAVOUR	22152t	00	22.5k	180.0m	366P	-	120L	BA2	BS	9181106
6	EUROPEAN HIGHLANDER	21128t	02	22.6k	162.7m	410P	315C	84T	BA2	BS	9244116
7F+	EUROPEAN SEAWAY	22986t	91	21.0k	179.7m	200P	-	120L	BA2	UK	9007283
8	NORBANK	17464t	93	22.5k	166.7m	114P	-	125T	A	NL	9056583
9	NORBAY	17464t	92	21.5k	166.7m	114P	-	125T	A	BM	9056595
10F	NORSKY	19992t	99	20.0k	180.0m	12P	-	194T	A	FI	9186182
11F	NORSTREAM	19992t	99	20.0k	180.0m	12P	-	194T	A	FI	9186194
12	PRIDE OF BRUGES	31598t	87	18.5k	179.0m	1050P	310C	185T	A	NL	8503797
13	PRIDE OF BURGUNDY	28138t	92	21.0k	179.7m	1420P	465C	120L	BA2	UK	9015254
14	PRIDE OF CANTERBURY	30635t	91	21.0k	179.7m	2000P	537C	120L	BA2	UK	9007295
15	PRIDE OF HULL	59925t	01	22.0k	215.4m	1360P	205C	263T	AS	BS	9208629
16	PRIDE OF KENT	30635t	92	21.0k	179.7m	2000P	537C	120L	BA2	UK	9015266
17	PRIDE OF ROTTERDAM	59925t	00	22.0k	215.4m	1360P	205C	263T	AS	NL	9208617
18	PRIDE OF YORK	31785t	87	18.5k	179.0m	1050P	310C	185T	A	BS	8501957
19	SPIRIT OF BRITAIN	47592t	11	22.0k-	212.0m	2000P	194C	180L	BA2	UK	9524231
20	SPIRIT OF FRANCE	47592t	12	22.0k-	212.0m	2000P	194C	180L	BA2	UK	9533816
21F	STENA CARRIER	21089t	04	22.0k	182.6m	12P	-	200T	A	DK	9138800

BORE SONG Built by Flensburger Schiffbau-Gesellschaft, Flensburg, Germany for *Bore Shipowners (Rettig Group Bore)* of Finland. In July 2011 chartered to *Mann Lines* to cover for the ESTRADEN'S refit. In September 2011 chartered to *P&O Ferries* and placed on the Middlesbrough - Zeebrugge route.

ELISABETH Container ship built by J.J. Sietas KG Schiffswerft GmbH & Co for *Holwerda Shipmanagement BV* of The Netherlands. In May 2017 introduced onto the Hull - Zeebrugge route to relive pressure on the two passenger ships.

ESTRADEN Built as the ESTRADEN by Aker Finnyards, Rauma, Finland for *Rederi Ab Engship* (later *Bore Shipowners*) of Finland and chartered to *ArgoMann*. Later in 1999 renamed the AMAZON. In 2001 the charter was taken over by *Mann Lines* and in August she resumed the name ESTRADEN. In 2006 *Rederi AB Engship* was taken over by *Rettig Group Bore* and she

87

European Endeavour *(George Holland)*

European Highlander *(Brian Maxted)*

Pride of Burgundy *(Darren Holdaway)*

Spirit of Britain *(Darren Holdaway)*

remained on charter to *Mann Lines*. In January 2015 chartered to *P&O Ferries* to replace the WILHELMINE of *Cobelfret Ferries* on the Rotterdam - Middlesbrough (Teesport) service. In June 2018 transferred to the Zeebrugge - Teesport service.

EUROPEAN CAUSEWAY Built by Mitsubishi Heavy Industries, Shimonoseki, Japan for *P&O Irish Sea* for the Cairnryan - Larne service.

EUROPEAN ENDEAVOUR Built as the MIDNIGHT MERCHANT by Astilleros Españoles SA, Sevilla, Spain for *Cenargo* (then owners of *NorseMerchant Ferries*). On delivery, chartered to *Norfolkline* to operate as second vessel on the Dover - Dunkerque (Ouest) service. In 2002 modified to allow two-deck loading. In 2006 chartered to *Acciona Trasmediterranea* of Spain and renamed the EL GRECO. Used on Mediterranean and Canary Island services. In 2007 sold to *P&O Ferries* and renamed the EUROPEAN ENDEAVOUR. Operated on The Dover - Calais route and as a re-fit relief vessel on Irish Sea routes. In May 2010 laid up. In February 2011 moved to the Liverpool - Dublin route.

EUROPEAN HIGHLANDER Built by Mitsubishi Heavy Industries, Shimonoseki, Japan for *P&O Irish Sea* for the Cairnryan - Larne service.

EUROPEAN SEAWAY Built by Schichau Seebeckwerft AG, Bremerhaven, Germany for *P&O European Ferries* for the Dover - Zeebrugge freight service. In 2000 a regular twice-daily freight-only Dover-Calais service was established, using this vessel which continued to operate to Zeebrugge at night. In 2001 car passengers (not foot or coach passengers) began to be conveyed on the Dover - Zeebrugge service. In 2003 the Zeebrugge service ended and she operated only between Dover and Calais in a freight-only mode. In 2004 withdrawn and laid up. In January 2005 returned to the Dover – Calais route. In July 2012 chartered to GLID, a joint venture between Centrica Renewable Energy Limited and EIG, for use by technicians working on the North Sea Lynn and Inner Dowsing wind farm array four miles off Skegness. In October 2012 returned to the Dover - Calais service. In April 2013 laid up at Tilbury. In August 2014 chartered as a wind farm accommodation and support vessel near the North German coast. In April 2015 returned to layup at Tilbury. In August 2015 returned to service on the Dover - Calais route.

NORBANK Built by Van der Giessen-de Noord, Krimpen aan den IJssel, Rotterdam, The Netherlands for *North Sea Ferries* for the Hull - Rotterdam service. She was originally built for and chartered to *Nedlloyd* but the charter was taken over by *P&O* in 1996 and she was bought by *P&O* in 2003. She retains Dutch crew and registry. In May 2001 moved to the Felixstowe - Europoort route. In January 2002 transferred to *P&O Irish Sea* and operated on the Liverpool – Dublin route.

NORBAY Built by Van der Giessen-de Noord, Krimpen aan den IJssel, Rotterdam, The Netherlands for *North Sea Ferries* for the Hull - Rotterdam service. Owned by *P&O*. In January 2002 transferred to *P&O Irish Sea* and operated on the Liverpool – Dublin route.

NORSKY, NORSTREAM Built by Aker Finnyards, Rauma, Finland for *Bore Line* of Finland and chartered to *P&O North Sea Ferries*. They generally operated on the Teesport - Zeebrugge service. In September 2011, the NORSTREAM was moved to the Tilbury - Zeebrugge route. In January 2013, the NORSKY was also moved to the Tilbury - Zeebrugge route.

PRIDE OF BRUGES Built as the NORSUN by NKK, Tsurumi, Japan for the Hull - Rotterdam service of *North Sea Ferries*. She was owned by *Nedlloyd* and was sold to *P&O* in 1996 but retains Dutch crew and registry. In May 2001 replaced by the PRIDE OF ROTTERDAM and in July 2001, after a major refurbishment, she was transferred to the Hull - Zeebrugge service, replacing the NORSTAR (26919t, 1974). In 2003 renamed the PRIDE OF BRUGES.

PRIDE OF BURGUNDY Built by Schichau Seebeckwerft AG, Bremerhaven, Germany for *P&O European Ferries* for the Dover - Calais service. When construction started she was due to be a sister vessel to the EUROPEAN SEAWAY (see Section 3) called the EUROPEAN CAUSEWAY and operate on the Zeebrugge freight route. However, it was decided that she should be completed as a passenger/freight vessel (the design allowed for conversion) and she was launched as the PRIDE OF BURGUNDY. In 1998, transferred to *P&O Stena Line* and renamed the P&OSL BURGUNDY. In 2002 renamed the PO BURGUNDY and in 2003 renamed the

Pride of Kent *(George Holland)*

PRIDE OF BURGUNDY. In 2004 she operated mainly in freight-only mode. In 2005 returned to full passenger service.

PRIDE OF CANTERBURY Built as the EUROPEAN PATHWAY by Schichau Seebeckwerft AG, Bremerhaven, Germany for *P&O European Ferries* for the Dover - Zeebrugge freight service. In 1998 transferred to *P&O Stena Line*. In 2001 car/foot passengers were again conveyed on the route. In 2002/03 rebuilt as a full passenger vessel and renamed the PRIDE OF CANTERBURY; now operates between Dover and Calais.

PRIDE OF HULL Built by Fincantieri-Cantieri Navali Italiani SpA, Venezia, Italy for *P&O North Sea Ferries* to replace (with the PRIDE OF ROTTERDAM) the NORSEA and NORSUN plus the freight vessels NORBAY and NORBANK on the Hull - Rotterdam service.

PRIDE OF KENT Built as the EUROPEAN HIGHWAY by Schichau Seebeckwerft AG, Bremerhaven, Germany for *P&O European Ferries* for the Dover - Zeebrugge freight service. In 1998 transferred to *P&O Stena Line*. In Summer 1999 she operated full-time between Dover and Calais. She returned to the Dover - Zeebrugge route in the autumn when the P&OSL AQUITAINE was transferred to the Dover - Calais service. In 2001 car/foot passengers were again conveyed on the route. In 2002/03 rebuilt as a full passenger vessel and renamed the PRIDE OF KENT; now operates between Dover and Calais.

PRIDE OF ROTTERDAM Built by Fincantieri-Cantieri Navali Italiani SpA, Venezia, Italy. Keel laid as the PRIDE OF HULL but launched as the PRIDE OF ROTTERDAM. Owned by Dutch interests until 2006 when she was sold to *P&O Ferries*. Further details as the PRIDE OF HULL.

PRIDE OF YORK Built as the NORSEA by Govan Shipbuilders Ltd, Glasgow, UK for the Hull - Rotterdam service of *North Sea Ferries* (jointly owned by *P&O* and *The Royal Nedlloyd Group* of The Netherlands until 1996). In December 2001 she was replaced by the new PRIDE OF HULL and, after a two-month refurbishment, in 2002 transferred to the Hull - Zeebrugge service, replacing the NORLAND (26290t, 1974). In 2003 renamed the PRIDE OF YORK.

SPIRIT OF BRITAIN, SPIRIT OF FRANCE Built by STX Europe, Rauma, Finland for the Dover - Calais service. Car capacity relates to dedicated car deck only; additional cars can be accommodated on the freight decks as necessary.

STENA CARRIER Laid down in 1998 by Societa Esercizio Cantieri SpA, Viareggio, Italy for *Stena RoRo*. In 1999 the builders went bankrupt and work ceased. The hull was purchased by *Enrico Bugazzi Shipmanagement*, named the ARONTE and in 2003 she was towed to Marina di Carrara, Italy for work to be completed. In 2003 she was sold to *Stena RoRo*; in 2004 she was transferred to *Stena Line* and was renamed the STENA CARRIER II. After further work at Göteborg she entered service on the Göteborg - Travemünde route. She was later renamed the STENA CARRIER. She replaced the STENA TRANSFER on Rotterdam - Harwich in September 2010. She left this route in September 2012 and subsequently operated a number of charters including *Transfennica, Corsica Linea*, and *Acciona Trasmediterranea*. In February 2018 she operated for *Stena Line* between Fishguard and Rosslare and in March for *P&O Ferries* between Liverpool and Dublin. Following a period of lay-up in Dun Laoghaire. in June 2018 she was chartered to *P&O Ferries* for three months to operate between Teesport and Rotterdam.

PENTLAND FERRIES

THE COMPANY *Pentland Ferries* is a UK private sector company.

MANAGEMENT Managing Director Andrew Banks, **Designated Person Ashore** Kathryn Scollie.

ADDRESS Pier Road, St Margaret's Hope, South Ronaldsay, Orkney KW17 2SW.

TELEPHONE Administration & Reservations +44 (0)1856 831226.

FAX Administration & Reservations +44 (0)1856 831697.

INTERNET Email sales@pentlandferries.co.uk **Website** www.pentlandferries.co.uk *(English)*,

ROUTE OPERATED Gills Bay (Caithness) - St Margaret's Hope (South Ronaldsay, Orkney) (1 hour; **PENTALINA**; up to 4 per day).

1	ORCADIA	899t	78	13.0k	69.5m	-	40C	-	AS	UK	7615490
2	PENTALINA	2382t	08	17.1k	59.0m	345P	70C	9L	A	UK	9437969

ORCADIA Built as the SATURN by Ailsa Shipbuilding, Troon for *Caledonian MacBrayne* and initially used on the Wemyss Bay - Rothesay services. Between 1986 and 2005 she usually rotated on this service and services from Gourock; until 2000 this, in summer, included Clyde cruising but this was not repeated in 2001. In the summers 2005 - 2010, she operated additional peak summer sailings between Ardrossan and Brodick with a maximum capacity of 250 passengers. In October 2010 she took over the Gourock - Dunoon service. In June 2011 replaced by *Argyll Ferries* passenger ferries. During Summer 2011 she operated additional sailings between Ardrossan and Brodick. In September returned to the Gourock - Dunoon route to provide additional capacity for the Cowal Games. She was then laid up. In February 2015 sold to *Pentland Ferries* and renamed the ORCADIA.

PENTALINA Catamaran built by FBMA Marine, Cebu, Philippines for *Pentland Ferries*.

Under construction

3	NEWBUILDING	-	18	16.0k	84.5m	430P	98C	12L	A	UK	

NEWBUILDING Catamaran under construction by the Strategic Marine Shipyard, Vũng Tàu, Vietnam.

RED FUNNEL FERRIES

THE COMPANY *Red Funnel Ferries* is the trading name of the *Southampton, Isle of Wight and South of England Royal Mail Steam Packet Company Limited*, a British private sector company owned by a consortium of British and Canadian pension funds led by the West Midland Pensions Fund and the Workplace Safety and Insurance Board of the Province of Ontario.

MANAGEMENT CEO Fran Collins, **Commercial Director** Colin Hetherington.

ADDRESS 12 Bugle Street, Southampton SO14 2JY.

TELEPHONE Administration +44 (0)23 8024 8500, **Reservations UK** 0844 844 9988, **Elsewhere** +44 (0)23 8001 9192.

FAX Administration & Reservations UK +44 (0)23 8024 8501.

INTERNET Email post@redfunnel.co.uk **Website** www.redfunnel.co.uk *(English),*

ROUTES OPERATED Conventional Ferries Southampton - East Cowes (55 mins; **RED EAGLE, RED FALCON, RED OSPREY**; hourly). **Fast Passenger Ferries** Southampton - Cowes (22 mins; **RED JET 4, RED JET 6, RED JET 7**; every hour or half hour).

1	RED EAGLE	3953t	96	13.0k	93.2m	895P	200C	18L	BA	UK	9117337
2	RED FALCON	3953t	94	13.0k	93.2m	895P	200C	18L	BA	UK	9064047
3»p●	RED JET 3	213t	98	33.0k	32.9m	190P	0C	0L	-	UK	9182758
4»p	RED JET 4	342t	03	35.0k	39.8m	277P	0C	0L	-	UK	9295854
5»p	RED JET 6	363t	16	35.0k	41.1m	275P	0C	0L	-	UK	9788083
6»p	RED JET 7	363t	18	35.0k	41.1m	275P	0C	0L	-	UK	
7	RED OSPREY	3953t	94	13.0k	93.2m	895P	200C	18L	BA	UK	9064059

RED EAGLE Built by Ferguson Shipbuilders, Port Glasgow, UK for the Southampton - East Cowes service. During Winter 2004/05 stretched by 10 metres and height raised by 3 metres at Gdansk, Poland. In spring 2018 she received an upgrade (as RED FALCON in 2014).

RED FALCON Built by Ferguson Shipbuilders, Port Glasgow, UK for the Southampton - East Cowes service. In 2004 stretched by 10 metres and height raised by 3 metres at Gdansk, Poland. In spring 2014 she received a £2m upgrade.

RED JET 3 Catamaran built by FBM Marine, Cowes, Isle of Wight, UK.

RED JET 4 Catamaran built North West Bay Ships Pty Ltd Hobart, Tasmania, Australia.

RED JET 6, RED JET 7 Catamaran built by Wight Shipyard, Cowes, Isle of Wight, UK.

RED OSPREY Built by Ferguson Shipbuilders, Port Glasgow, UK for the Southampton - East Cowes service. In 2003 stretched by 10 metres and height raised by 3 metres at Gdansk, Poland. In spring 2015 she received an upgrade (as RED FALCON in 2014).

Under Construction

| 8F | RED KESTREL | 1070t | 19 | 12.5k | 74.3m | 12P | - | 12L | BA | UK | - |

RED KESTREL Under construction by Cammell Laird, Birkenhead. This new vessel is designed to provide additional year-round freight capacity for the Southampton - East Cowes route.

SHETLAND ISLANDS COUNCIL

THE COMPANY *Shetland Islands Council* is a British local government authority.

MANAGEMENT Ferry Services Manager Craig Robertson, **Marine Superintendent** Ian Pearson.

ADDRESS Port Administration Building, Sella Ness, Mossbank, Shetland ZE2 9QR.

TELEPHONE Administration +44 (0)1806 244234, 244266, **Reservations** *Yell Sound & Bluemull* +44 (0)1595 745804, *Fair Isle* +44 (0)1595 760363, *Whalsay* +44(0)1595 745804, *Skerries* +44 (0)1595 745804, *Papa Stour* +44 (0)1595 745804.

FAX +44 (0)1806 244232.

INTERNET Email ferries@shetland.gov.uk **Website:** www.shetland.gov.uk/ferries *(English)*

ROUTES OPERATED Yell Sound Service Toft (Mainland) - Ulsta (Yell) (20 mins; *DAGALIEN, DAGGRI*; up to 26 per day), **Bluemull Sound Service** (Gutcher (Yell) - Belmont (Unst) (10 mins; *BIGGA, FIVLA, GEIRA*; up to 28 per day), Gutcher – Hamars Ness (Fetlar) (25 mins; *BIGGA, FIVLA, GEIRA*; up to 8 per day), **Bressay** Lerwick (Mainland) - Maryfield (Bressay) (5 mins; *LEIRNA*; up to 23 per day), **Whalsay** Laxo/Vidlin (Mainland) - Symbister (Whalsay) (30-45 mins; *HENDRA, LINGA*; up to 18 per day), **Skerries** Vidlin (Mainland) – Out Skerries (1 hr 30 mins; *FILLA*; up to 10 per week), Out Skerries – Lerwick (3 hours; *FILLA*; 2 per week), **Fair Isle** (Grutness (Mainland) - Fair Isle (3 hrs; *GOOD SHEPHERD IV*; 2 per week), **Papa Stour** West Burrafirth (Mainland) – Papa Stour (40 mins; *SNOLDA*; up to 7 per week).

1	BIGGA	274t	91	11.0k	33.5m	96P	21C	2L	BA	UK	9000821
2	DAGALIEN	1861t	04	12.0k	65.4m	144P	30C	4L	BA	UK	9291626
3	DAGGRI	1861t	04	12.0k	65.4m	144P	30C	4L	BA	UK	9291614
4	FILLA	356t	03	12.0k	35.5m	30P	10C	2L	BA	UK	9269192
5	FIVLA	230t	85	11.0k	29.9m	95P	15C	2L	A	UK	8410237
6	GEIRA	226t	88	10.8k	29.9m	95P	15C	2L	BA	UK	8712489
7	GOOD SHEPHERD IV	76t	86	10.0k	18.3m	12P	2C	0L	C	UK	
8	HENDRA	248	82	11.0k	30.2m	95P	18C	2L	BA	UK	8200254
9	LEIRNA	420t	92	9.0k	35.1m	124P	20C	2L	BA	UK	9050199
10	LINGA	658t	01	11.0k	36.2m	100P	16C	2L	BA	UK	9242170
11	SNOLDA	130t	83	9.0k	24.4m	12P	6C	1L	A	UK	8302090

BIGGA Built by JW Miller & Sons Ltd, St Monans, Fife, UK. Used on the Toft - Ulsta service. In 2005 moved to the Bluemull Sound service.

DAGALIEN, DAGGRI Built by Stocznia Polnócna, Gdansk, Poland to replace the BIGGA and HENDRA on Toft - Ulsta service.

FILLA Built by Stocznia Polnócna, Gdansk, Poland for the Lerwick /Vidlin - Out Skerries service. She looks like an oil rig supply vessel and is capable of transporting fresh water for replenishing the tanks on the Skerries in case of drought.

Red Eagle *(Andrew Cooke)*

Hendra *(Miles Cowsill)*

FIVLA Built by Ailsa Shipbuilding, Troon, UK. Now a spare vessel, though often used on the Bluemull service.

GEIRA Built by Richard Dunston (Hessle), Hessle, UK. Formerly used on the Laxo - Symbister route. Replaced by the HENDRA in 2005 and moved to the Bluemull Sound service.

GOOD SHEPHERD IV Built by JW Miller & Sons Ltd, St Monans, Fife, UK. Used on the service between Grutness (Mainland) and Fair Isle. This vessel is not roll-on roll-off; vehicles are conveyed by special arrangement and generally consist of agricultural vehicles. She is pulled up on the marine slip on Fair Isle at the conclusion of each voyage.

HENDRA Built by McTay Marine, Bromborough, Wirral, UK for the Laxo - Symbister service. In 2002 transferred to the Toft - Ulsta service. In 2004 replaced by new vessels DAGGRI and DAGALIEN and moved to the Bluemull Sound service. In May 2005 returned to the Laxo - Symbister service as second vessel.

LEIRNA Built by Ferguson Shipbuilders, Port Glasgow, UK. Used on the Lerwick - Maryfield (Bressay) service.

LINGA Built by Stocznia Polnócna, Gdansk, Poland. Used on the Laxo - Symbister service.

SNOLDA Built as the FILLA by Sigbjorn Iversen, Flekkefjord, Norway. Used on the Lerwick (Mainland) - Out Skerries and Vidlin (Mainland) - Out Skerries services. At other times she operated freight and charter services around the Shetland Archipelago. She resembles a miniature oil rig supply vessel. Passenger capacity was originally 20 from 1st April to 31st October inclusive but is now 12 all year. In 2003 renamed the SNOLDA; replaced by the new FILLA and, in 2004, transferred to the West Burrafirth - Papa Stour route.

STENA LINE

MANAGEMENT Chief Executive Niclas Mårtensson, **Trade Director North Sea** Annika Hult, **Trade Director Irish Sea North** Paul Grant, **Trade Director Irish Sea South** Ian Davies.

ADDRESS *UK* Stena House, Station Approach, Holyhead, Anglesey LL65 1DQ, ***The Netherlands*** PO Box 2, 3150 AA, Hoek van Holland, The Netherlands.

TELEPHONE Administration *UK* +44 (0)1407) 606631, ***The Netherlands*** +31 (0)174 389333, **Reservations *UK*** 0844 7707070 (from UK only), ***The Netherlands*** +31 (0)174 315811.

FAX Administration & Reservations *UK* +44 (0)1407 606811, ***The Netherlands*** +31 (0)174 387045, **Telex** 31272.

INTERNET Email info@stenaline.com **Website** www.stenaline.co.uk *(English),*

ROUTES OPERATED Conventional Ferries Cairnryan - Belfast (2 hrs 15 mins; *STENA SUPERFAST VII*, *STENA SUPERFAST VII*; up to 6 per day, Port of Liverpool (Twelve Quays River Terminal, Birkenhead) - Belfast (8 hrs; *STENA FORERUNNER*, (freight only), *STENA LAGAN*, *STENA MERSEY*; 1 per day (Mon), 2 per day (Sun, Tue-Sat)), Holyhead - Dublin (3 hrs 15 mins; *STENA ADVENTURER*, *STENA SUPERFAST X*; 4 per day), Fishguard - Rosslare (3 hrs 15 mins on day sailings *STENA EUROPE*; 2 per day), Rosslare - Cherbourg (17 - 20 hrs; *STENA HORIZON*; 3 per week), Harwich - Hoek van Holland (The Netherlands) (7 hrs 30 mins; *STENA BRITANNICA*, *STENA HOLLANDICA*; 2 per day), **Freight Ferries** Heysham - Belfast (7 hrs; *STENA HIBERNIA*, *STENA SCOTIA*; 2 per day), Harwich - Rotterdam (8 hrs; *MISTRAL*, *UNKNOWN*; 11 per week), Killingholme - Hoek van Holland (11 hrs; *STENA TRANSIT*, *STENA TRANSPORTER*; 1 per day), Killingholme - Rotterdam (13 hrs; *MISANA*, *MISIDA*; 6 per week).

1F	MISANA	14100t	07	20.0k	163.9m	12P	-	150T	A	FI	9348936
2F	MISIDA	14100t	07	20.0k	163.9m	12P	-	150T	A	FI	9348948
3F	MISTRAL	10471t	98	22.0k	153.5m	12P	-	112T	A	FI	9183788
4	STENA ADVENTURER	43532t	03	22.0k	210.8m	1500P	-	210L	BA2	UK	9235529
5	STENA BRITANNICA	63600t	10	22.0k	240.0m	1200P	-	300T	BA2	UK	9419175

Stena Horizon *(Gordon Hislip)*

Stena Europe *(Gordon Hislip)*

6	STENA EUROPE	24828t	81	20.5k	149.0m	2076P	456C	60T	BA	UK	7901760
7F	STENA FORERUNNER	24688t	02	22.0k	195.3m	12P	-	210T	A2	SE	9227259
8F	STENA HIBERNIA	13017t	96	18.6k	142.5m	12P	-	114T	A	UK	9121637
9	STENA HOLLANDICA	63600t	10	22.5k	240.0m	1200P	-	300T	BA2	NL	9419163
10	STENA HORIZON	26500t	06	23.5k	186.5m	720P	160C	135L	A	IT	9332559
11	STENA LAGAN	27510t	05	23.5k	186.5m	720P	160C	135T	A	UK	9329849
12	STENA MERSEY	27510t	05	23.5k	186.5m	720P	160C	135T	A	UK	9329851
13F	STENA SCOTIA	13017t	96	18.6k	142.5m	12P	-	114T	A	NL	9121625
14	STENA SUPERFAST VII	30285t	01	22.0k	203.3m	1200P	660C	110L	BA2	UK	9198941
15	STENA SUPERFAST VIII	30285t	01	22.0k	203.3m	1200P	660C	110L	BA2	UK	9198953
16	STENA SUPERFAST X	30285t	02	22.0k	203.3m	1200P	660C	110L	BA2	UK	9211511
17F+	STENA TRANSIT	34700t	11	22.2k	212.0m	300P	-	290T	A2	NL	9469388
18F+	STENA TRANSPORTER	34700t	11	22.2k	212.0m	300P	-	290T	A2	NL	9469376

MISANA, MISIDA Built by J J Sietas, Hamburg, Germany for *Godby Shipping AB* of Finland and time-chartered to *UPM-Kymmene* of Finland to operate between Finland, Spain and Portugal. In July 2013 charter taken over by *Finnlines*. In January 2016 long-term chartered to *Stena RoRo*, who then sub-chartered them to *Transfennica*. In January 2018 chartered to *Stena Line* and placed on the Harwich - Rotterdam service.

MISTRAL Built by J J Sietas KG, Hamburg, Germany for *Godby Shipping AB* of Finland. Chartered to *Transfennica*. In 2003 chartered to *UPM-Kymmene Oy* of Finland and operated between Rauma and Santander. In 2005 chartered to *Finnlines*. Until the end of 2007 used on a Helsinki - Hamina - Zeebrugge service only available northbound for general traffic. From January 2008 operated on *UPM-Kymmene Seaways'* service from Hamina to Lübeck, Amsterdam and Tilbury. In June 2013 charter ended. During the ensuing period she undertook several short charters. In October 2014 chartered to *P&O Ferries* as second ship on the Zeebrugge - Middlesbrough (Teesport) service; she has also operated between Tilbury and Zeebrugge. In early June 2018 replaced by the *Estraden* and at the end of the month sub-chartered to *Stena Line* to operate between Rotterdam and Harwich.

STENA ADVENTURER Ro-pax vessel built by Hyundai Heavy Industries, Ulsan, South Korea, for *Stena RoRo* and chartered to *Stena Line* to operate between Holyhead and Dublin.

STENA BRITANNICA Built by Waden Yards in Wismar and Warnemünde, Germany, for *Stena Rederi* (bow sections constructed at Warnemünde and stern and final assembly at Wismar). Replaced the 2003 built STENA BRITANNICA on the Harwich - Hoek van Holland service.

STENA EUROPE Built as the KRONPRINSESSAN VICTORIA by Götaverken Arendal AB, Göteborg, Sweden for *Göteborg-Frederikshavn Linjen* of Sweden (trading as *Sessan Linjen*) for their Göteborg - Frederikshavn service. Shortly after delivery, the company was taken over by *Stena Line* and services were marketed as *Stena-Sessan Line* for a period. In 1982 she was converted to an overnight ferry by changing one vehicle deck into two additional decks of cabins and she was switched to the Göteborg - Kiel route (with, during the summer, daytime runs from Göteborg to Frederikshavn and Kiel to Korsør (Denmark)). In 1989 she was transferred to the Oslo - Frederikshavn route and renamed the STENA SAGA. In 1994, transferred to *Stena Line BV*, renamed the STENA EUROPE and operated between Hoek van Holland and Harwich. She was withdrawn in June 1997, transferred to the *Lion Ferry* (a *Stena Line* subsidiary) Karlskrona - Gdynia service and renamed the LION EUROPE. In 1998 she was transferred back to *Stena Line* (remaining on the same route) and renamed the STENA EUROPE. In early 2002 the cabins installed in 1982 were removed and other modifications made and she was transferred to the Fishguard - Rosslare route.

STENA FORERUNNER Built by Dalian Shipyard Co Ltd, Dalian, China for *Stena RoRo* and chartered to *Transfennica*. In January 2018 chartered to *Stena Line* and placed on the Rotterdam - Harwich service. In August moved to Birkenhead-Belfast.

STENA HIBERNIA Built as the MAERSK IMPORTER by Miho Shipyard, Shimizu, Japan for *Norfolkline*. Used on the Scheveningen (from 2007 Vlaardingen) - Felixstowe service. In October 2009 moved to the Heysham-Belfast service. In July 2010 renamed the HIBERNIA SEAWAYS. In July 2011 renamed the STENA HIBERNIA. In September 2012 transferred to

Stena Britannica *(Rob de Visser)*

Stena Superfast VII *(Stuart Mackillop)*

Stena Superfast VIII *(George Holland)*

Stena Scotia *(Rob de Visser)*

Stena RoRo. In November chartered to *Stena Line* and placed on the Birkenhead - Belfast service. In September 2015 moved to the Heysham - Belfast route.

STENA HOLLANDICA Built by Nordic Yards in Wismar and Warnemünde, Germany, for *Stena Rederi* (bow sections constructed at Warnemünde and stern and final assembly at Wismar) to replace the previous STENA HOLLANDICA on the Harwich - Hoek van Holland service. Entered service May 2010.

STENA HORIZON Built as the CARTOUR BETA by CN Visentini, Porto Viro, Italy for Levantina Trasporti of Italy. Chartered to *Caronte & Tourist* of Italy and operated between Messina and Salerno (Sicily). In October 2011 chartered to *Celtic Link Ferries*, renamed the CELTIC HORIZON and placed on the Rosslare - Cherbourg route. In March 2014 service and charter taken over by *Stena Line*. Renamed the STENA HORIZON.

STENA LAGAN, STENA MERSEY Built as the LAGAN VIKING and MERSEY VIKING by CN Visentini, Donada, Italy for *Levantina Trasporti* of Italy. Chartered to *NorseMerchant Ferries* and placed on the Birkenhead - Belfast route. In 2008 sold to *Norfolkline*, then resold to *Epic Shipping* and chartered back. In August 2010, following *Norfolkline's* purchase by *DFDS Seaways*, they were renamed the LAGAN SEAWAYS and MERSEY SEAWAYS respectively. Between January and July 2011 they were operated by *Stena Line Irish Sea Ferries*, a 'stand-alone' company pending consideration of a take-over by *Stena Line* by the UK and Irish competition authorities. In July 2011 the take-over was confirmed and in August 2011 they were renamed the STENA LAGAN and STENA MERSEY. In April 2012 they were sold to *Stena RoRo* and chartered back by *Stena Line*.

STENA SCOTIA Built as the MAERSK EXPORTER by Miho Shipyard, Shimizu, Japan for *Norfolkline*. Used on the Scheveningen (from 2007 Vlaardingen) - Felixstowe service until March 2009 when she was moved to the Heysham - Belfast route. In July 2010 renamed the SCOTIA SEAWAYS. In July 2011 renamed the STENA SCOTIA. In September 2013 transferred to *Stena RoRo* and placed on the charter market. In September 2014 chartered to *Stena Line* and inaugurated a new service between Rotterdam and Killingholme. In January 2018 transferred to Rotterdam - Harwich service. In August 2018 transferred to the Heysham - Belfast service.

STENA SUPERFAST VII, STENA SUPERFAST VIII Built as the SUPERFAST VII and SUPERFAST VIII by Howaldtswerke Deutsche Werft AG, Kiel, Germany for *Attica Enterprises* (now *Attica Group*) for use by *Superfast Ferries* between Rostock and Hanko. In 2006 sold to *Tallink*. The Finnish terminal was transferred to Helsinki and daily return trips between Helsinki and Tallinn were introduced. These ceased in September 2008. The operation was ceased for the winter season in December 2009 and 2010. Service resumed at the end of April 2010 and 2011. In August 2011 chartered to *Stena Line* and renamed the STENA SUPERFAST VII, STENA SUPERFAST VIII. In November 2011, after a major refit, they were placed on a service between Cairnryan and Belfast (replacing the Stranraer - Belfast service). In December 2017 purchased by *Stena Ropax*.

STENA SUPERFAST X Built as the SUPERFAST X by Howaldtswerke Deutsche Werft AG, Kiel, Germany for *Attica Enterprises* (now *Attica Group*) for use by *Superfast Ferries*. In May 2002 she and the SUPERFAST IX (see ATLANTIC VISION, *Tallink*, Section 6) began operating between Rosyth (Scotland) and Zeebrugge. In 2004 fitted with additional cabins and conference/seating areas. In 2007 sold to *Veolia Transportation* and renamed the JEAN NICOLI. Chartered to *CoTuNav* of Tunisia and operated between France/Italy and Tunisia. Later chartered to *ANEK Lines* of Greece and operated on the Patras - Corfu - Igoumenitsa - Venezia route. In July 2008 chartered to *SeaFrance* and renamed the SEAFRANCE MOLIERE. After modifications she was placed on the Dover - Calais route. In November 2011 laid up. In January 2012 offered for sale or charter. In July 2012 sold to *Scapino Shipping Ltd* of Monaco and renamed the MOLIERE. In October 2012 chartered to the *DFDS/LD Lines* joint venture and, in November, renamed the DIEPPE SEAWAYS and introduced onto the Dover - Calais service. In May 2014 sold to *Stena Line North Sea Ltd*. In December 2014 charter ended. Refurbished and, in March 2015, chartered to *Stena Line*, renamed the STENA SUPERFAST X and placed on the Holyhead - Dublin route.

Sound of Soay *(Brain Maxted)*

Hunters Quay, Dunoon *(Brain Maxted)*

STENA TRANSIT, STENA TRANSPORTER Built by Samsung Heavy Industries, Koje, South Korea. Used on the Hoek van Holland - Killingholme service.

Under Construction

19	NEWBUILDING 1	42000t	19	22k	214.5m	927P	300C	180L	BA2	-	-
20	NEWBUILDING 2	42000t	20	22k	214.5m	927P	300C	180L	BA2	-	-
21	NEWBUILDING 4	42000t	20	22k	214.5m	927P	300C	180L	BA2	-	-
22	NEWBUILDING 7	-	22	22k	239.7m	1200P	300C	220L	BA2	-	-
23	NEWBUILDING 8	-	22	22k	239.7m	1200P	300C	220L	BA2	-	-

NEWBUILDING 1, NEWBUILDING 2, NEWBUILDING 4 Under construction for *Stena Line* by AVIC International Maritime Holdings, Weihai, China. They are designed to run traditional fuel but are under the class notation "gas ready" and can be converted to run on natural gas. NEWBUILDING 1 is planned to operated on Holyhead-Dublin. NEWBUILDING 2 and 4 are planned to operate on the Liverpool - Belfast route. There are also a NEWBUILDING 3 and a NEWBUILDING 6 which are to be chartered to *Brittany Ferries* on delivery and are listed under that heading (under their chosen names) and a NEWBUILDING 5 which is to be chartered to *DFDS Seaways* on delivery and is listed under that heading.

NEWBUILDING 7, NEWBUILDING 8 A lengthened version of NEWBUILDING 1-6. It has been announced they will operate for *Stena Line* but whether this is in UK waters or in the Baltic is not known. *Stena Line* have an option for four more similar vessels.

WESTERN FERRIES

THE COMPANY *Western Ferries (Clyde) Ltd* is a British private sector company.

MANAGEMENT Managing Director Gordon Ross.

ADDRESS Hunter's Quay, Dunoon, Argyll PA23 8HJ.

TELEPHONE Administration +44 (0)1369 704452, **Reservations** Not applicable.

INTERNET Email enquiries@western-ferries.co.uk **Website** www.western-ferries.co.uk *(English)*,

ROUTE OPERATED McInroy's Point (Gourock) - Hunter's Quay (Dunoon) (20 mins; *SOUND OF SCARBA*, *SOUND OF SEIL*, *SOUND OF SHUNA*, *SOUND OF SOAY*; every 20 mins (15 mins in peaks)).

1	SOUND OF SCARBA	489t	01	11.0k	49.95m	220P	40C	4/5L	BA	UK	9237424
2	SOUND OF SEIL	497t	13	11.0k	49.95m	220P	40C	4/5L	BA	UK	9665217
3	SOUND OF SHUNA	489t	03	11.0k	49.95m	220P	40C	4/5L	BA	UK	9289441
4	SOUND OF SOAY	497t	13	11.0k	49.95m	220P	40C	4/5L	BA	UK	9665229

SOUND OF SCARBA, SOUND OF SHUNA Built by Ferguson Shipbuilders, Port Glasgow, UK for *Western Ferries*.

SOUND OF SEIL, SOUND OF SOAY Built by Cammell Laird Shiprepairers & Shipbuilders, Birkenhead, UK for *Western Ferries*.

WIGHTLINK

THE COMPANY *Wightlink* is a British private sector company, owned by *Basalt Infrastructure Partners LLP*, formerly known as *Balfour Beatty Infrastructure Partners (BBIP)*. The routes and vessels were previously part of *Sealink (British Rail)* but were excluded from the purchase of most of the *Sealink* operations by *Stena Line AB* in 1990. They remained in *Sea Containers'* ownership until purchased by *CINVen* Ltd, a venture capital company in 1995. The company was the subject of a management buy-out financed by the *Royal Bank of Scotland* in 2001 and was sold to the *Macquarie Group* of Australia in 2005. It was purchased by *Balfour Beatty Infrastructure Partners LLP* in February 2015.

MANAGEMENT Chief Executive Keith Greenfield, **Finance Director** Jonathan Pascoe **Operations Director** Daryl Palmer, **Marketing and Innovation Director** Stuart James,

SECTION 1 – GB & IRELAND PASSENGER OPERATIONS

Ferries 2019

Project Director John Burrows, **Business Development Director** Clive Tilley, **Interim Human Resources Director** Karen Wellman.

ADDRESS Gunwharf Road, Portsmouth PO1 2LA.

TELEPHONE Administration and Reservations +44 (0)333 999 7333.

INTERNET Email bookings@wightlink.co.uk **Website** www.wightlink.co.uk *(English, Dutch, French, German),*

ROUTES OPERATED Conventional Ferries Lymington - Yarmouth (Isle of Wight) (approx 40 mins; *WIGHT LIGHT, WIGHT SKY*; hourly), Portsmouth - Fishbourne (Isle of Wight) (approx 45 mins; *ST. CECILIA, ST. CLARE, ST. FAITH, VICTORIA OF WIGHT, WIGHT SUN*; half-hourly or hourly depending on time of day). **Fast Cats** Portsmouth - Ryde (Isle of Wight) (passenger-only) (under 22 mins; *WIGHT RYDER I, WIGHT RYDER II*; 2 per hour).

1	ST. CECILIA	2968t	86	12.0k	77.0m	771P	142C	12L	BA	UK	8518546
2	ST. CLARE	5359t	01	13.0k	86.0m	878P	186C	-	BA2	UK	9236949
3	ST. FAITH	3009t	89	12.5k	77.0m	771P	142C	12L	BA	UK	8907228
4	VICTORIA OF WIGHT	8200t	18	13.0k	89.7m	1208P	178C	-	BA2	UK	9791028
5	WIGHT LIGHT	2546t	08	11.0k	62.4m	360P	65C	-	BA	UK	9446972
6»p	WIGHT RYDER I	520t	09	20.0k	40.9m	260P	0C	-	-	UK	9512537
7»p	WIGHT RYDER II	520t	09	20.0k	40.9m	260P	0C	-	-	UK	9512549
8	WIGHT SKY	2456t	08	11.0k	62.4m	360P	65C	-	BA	UK	9446984
9	WIGHT SUN	2546t	09	11.0k	62.4m	360P	65C	-	BA	UK	9490416

ST. CECILIA, ST FAITH Built by Cochrane Shipbuilders, Selby, UK for *Sealink British Ferries* for the Portsmouth - Fishbourne service.

ST. CLARE Built by Stocznia Remontowa, Gdansk, Poland for the Portsmouth - Fishbourne service. She is a double-ended ferry with a central bridge. During winter 2015/16 modified for double deck loading.

VICTORIA OF WIGHT Built by the Cemre Shipyard, Yalova, Turkey. She is a hybrid diesel/battery electric vessel.

WIGHT LIGHT, WIGHT SKY, WIGHT SUN Built by Brodogradilište Kraljevica, Croatia for the Lymington - Yarmouth route. One of these ships now operates on the Portsmouth - Fishbourne route.

WIGHT RYDER I, WIGHT RYDER II Catamarans built by FBMA Marine, Balamban, Cebu, Philippines. Operate on the Portsmouth - Ryde service.

Wight Sky *(Andrew Wood)*

St Clare and Normandie Express *(Andrew Cooke)*

Glenbrook *(Brian Maxted)*

Morvern *(Brian Maxted)*

Corran *(Brian Maxted)*

SECTION 2 – MINOR PASSENGER OPERATORS
ARGYLL AND BUTE COUNCIL

THE COMPANY *Argyll and Bute Council* is a British local government authority.

Head of Economic Development and Strategic Transportation Jim Smith,

Marine Operations Manager Stewart Clark.

ADDRESS 1A Manse Brae, Lochgilphead, Argyll PA31 8RD.

TELEPHONE Administration +44 (0)1546 604673.

FAX Administration +44 (0)1546 604738.

INTERNET Email stewart.clark@argyll-bute.gov.uk **Website** www.argyll-bute.gov.uk/transport-and-streets/ferry-travel

ROUTES OPERATED Vehicle ferries Seil - Luing (5 mins; *BELNAHUA*; approx half-hourly), Port Askaig (Islay) - Feolin (Jura) (5 mins; *EILEAN DHIURA*; approx half-hourly). **Passenger-only ferries** Port Appin – Lismore (10 mins; *THE LISMORE*; approx hourly), Ellenabeich – Easdale (5 mins; *EASDALE*; approx quarter-hourly).

1	BELNAHUA	35t	72	8.0k	17.1m	40P	5C	1L	BA	UK	
2p	EASDALE	-	93	6.5k	6.4m	11P	0C	0L	-	UK	
3	EILEAN DHIURA	86t	98	9.0k	25.6m	50P	13C	1L	BA	UK	
4p	THE LISMORE	12t	88	8.0k	9.7m	20P	0C	0L	-	UK	

BELNAHUA Built by Campbeltown Shipyard, Campbeltown, UK for *Argyll County Council* for the Seil - Luing service. In 1975, following local government reorganisation, transferred to *Strathclyde Regional Council*. In 1996, transferred to *Argyll and Bute Council*.

EASDALE Built for *Strathclyde Regional Council* for the Ellenabeich - Easdale passenger-only service. In 1996, following local government reorganisation, transferred to *Argyll and Bute Council*.

EILEAN DHIURA Built by McTay Marine, Bromborough, Wirral, UK for *Argyll and Bute Council* to replace the *Western Ferries (Argyll)* SOUND OF GIGHA on the Islay - Jura route. *ASP Ship Management* manage and operate this vessel on behalf of *Argyll and Bute Council*.

THE LISMORE Built for *Strathclyde Regional Council* for the Port Appin – Lismore passenger-only service. In 1996, following local government reorganisation, transferred to *Argyll and Bute Council*.

ARRANMORE FAST FERRIES

THE COMPANY *Arranmore Fast Ferries*, trading as *Arranmore Blue Ferry and Tory Ferry*, is a Republic of Ireland private sector company.

MANAGEMENT Managing Director Seamus Boyle.

ADDRESS Blue Ferry Office, Burtonport, Letterkenny, Co. Donegal, Republic of Ireland.

TELEPHONE Administration & Reservations +353 (0)87 3171810.

INTERNET Email: info.fastferry@gmail.com **Website** www.arranmorefastferry.com *(English)*.

ROUTES OPERATED Arranmore Blue Ferry Burtonport (County Donegal) - Leabgarrow (Arranmore Island) (20 mins; *MORVERN*; up to 8 per day), **Tory Ferry** Magheroarty (County Donegal) - Tory Island (45 mins; *QUEEN OF ARAN*; up to 4 per day).

1	MORVERN	83t	73	8.0k	26.6m	96P	10C	-	B	IR	7235501
2p	OCEAN WARRIOR	18t	89	18.0k	14.3m	12P	0C	-	-	IR	
3p	QUEEN OF ARAN	113t	76		20.1m	96P	-	-	IR	7527928),	

MORVERN Built by James Lamont & Co Ltd, Port Glasgow, UK for *Caledonian MacBrayne*. After service on a number of routes she was, after 1979, the main vessel on the Fionnphort (Mull) - Iona service. In 1992 she was replaced by the LOCH BUIE and became a spare vessel. In 1995 sold to *Arranmore Island Ferry Services*. In 2001 sold to *Bere Island Ferries*. In February 2010 refurbished by Bere Island Boatyard and sold to *Arranmore Charters* (now *Arranmore Fast Ferries*). Extended in June 2012.

OCEAN WARRIOR Built by FBM Marine, Cowes, Isle of Wight as an RNLI Tyne class lifeboat ALEXANDER COUTANACHE (No1157) and operated at St Helier, Channel Islands until June 2009 when she became a relief vessel. Bought by *Arranmore Fast Ferries* in December 2014 and renamed the OCEAN WARRIOR.

QUEEN OF ARAN built in 1976 as the SHONAG OF KISHORN to work at the oil rig construction site in Loch Kishorn in Scotland. Moved to Ireland in1985 and eventually became the QUEEN OF ARAN. In 2017 sold to *Arranmore Fast Ferries* and, after a major refit, placed on the Tory island service.

ARRANMORE ISLAND FERRY SERVICES

THE COMPANY *Arranmore Island Ferry Services (Bád Farrantoireacht Arainn Mhór)*, trading as *Arranmore Red Ferry*, is a Republic of Ireland company, supported by *Roinn na Gaeltachta (The Gaeltacht Authority)*, a semi-state-owned body responsible for tourism and development in the Irish-speaking areas of The Republic of Ireland. They also operate the summer only Lough Swilly service.

MANAGEMENT Managing Director Dominic Sweeney.

ADDRESS Cara na nOilean, Burtonport Pier, Letterkenny, Co. Donegal, Republic of Ireland.

TELEPHONE Administration & Reservations *Arranmore Island Service* +353 (0)7495 20532, +353 (0)7495 42233, *Lough Swilly Service* +353 (0)87 2112331.

INTERNET Email arranmoreferry@gmail.com loughswillyferry@gmail.com **Websites** www.arranmoreferry.com swillyferry.com *(English)*

ROUTES OPERATED *Arranmore Island Service* Burtonport (County Donegal) - Leabgarrow (Arranmore Island) (15 mins; **COLL or RHUM**; up to 8 per day (Summer), 6 per day (Winter)), **Lough Swilly Service (summer only)** Buncrana (County Donegal) - Rathmullan (County Donegal) (20 mins; **SPIRIT OF LOUGH SWILLY**; up to 8 per day).

1	COLL	69t	74	8.0k	25.3m	96P	6C	-	B	IR	7327990
2	RHUM	69t	73	8.0k	25.3m	96P	6C	-	B	IR	7319589
3	SPIRIT OF LOUGH SWILLY	110t	59	-	32.0m	57P	12C	-	BA	IR	

COLL Built by James Lamont & Co Ltd, Port Glasgow, UK for *Caledonian MacBrayne*. For several years she was employed mainly in a relief capacity. In 1986 she took over the Tobermory (Mull) - Kilchoan service from a passenger-only vessel; the conveyance of vehicles was not inaugurated until 1991. In 1996 she was transferred to the Oban - Lismore route. In 1998 she was sold to *Arranmore Island Ferry Services*.

RHUM Built by James Lamont & Co Ltd, Port Glasgow, UK for *Caledonian MacBrayne*. Until 1987, she was used primarily on the Claonaig - Lochranza (Arran) service. After that time she served on various routes. In 1994 she inaugurated a new service between Tarbert (Loch Fyne) and Portavadie. In 1997 she operated between Kyles Scalpay and Scalpay until the opening of the new bridge on 16th December 1997. In 1998 she was sold to *Arranmore Island Ferry Services*.

SPIRIT OF LOUGH SWILLY Built as the LORELEY V by Ruthof, Mainz, Germany to operate between St Goarshausen and St Goar on the River Rhine. In 2004 replaced by a new vessel (the LORELEY VI) and became a reserve vessel. In 2007, sold to the *Waterford Castle Hotel* and renamed the LORELEY and, in 2008, replaced the previous ferry. Modified for cable guidance. In August 2014 replaced by the MARY FITZGERALD and laid up. In July 2017 sold to sold to *Arranmore Island Ferry Services*, changed back to self steering and renamed the SPIRIT OF LOUGH SWILLY. Placed on the Lough Swilly service.

BERE ISLAND FERRIES

THE COMPANY *Bere Island Ferries Ltd* is a Republic of Ireland private sector company.

MANAGEMENT Operator Colum Harrington.

ADDRESS Ferry Lodge, West End, Bere Island, Beara, County Cork, Republic of Ireland.

TELEPHONE Administration +353 (0)27 75009, **Reservations** Not applicable, **Mobile** +353 (0)86 2423140.

FAX Administration +353 (0)27 75000, **Reservations** Not applicable.

INTERNET Email biferry@eircom.net **Website** www.bereislandferries.com (English)

1	HOUTON LASS	58t	60	9.0k	22.9m	12P	10C	1L	B	IR
2F	KIRSTY M	109t	66	10.5k	23.7m	0P	-	1L	B	IR
3	OILEAN NA H-OIGE	69t	80	7.0k	18.6m	75P	4C	-	B	IR
4	SANCTA MARIA	67t	83	7.0k	18.6m	75P	4C	-	B	IR

HOUTON LASS Built by Magnaport Marine Ltd, Poole, UK for Flotta Oil Terminals, Stromness, Orkney Islands. Later sold for use as an antipollution vessel on the Black Isle, near Inverness. In November 2013 delivered to *Bere Island Ferries Ltd*. During 2014-2016 refurbished and lengthened in Galway. Mainly in use for transporting lorries but is also used for taking (up to) 10 cars during busy times.

KIRSTY M Landing craft (Klasse 521) built as the LCM 12 SPROTTE by Rheinwerft Walsum, Walsum, Germany for the German Navy. In 1993 withdrawn and sold to a German firm and converted to a civilian ferry. She was later sold to *Mainstream Salmon Farm (Aquascot Seafarms Ltd)*, Orkney, renamed the KIRSTY M and used as a work boat. In December 2009 sold to *Bere Island Ferries* and converted back to ferry operation. She is used in a freight-only mode and has no licence to carry passengers.

OILEAN NA H-OIGE Built as the EILEAN NA H-OIGE by Lewis Offshore Ltd, Stornoway, UK for *Western Isles Islands Council* (from 1st April 1996 the *Western Isles Council* and from 1st January 1998 *Comhairle Nan Eilean Siar*) for their Ludaig (South Uist) - Eriskay service. From 2000 operated from a temporary slipway at the Eriskay causeway. This route ceased in July 2001 following the full opening of the causeway and she was laid up. In 2002 she was moved to the Eriskay - Barra service. In 2003 replaced by the LOCH BHRUSDA of *Caledonian MacBrayne* and laid up. Later sold to *Bere Island Ferries* and renamed the OILEAN NA H-OIGE (same name - "The Island of Youth" - in Irish rather than Scots Gaelic).

SANCTA MARIA Built as the EILEAN BHEARNARAIGH by George Brown & Company, Greenock, UK for *Western Isles Islands Council* for their Otternish (North Uist) - Berneray service. From 1996 until 1999 she was operated by *Caledonian MacBrayne* in conjunction with the LOCH BHRUSDA on the service between Otternish and Berneray and during the winter she was laid up. Following the opening of a causeway between North Uist and Berneray in early 1999, the ferry service ceased and she became reserve vessel for the Eriskay route. This route ceased in July 2001 following the opening of a causeway and she was laid up. In 2002 operated between Eriskay and Barra as reserve vessel. In 2003 sold to *Transalpine Redemptorists Inc*, a community of monks who live on Papa Stronsay, Orkney. Used for conveying supplies to the island - not a public service. In 2008 sold to *Bere Island Ferries*. Entered service in May 2009.

SECTION 2 – MINOR FERRY OPERATORS

BK MARINE

THE COMPANY *BK Marine* is a UK company.

MANAGEMENT Managing Director Donald Gordon Fraser Ross.

ADDRESS Herrislea House Hotel, Veensgarth, Tingwall, Shetland ZE2 9SB.

TELEPHONE Administration & Reservations +44 (0)1595 840208.

INTERNET Website www.bkmarine.co.uk *(English)*,

ROUTE OPERATED *All year* Foula - Walls (Mainland) (2 hours; *NEW ADVANCE*; 2 per week (Winter), 3 per week (Summer)), *Summer only* Foula - Scalloway (3 hrs 30 mins; *NEW ADVANCE*; alternate Thursdays).

1	NEW ADVANCE	25t	96	8.7k	9.8m	12P	1C	0L	C	UK

NEW ADVANCE Built by Richardson's, Stromness, Orkney, UK for *Shetland Islands Council* for the Foula service. Although built at Penryn, Cornwall, she was completed at Stromness. She has a Cygnus Marine GM38 hull and is based on the island where she can be lifted out of the water. Vehicle capacity is to take residents' vehicles to the island - not for tourist vehicles. In 2004 it was announced that the vessel and service would be transferred to the *Foula Community*. However, it was then found that under EU rules the route needed to be offered for competitive tender. In July 2006 the contract was awarded to *Atlantic Ferries Ltd* who began operations in October 2006. In August 2011 replaced by *BK Marine*.

CLARE ISLAND FERRY COMPANY

THE COMPANY *Clare Island Ferry Company* is owned and operated by the O'Grady family, natives of Clare Island, Republic of Ireland, who have been operating the Clare Island Mail Boat Ferry service since 1880.

MANAGEMENT Managing Director Chris O'Grady.

ADDRESS Clare Island Ferry Co Ltd, Clare Island, Co Mayo, F28 AT04, Republic Of Ireland.

TELEPHONE/FAX *May-September* +353 (0)98 23737 *Winter* +353 (0)98 25212, +353 (0)86 8515003.

INTERNET Email clareislandferry@anu.ie **Website** www.clareislandferry.com *(English)*,

ROUTE OPERATED Roonagh (Co Mayo) - Clare Island (15 mins; *CLEW BAY QUEEN*, *EIGG*, *PIRATE QUEEN*, *SEA SPRINTER*; *Winter* 1 to 2 trips per day, *Summer* up to 5 per day, Roonagh - Inishturk (50 mins; *CLEW BAY QUEEN*, *EIGG*, *PIRATE QUEEN*, *SEA SPRINTER*; *Winter* 1 per day *Summer* up to 2 per day. Tourist vehicles are not normally carried.

1	CLEW BAY QUEEN	64t	72	10.0k	21.9m	96P	6C	-	B	IR	
2	EIGG	69t	75	8.0k	24.3m	75P	6C	-	B	IR	7340411
3p	PIRATE QUEEN	73t	96	10.5k	19.8m	96P	0C	-	-	IR	
4p	SEA SPRINTER	16t	93	22.0k	11.6m	35P	0C	-	-	IR	

CLEW BAY QUEEN Built as the KILBRANNAN by James Lamont & Co Ltd, Port Glasgow, UK for *Caledonian MacBrayne*. Used on a variety of routes until 1977, she was then transferred to the Scalpay (Harris) - Kyles Scalpay service. In 1990 she was replaced by the CANNA and, in turn, replaced the CANNA in her reserve/relief role. In 1992 sold to *Arranmore Island Ferry Services* and renamed the ÁRAINN MHÓR. She was subsequently sold to *Údarás na Gaeltachta* and leased back to *Arranmore Island Ferry Services*. In 2008 she was sold to *Clare Island Ferry Company* and renamed the CLEW BAY QUEEN. She operates a passenger and heavy freight service to both Clare Island and Inishturk all year round. In winter passenger capacity is reduced to 47 with 3 crew. Fitted with crane for loading and unloading cargo.

EIGG *(EILEAN EIGE)* Built by James Lamont & Co, Port Glasgow, UK. Since 1976 she has been employed mainly on the Oban - Lismore service. In 1996 she was transferred to the

Maid of Glencoul (Brian Maxted)

Clew Bay Queen (Nick Widdows)

Tobermory (Mull) - Kilchoan route, very occasionally making sailings to the Small Isles (Canna, Eigg, Muck and Rum) for special cargoes. In 1999 her wheelhouse was raised to make it easier to see over taller lorries and she returned to the Oban - Lismore route. In June 2018 sold to *Clare Island Ferry Company*.

PIRATE QUEEN Built by Arklow Marine Services in 1996 for *Clare Island Ferry Company*. She operates a daily passenger and light cargo service to Clare Island and Inishturk all year round. In winter passenger capacity is reduced to 47 with 3 crew. Fitted with crane for loading and unloading cargo.

SEA SPRINTER Built by Lochin Marine, East Sussex, UK for *Island Ferries* (now *Aran Island Ferries*) of the Irish Republic. In June 2015 sold to *Clare Island Ferries*.

CROSS RIVER FERRIES

THE COMPANY *Cross River Ferries Ltd* is a Republic of Ireland company, part of the *Doyle Shipping Group*.

MANAGEMENT Operations Manager Eoin O'Sullivan.

ADDRESS Westlands House, Rushbrooke, Cobh, County Cork, P24 H940, Republic of Ireland.

TELEPHONE Administration +353 (0)21 481 1485 **Reservations** Not applicable.

INTERNET Website crossriverferries.ie *(English)*,

ROUTE OPERATED Carrigaloe (near Cobh, on Great Island) - Glenbrook (Co Cork) (4 mins; **CARRIGALOE**, **GLENBROOK**; frequent service 07.00 - 00.15 (one or two vessels used according to demand)).

1	CARRIGALOE	225t	70	8.0k	49.1m	200P	27C	-	BA	IR	7028386
2	GLENBROOK	225t	71	8.0k	49.1m	200P	27C	-	BA	IR	7101607

CARRIGALOE Built as the KYLEAKIN by Newport Shipbuilding and Engineering Company, Newport (Gwent), UK for the *Caledonian Steam Packet Company* (later *Caledonian MacBrayne*) for the Kyle of Lochalsh - Kyleakin service. In 1991 sold to *Marine Transport Services Ltd* and renamed the CARRIGALOE. She entered service in March 1993. In Summer 2002 chartered to the *Lough Foyle Ferry Company*, returning in Spring 2003.

GLENBROOK Built as the LOCHALSH by Newport Shipbuilding and Engineering Company, Newport (Gwent), UK for the *Caledonian Steam Packet Company* (later *Caledonian MacBrayne*) for the Kyle of Lochalsh - Kyleakin service. In 1991 sold to *Marine Transport Services Ltd* and renamed the GLENBROOK. She entered service in March 1993.

FRAZER FERRIES

THE COMPANY *Frazer Ferries Ltd*, is a Republic of Ireland company. In June 2016 it took over *Passage East Ferries* and *Lough Foyle Ferry Service*. The *Carlingford Ferry* started in June 2017.

MANAGEMENT Director John Driscol, **Chief Executive** Pamela Houston **Manager, Passage East Ferry** Gary O Hanlon.

ADDRESSES Registered Office Riverfront, Howley's Quay, Limerick, V94 WTK7, Republic of Ireland, **Lough Foyle Ferry** The Pier, Greencastle, Co Donegal, Republic of Ireland, **Carlingford Ferry** Greenore Port, The Harbour, Greenore, Co. Louth, A91 A0V1, Republic of Ireland. **Passage East Ferry** Barrack Street, Passage East, Co Waterford, X91 C52E, Republic of Ireland.

TELEPHONE Passage East Ferry +353 (0)51 382480.

FAX Passage East Ferry +353 (0)51 382598.

INTERNET Carlingford Ferry Website carlingfordferry.com *(English)* **Lough Foyle Ferry** www.loughfoyleferry.com *(English)* **Passage East Ferry Email** passageferry@eircom.net **Website** www.passageferry.ie *(English)*,

ROUTES OPERATED *All Year Service* **Carlingford Ferry** Greenore, Co Louth, Republic of Ireland - Greencastle, Co Down, Northern Ireland (15 minutes; *AISLING GABRIELLE*; hourly), **Passage East Ferry** Passage East (County Waterford) - Ballyhack (County Wexford) (7 mins; *FBD TINTERN*; frequent service), *Summer Service* **Lough Foyle Ferry** *July - September* Greencastle (Inishowen, Co Donegal, Republic of Ireland) - Magilligan (Co Londonderry, Northern Ireland) (15 mins; *FRAZER MARINER*; frequent service),

1	AISLING GABRIELLE	324t	78	10.0k	47.9m	300P	44C	-	BA	IR	7800033
2	FRAZER MARINER	-	83	7.2k	43.0m	100P	20C	-	BA	IR	
3	FRAZER TINTERN	236t	71	9.0k	54.8m	130P	30C	-	BA	IR	
4	STRANGFORD 1	186t	69	10.0k	32.9m	263P	20C	-	BA	UK	6926311

AISLING GABRIELLE Built as the SHANNON WILLOW by Scott & Sons (Bowling) Ltd, Bowling, Glasgow, UK for *Shannon Ferry Ltd*. In 2000 replaced by the SHANNON BREEZE and laid up for sale. In 2003 sold to the *Lough Foyle Ferry Company Ltd* and renamed the FOYLE VENTURE. In November 2015 sold to *Frazer Ferries*. In July 2016 re-opened the *Lough Foyle Ferry;* this ceased in October. In February 2017 renamed the AISLING GABRIELLE. In July 2017 inaugurated a new Carlingford Lough service.

FRAZER MARINER Built as the BERNE-FARGE for *Schnellastfähre Berne-Farge GmbH* (from 1993 *Fähren Bremen-Stedingen GmbH*) to operate across the River Weser (Vegesack - Lemwerder and Berne - Farge). In January 2017 sold to *Frazer Ferries*. In July 2017 renamed the FRAZER MARINER and began operating between Greencastle and Magilligan.

FRAZER TINTERN Built as the STADT LINZ by Schiffswerft Oberwinter, Oberwinter, Rhein, Germany for *Rheinfähre Linz - Remagen GmbH* of Germany and operated on the Rhine between Linz and Remagen. In 1990 renamed the ST JOHANNES. In 1997 sold to *Fähren Bremen-Stedingen GmbH*, renamed the VEGESACK and operated across the Weser between Lemwerder and Vegesack. In 2003 she became a reserve vessel and in 2004 was renamed the STEDINGEN. Later sold to *Schraven BV* of The Netherlands and refurbished. In Autumn 2005 sold to *Passage East Ferry* and renamed the FBD TINTERN. During 2017 renamed the FRAZER TINTERN

STRANGFORD 1 Built as the STRANGFORD FERRY by Verolme Dockyard Ltd, Cork, Republic of Ireland for *Down County Council*. Subsequently transferred to the *DOE (Northern Ireland)* and then the *DRD (Northern Ireland)*. Following entry into service of the STRANGFORD II in February 2016, she was withdrawn. In December 2017 sold to *Arranmore Island Ferry Services* and renamed the STRANGFORD 1. In June 2018 sold to *Frazer Ferries*. Used as a reserve vessel.

THE HIGHLAND COUNCIL

THE COMPANY *The Highland Council* is a Scottish local authority.

MANAGEMENT Area Roads Operations Manager Richard Porteous, **Ferry Foremen** Allan McCowan and Donald Dixon.

ADDRESS *Area Office* Lochybridge Depot, Carr's Corner Industrial Estate, Fort William PH33 6TQ, *Ferry Office* Ferry Cottage, Ardgour, Fort William PH33 7AA.

TELEPHONE Administration *Area Office* +44 (0)1397 709000, *Corran* +44 (0)1855 841243.

INTERNET Email communityservices@highland.gov.uk **Website** www.highland.gov.uk/info/1526/public_and_community_transport/776/corran_ferry/1 *(English),*

ROUTES OPERATED Vehicle Ferries Corran - Ardgour (5 mins; *CORRAN, MAID OF GLENCOUL*; half-hourly).

| 1 | CORRAN | 351t | 01 | 10.0k | 42.0m | 150P | 30C | 2L | BA | UK | 9225990 |
| 2 | MAID OF GLENCOUL | 166t | 75 | 8.0k | 32.0m | 116P | 16C | 1L | BA | UK | 7521613 |

CORRAN Built by George Prior Engineering Ltd, Hull, UK for *The Highland Council* to replace the MAID OF GLENCOUL as main vessel.

MAID OF GLENCOUL Built by William McCrindle Ltd, Shipbuilders, Ardrossan, UK for *Highland Regional Council* for the service between Kylesku and Kylestrome. In 1984 the ferry service was replaced by a bridge and she was transferred to the Corran - Ardgour service. In April 1996, ownership transferred to *The Highland Council*. In 2001 she became the reserve vessel.

The *Highland Council* also supports both services operated by *Highland Ferries*.

HIGHLAND FERRIES

THE COMPANY *Highland Ferries* is a UK private sector operation. Services are operated under contract to *The Highland Council*.

MANAGEMENT Operator Dougie Robertson.

TELEPHONE Administration +44(0)7468 417137 **Reservations** Not applicable.

INTERNET Email southuist24@hotmail.co.uk

Facebook www.facebook.com/CamusnagaulFerry

1p	BHOY TAYLOR	-	80	7.5k	9.8m	26P	0C	0L	-	UK	
2	RENFREW ROSE	65t	84	7.6k	17.5m	12P	3C	0L	B	UK	

ROUTES OPERATED Vehicle Ferry 1st June - 30th September Cromarty - Nigg (Ross-shire) (10 mins; *RENFREW ROSE*; half-hourly), **Passenger-only Ferry** Fort William - Camusnagaul (10 mins; *BHOY TAYLOR*; up to 5 per day).

BHOY TAYLOR Built as the CAILIN AN AISEAG by Buckie Shipbuilders Ltd, Buckie, UK for *Highland Regional Council* and used on the Fort William - Camusnagaul passenger-only service. In 2006 the service transferred to *Geoff Ward* under contract with a different vessel. In 2013 the CAILIN AN AISEAG resumed service with *Highland Ferries* as contractor. In April 2013 renamed the BHOY TAYLOR.

RENFREW ROSE Built by MacCrindle Shipbuilding Ltd, Ardrossan for *Strathclyde PTE* (later *Strathclyde Partnership for Transport*). Built as a small car ferry but operated passenger only between Renfrew and Yoker (apart from occasionally carrying ambulances in earlier days before they became too heavy). In March 2010 laid up. In June 2012 sold to *Arranmore Fast Ferries* for use as a passenger/car ferry. In June 2016 sold to *Highland Ferries* to reopen the Cromarty - Nigg service.

ISLES OF SCILLY STEAMSHIP COMPANY

THE COMPANY *Isles of Scilly Steamship Company* is a British private sector company.

MANAGEMENT Chief Executive Robert Goldsmith, **Marketing & Communications Manager** Sharon Sandercock, **Chief Operating Officer** Stuart Ried.

ADDRESS Scilly PO Box 10, Hugh Town, St Mary's, Isles of Scilly TR21 0LJ, *Penzance* Steamship House, Quay Street, Penzance, Cornwall, TR18 4BZ.

TELEPHONE Administration & Reservations +44 (0) 1736 334220.

INTERNET Email sales@islesofscilly-travel.co.uk **Website** www.islesofscilly-travel.co.uk *(English).*

ROUTES OPERATED Passenger services: Penzance - St Mary's (Isles of Scilly) (2 hrs 40 mins; *SCILLONIAN III*; 1 per day), St Mary's - Tresco/St Martin's/St Agnes/Bryher; *LYONESSE LADY*, *SWIFT LADY (inter-island boats)*; irregular), *Freight service*: GRY *MARITHA*; Freight from Penzance Monday, Wednesday and Fridays (weather dependant, all year round).

1F	GRY MARITHA	590t	81	10.5k	40.3m	6P	5C	1L	C	UK	8008462

Renfrew Rose *(Brian Maxted)*

Spirit of Rathlin *(Nick Widdows)*

2	LYONESSE LADY	40t	91	9.0k	15.5m	4P	1C	0L	AC	UK	
3F	MALI ROSE	768t	92	-	50.2m	6P	10C	1L	SC	NO	9065144
4	SCILLONIAN III	1346t	77	15.5k	67.7m	485P	5C	-	C	UK	7527796
5F	SWIFT LADY	-	04	30.0k	8.4m	0P	0C	0L	-	UK	

GRY MARITHA Built by Moen Slip AS, Kolvereid, Norway for *Gjofor* of Norway. In design she is a coaster rather than a ferry. In 1990 she was sold to the *Isles of Scilly Steamship Company*. She operates a freight and passenger service all year (conveying most goods to and from the Islands). During the winter she provides the only sea service to the islands, the SCILLONIAN III being laid up.

LYONESSE LADY Built Lochaber Marine Ltd of Corpach, Fort William, Scotland, for inter-island ferry work.

MALI ROSE Pallet and deck cargo carrier built by Halsnøy Verft, Halsnøy, Norway. Passed through various hands until June 2016 when she was sold to *Isles of Scilly Steamship Company* to replace the GRY MARITHA.

SCILLONIAN III Built by Appledore Shipbuilders Ltd, Appledore, UK for the Penzance - St Mary's service. She operates from late March to November and is laid up in the winter. She is the last major conventional passenger/cargo ferry built for UK waters and probably Western Europe. Extensively refurbished during Winter 1998/99 and 2012/13. She can carry cars in her hold and on deck, as well as general cargo/perishables, boats, trailer tents and passenger luggage.

SWIFT LADY Stormforce 8.4 RIB (Rigid Inflatable Boat) built by Redbay Boats of Cushendall, Co Antrim, Northern Ireland for inter-island ferry work conveying mail and as back-up to the LYONESSE LADY.

MURPHY'S FERRY SERVICE

THE COMPANY *Murphy's Ferry Service* is privately operated.

MANAGEMENT Operator Brendan Murphy.

ADDRESS Lawrence Cove, Bere Island, Co Cork, Republic of Ireland.

TELEPHONE Administration +353 (0)87 2386095.

INTERNET Email edel@bereislandlodge.com **Website** www.murphysferry.com *(English)*,

ROUTE OPERATED Castletownbere (Pontoon - 3 miles to east of town centre) - Bere Island (Lawrence Cove, near Rerrin) (20 mins; *IKOM K*; up to 8 per day).

1	IKOM K	55t	99	10.0k	16.0m	60P	4C	1L	B	IR

IKOM K Built by Arklow Marine Services, Arklow, Republic of Ireland for *Murphy's Ferry Service*.

RATHLIN ISLAND FERRY

THE COMPANY *Rathlin Island Ferry Ltd* is a UK private sector company owned by Ciarán and Mary O'Driscoll of County Cork, Republic of Ireland.

MANAGEMENT Managing Director Ciarán O'Driscoll.

ADDRESS Ballycastle Ferry Terminal, 18 Bayview Road, Ballycastle, County Antrim BT54 6BT.

TELEPHONE Administration & Reservations +44 (0)28 2076 9299.

INTERNET Email info@rathlinballycastleferry.com **Website** www.rathlinballycastleferry.com *(English)*,

ROUTE OPERATED Vehicle Ferry Ballycastle - Rathlin Island (45 min; *SPIRIT OF RATHLIN*; up to 4 per day). **Passenger-only Fast Ferry** (20 min; *RATHLIN EXPRESS*; up to 6 per day). The service is operated on behalf of the *Northern Ireland Department of Regional Development*.

| 1»p | RATHLIN EXPRESS | 31t | 09 | 18.0k | 17.7m | 98P | 0C | 0L | - | UK | |
| 2 | SPIRIT OF RATHLIN | 105t | 17 | - | 25.0m | 125P | 5C | 1L | B | UK | 9780122 |

RATHLIN EXPRESS Built by Arklow Marine Services, Arklow, Republic of Ireland for *Rathlin Island Ferry Ltd.*

SPIRIT OF RATHLIN Built by Arklow Marine Services, Arklow, Irish Republic for *DRD (Northern Ireland)*, UK to replace the CANNA. Chartered to *Rathlin Island Ferry Ltd.*

SHANNON FERRY

THE COMPANY *Shannon Ferry Group Ltd* is a Republic of Ireland private company owned by eighteen shareholders on both sides of the Shannon Estuary.

MANAGEMENT Managing Director Eugene Maher.

ADDRESS Ferry Terminal, Killimer, County Clare, V15 FK09, Republic of Ireland.

TELEPHONE Administration +353 (0)65 9053124, **Reservations** Phone bookings not available; Online booking available at www.shannonferries.com

FAX Administration +353 (0)65 9053125, **Reservations** Fax bookings not available; Online booking available at www.shannonferries.com

INTERNET Email enquiries@shannonferries.com **Website** www.shannonferries.com *(English),*

ROUTE OPERATED Killimer (County Clare) - Tarbert (County Kerry) (20 mins; *SHANNON BREEZE*, *SHANNON DOLPHIN*; hourly (half-hourly during June, July, August and September)).

| 1 | SHANNON BREEZE | 611t | 00 | 10.0k | 80.8m | 350P | 60C | - | BA | IR | 9224910 |
| 2 | SHANNON DOLPHIN | 501t | 95 | 10.0k | 71.9m | 350P | 52C | - | BA | IR | 9114933 |

SHANNON BREEZE, SHANNON DOLPHIN Built by Appledore Shipbuilders, Appledore, UK for *Shannon Ferry Group Ltd.*

SHERKIN ISLAND FERRY

THE COMPANY The *Sherkin Island Ferry* is privately operated in the Republic of Ireland.

MANAGEMENT Operator: Vincent O'Driscoll.

ADDRESS Sherkin Ferry, The Cove, Baltimore, Skibbereen, Co Cork, P81 RW71, Republic of Ireland.

TELEPHONE Administration +353 (0)87 244 7828. **Ferry Boat** +353 (0)87 911 7377.

INTERNET Email info@sherkinferry.com **Website** www.sherkinferry.com *(English),*

ROUTE OPERATED Passenger only Baltimore (Co Cork) - Sherkin Island (10 minutes; *MYSTIC WATERS*; up to 10 per day). **Note:** No vehicle service advertised.

| 1p | MYSTIC WATERS | 100t | 72 | | 19.8m | 99P | 0C | 0L | - | IR | 8943038 |
| 2 | YOKER SWAN | 65t | 84 | | 21.9m | 50P | 3C | 0L | B | IR | |

MYSTIC WATERS Built by Ryton Marine Ltd, Wallsend, UK as the FREDA CUNNINGHAM for *Tyne & Wear PTE* and operated between North Shields and South Shields. Withdrawn in 1993 and sold to *Tyne Towage Ltd*, Newcastle and renamed the ANYA DEV. Later sold and renamed the LADY LAURA. In 2006 sold to *Sherkin Island Ferry* and renamed the MYSTIC WATERS.

YOKER SWAN Built by MacCrindle Shipbuilding Ltd, Ardrossan for *Strathclyde PTE* (later *Strathclyde Partnership for Transport*). Built as a small car ferry but operated passenger only between Renfrew and Yoker (apart from carrying ambulances in earlier days before they became too heavy). In March 2010 laid up. Later sold to *Sherkin Island Ferry* for use as a

SECTION 2 – MINOR FERRY OPERATORS

Belnahua *(Brian Maxted)*

Portaferry II *(Brian Maxted)*

passenger/car ferry. She is used as required to convey vehicles and freight to and from the island, and sometimes conveys passengers. No public vehicle service is advertised.

SKYE FERRY

THE COMPANY The *Skye Ferry* is owned by the *Isle of Skye Ferry Community Interest Company*, a company limited by guarantee.

MANAGEMENT Ferry Development Manager Jo Crawford.

ADDRESS 6 Coulindune, Glenelg, Kyle, Ross-shire, IV40 8JU.

TELEPHONE Administration +44 (0)7881 634726.

INTERNET Email info@skyeferry.co.uk **Website** skyeferry.co.uk *(English)*,

ROUTE OPERATED *Easter - October only* Glenelg - Kylerhea (Skye) (10 mins; *GLENACHULISH*; frequent service).

1	GLENACHULISH	44t	69	9.0k	20.0m	12P	6C	-	BSt	UK

GLENACHULISH Built by Ailsa Shipbuilding Company, Troon, UK for the *Ballachulish Ferry Company* for the service between North Ballachulish and South Ballachulish, across the mouth of Loch Leven. In 1975 the ferry was replaced by a bridge and she was sold to *Highland Regional Council* and used on a relief basis on the North Kessock - South Kessock and Kylesku - Kylestrome routes. In 1983 she was sold to *Murdo MacKenzie*, who had operated the Glenelg – Skye route as ferryman since 1959. The vessel was eventually bought by *Roddy MacLeod* and the service resumed in September 1990. The *Isle of Skye Ferry Community Interest Company* reached agreement with *Mr MacLeod* that he would operate the ferry in 2006. In 2007 she was sold to the Company. During winter 2012 she was chartered to *The Highland Council* to operate between North and South Strome following a road closure due to a rock fall. She is the last turntable ferry in operation.

STRANGFORD LOUGH FERRY SERVICE

THE COMPANY The *Strangford Lough Ferry Service* is operated by the *DFI Transport NI*, a Northern Ireland Government Department (formerly operated by *Department of the Environment (Northern Ireland)*).

MANAGEMENT Ferry Manager Tim Tew.

ADDRESS Strangford Lough Ferry Service, The Slip, Strangford, Co Down BT30 7NE.

TELEPHONE Administration +44 0300 200 7898, **Reservations** Not applicable.

INTERNET Website www.nidirect.gov.uk/strangford-ferry-timetable *(English)*,

ROUTE OPERATED Strangford - Portaferry (County Down) (10 mins; *PORTAFERRY II*, *STRANGFORD II*; half-hourly).

1	PORTAFERRY II	312t	01	12.0k	38.2m	260P	28C	-	BA	UK	9237436
2	STRANGFORD II	405t	16	12.0k	64.0m	260P	28C	-	BA	UK	9771561

PORTAFERRY II Built by McTay Marine, Bromborough, Wirral, UK for *DRD (Northern Ireland)*.

STRANGFORD II Built by Cammell Laird, Birkenhead for *DRD (Northern Ireland)*, UK to replace the STRANGFORD FERRY. Entered service February 2017.

C TOMS & SON LTD

THE COMPANY *C Toms & Son Ltd* is a British private sector company.

MANAGEMENT Managing Director Allen Toms.

ADDRESS East Street, Polruan, Fowey, Cornwall PL23 1PB.

TELEPHONE Administration +44 (0)1726 870232.

INTERNET Email enquiries@ctomsandson.co.uk **Website** www.ctomsandson.co.uk *(English)*,

ROUTE OPERATED *Car Ferry* Fowey - Bodinnick (Cornwall) (5 mins; *GELLAN*, *JENACK*; frequent), *Passenger Ferry* Fowey - Polruan (Cornwall) (5 mins; *KALEY*, *LADY DIANA*, *LADY JEAN*, *TAMSIN*, *THREE COUSINS*; frequent).

1	GELLAN	50t	03	4.5k	36.0m	50P	10C	-	BA	UK
2	JENACK	60t	00	4.5k	36.0m	50P	15C	-	BA	UK
3p	KALEY	7.6t	03	-	9.5m	48P	0C	-	-	UK
4p	LADY DI	-	81	-	8.2m	36P	0C	-	-	UK
5p	LADY JEAN	-	-	-	-	12P	0C	-	-	UK
6p	THREE COUSINS	-	14	-	-	12P	0C	-	-	UK

GELLAN, JENACK Built by C Toms & Sons Ltd, Fowey, UK.

KALEY, LADY DIANA, LADY JEAN, THREE COUSINS Built by C Toms & Sons Ltd, Fowey, UK.

VALENTIA ISLAND CAR FERRY

THE COMPANY *Valentia Island Car Ferry* is the trading name of *Valentia Island Ferries Ltd*, an Republic of Ireland private sector company.

MANAGEMENT Manager Richard Foran.

ADDRESS Valentia Island, County Kerry, Republic of Ireland.

TELEPHONE Administration +353 (0)87 241 8973, **Reservations** Not applicable.

FAX Administration +353 (0)66 76377, **Reservations** Not applicable.

INTERNET Email reforan@indigo.ie **Website** www.facebook.com (search for Valentia Island Car Ferry *(English)*,

ROUTE OPERATED Reenard (Co Kerry) - Knightstown (Valentia Island) (5 minutes; *GOD MET ONS III*; frequent service, 1st April - 30th September).

1	GOD MET ONS III	95t	63	-	43.0m	95P	18C	-	BA	IR

GOD MET ONS III Built by BV Scheepswerven Vh HH Bodewes, Millingen, The Netherlands for *FMHE Res* of The Netherlands for a service across the River Maas between Cuijk and Middelaar. In 1987 a new bridge was opened and the service ceased. She was latterly used on contract work in the Elbe and then laid up. In 1996 acquired by *Valentia Island Ferries* and inaugurated a car ferry service to the island. **Note** This island never had a car ferry service before. A bridge was opened at the south end of the island in 1970; before that a passenger/cargo service operated between Reenard Point and Knightstown.

WOOLWICH FREE FERRY

THE COMPANY The *Woolwich Free Ferry* is operated by *Briggs Marine*, a British private sector company on behalf of *Transport for London*.

ADDRESS New Ferry Approach, Woolwich, London SE18 6DX.

TELEPHONE Administration +44 (0)20 8853 9400, **Reservations** Not applicable.

FAX Administration +44 (0)20 8316 6096, **Reservations** Not applicable.

INTERNET Website www.tfl.gov.uk/modes/river/woolwich-ferry *(English)*,

ROUTE OPERATED Woolwich - North Woolwich (free ferry) (5 mins; *ERNEST BEVIN*, *JAMES NEWMAN*, *JOHN BURNS*; every 10 mins (weekdays - two ferries in operation), every 15 mins (weekends - one ferry in operation)). **Note** One ferry is always in reserve/under maintenance.

1	ERNEST BEVIN	1194t	63	8.0k	56.7m	310P	32C	6L	BA	UK	5426998
2	JAMES NEWMAN	1194t	63	8.0k	56.7m	310P	32C	6L	BA	UK	5411905
3	JOHN BURNS	1194t	63	8.0k	56.7m	310P	32C	6L	BA	UK	5416010

John Burns (Brian Maxted)

ERNEST BEVIN, JAMES NEWMAN, JOHN BURNS Built by Robb Caledon Shipbuilders Ltd, Dundee, UK for the *London County Council* who operated the service when the vessels were new. In 1965 ownership was transferred to the *Greater London Council*. Following the abolition of the *GLC* in April 1986, ownership was transferred to the *Department of Transport* and in 2001 to *Transport for London*. The *London Borough of Greenwich* operated the service on their behalf. In 2008 the operation of the service was transferred to Serco and subsequently to Briggs Marine in 214. An alternative loading is 6 x 18m articulated lorries and 14 cars; lorries of this length are too high for the nearby northbound Blackwall Tunnel.

Under Construction

| 4 | BEN WOOLLACOTT | 1538t | 18 | 8.0k | 62.2m | 150P | 42C | 12L | BA | UK | 9822011 |
| 5 | DAME VERA LYNN | 1539t | 18 | 8.0k | 62.2m | 150P | 42C | 12L | BA | UK | 9822023 |

Under Construction

BEN WOOLLACOTT, DAME VERA LYNN Under construction by Remontowa Shipbuilding, Gdansk, Poland. They will be diesel electric battery hybrid vessels. They are expected to enter service in December 2018.

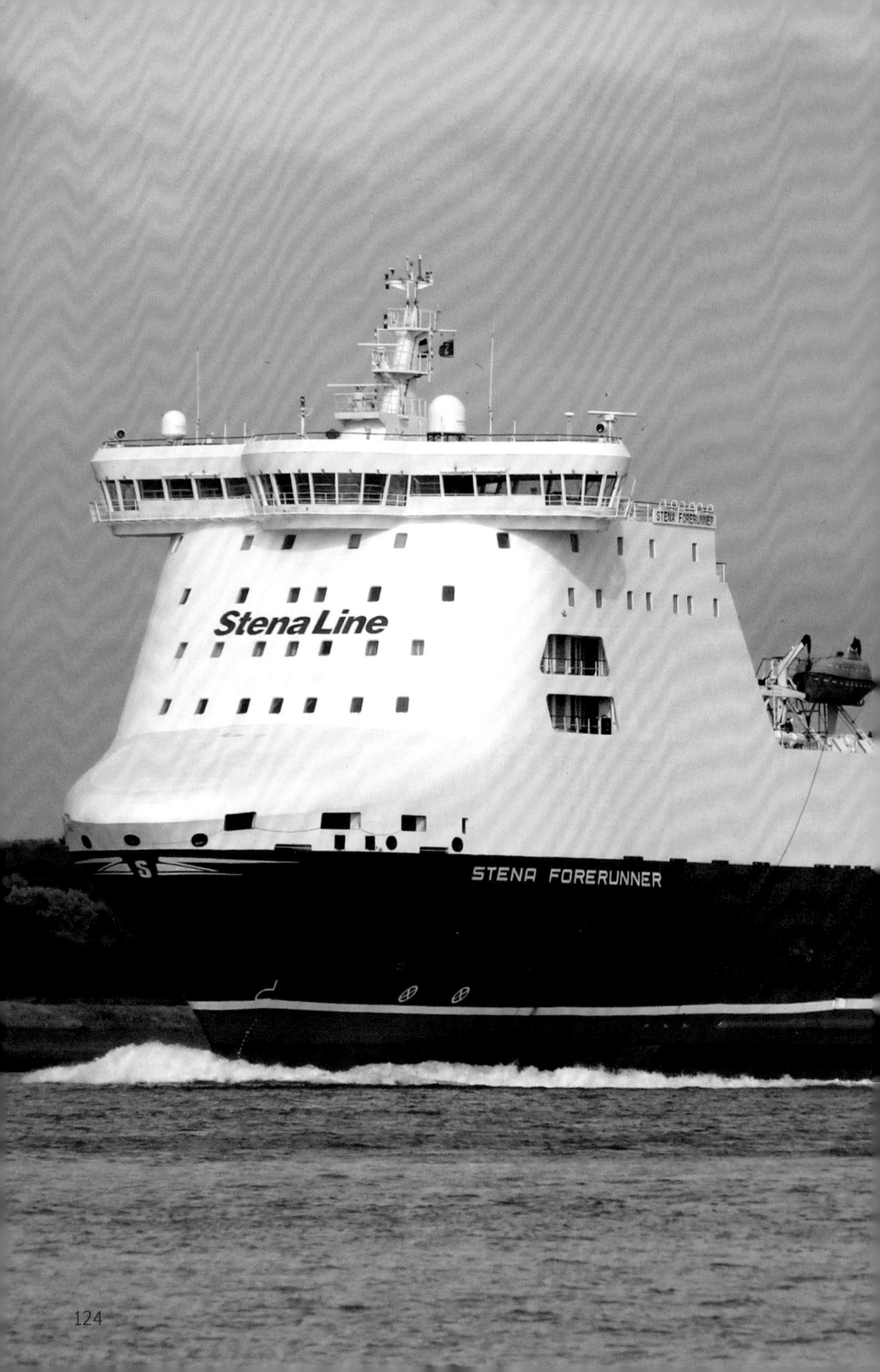
Stena Line
STENA FORERUNNER

Stena Forerunner *(Rob de Visser)*

SECTION 3 - GB & IRELAND - RO-RO FREIGHT-FERRIES
CLDN/COBELFRET FERRIES

THE COMPANIES CLdN Cobelfret SA is a Luxembourg private sector company. There are a number of subsidiary companies. CLdN stands for Compagnie Luxembourgouise de Navigation.

MANAGEMENT CLdN Ro-Ro SA (Luxembourg) Caroline Dubois, **Cobelfret Waterways SA (Vlissingen)** Geert Bogaerts, **CLdN ro-ro Agencies Ltd (UK)** Karla Fairway.

ADDRESSES *Luxembourg* CLdN Cobelfret SA & CLdN ro-ro SA, 3-7 rue Schiller, 2519 Luxembourg, *UK* CLdN ro-ro UK Ltd, Long Reach House, London Road, Purfleet, Essex RM19 1RP UK, *UK - Irish Republic* CLdN ro-ro SA, Port Centre, 2nd Floor, Alexandra Road, Dublin Port, Dublin 1, D01 H4C6, Republic of Ireland.

TELEPHONE *Luxembourg* CLdN Cobelfret SA +352 (0)26 44 631, **CLdN ro-ro SA** +352 (0)26 44 661 *UK* +44 (0)1708 865522, *Irish Republic* +353 (0)1 856 1608.

FAX *Luxembourg* CLdN Cobelfret SA +352 (0)26 44 63 298, **CLdN ro-ro SA** +352 (0)26 44 66 299 *UK* +44 (0)1708 866419, *Irish Republic* +353 (0)1 704 0164.

INTERNET Email admin.roro@cldn.com **Websites** www.cldn.com *(English)*

ROUTES OPERATED Cobelfret Ferries Services Zeebrugge - Purfleet (9 hrs; **WILHELMINE, CELESTINE CLASS**; 2/3 per day), Zeebrugge - Killingholme (13 hrs; **CELINE, DELPHINE, MAZARINE CLASS**; 6 per week), **CLdN Services** Rotterdam - Purfleet (14 hrs 30 mins; **MAZARINE CLASS, OPALINE CLASS**); 6 per week), Rotterdam - Killingholme (14 hrs; **PAULINE, YASMINE**; 6 per week), Zeebrugge - Esbjerg (24hrs; **CELESTINE CLASS**; 1 per week), Zeebrugge - Dublin (35-41 hrs; **MAZARINE CLASS, CELESTINE CLASS, CELINE, DELPHINE**; 4 per week), Rotterdam - Dublin (41-47 hrs; **CELESTINE CLASS, MAZARINE CLASS, OPALINE CLASS**; 3 per week), Rotterdam - Leixoes (Portugal) (64-69 hrs; **CATHERINE, MAZARINE CLASS**; 3 per week), Zeebrugge - Santander (50 hrs; **CELESTINE CLASS, MAZARINE CLASS**; 2 per week, Zeebrugge - Göteborg (32-33 hrs; **CELESTINE CLASS, SOMERSET**; 4 per week (1 weekly call at Hirtshals in both directions), (CELESTINE CLASS = CELESTINE, CELANDINE, CLEMENTINE, MELUSINE, VALENTINE and VICTORINE, MAZARINE CLASS = MAZARINE, PALATINE, PEREGRINE and VESPERTINE; OPALINE CLASS = AMANDINE and OPALINE). **CLdN Container service** Rotterdam - Dublin (43/47 hrs; **ARX** ; 1 per week).

Contract Services for Ford Motor Company Vlissingen - Dagenham (11 hrs; **CELESTINE, CYMBELINE, UNDINE**; 2 per day).

1	ADELINE	21020t	12	15.8k	150.0m	12P	-	170T	A	MT	9539092
2	AMANDINE	33960t	11	18.5k	195.4m	12P	-	270T	A	MT	9424871
3	ARX	6901t	05	13.8k	139.8m	0P		707 TEU	C	MT	9328625
4	CAPUCINE	16342t	11	16.0k	150.0m	12P	-	140T	A	UK	9539066
5	CATHERINE	21287t	02	18.0k	182.2m	12P	-	200T	A2	MT	9209453
6	CELANDINE	23987t	00	17.9k	162.5m	12P	630C	157T	A	MT	9183984
7	CELESTINE	23986t	96	17.8k	162.5m	12P	630C	157T	A	MT	9125372
8	CELINE	74273t	17	17.9k	235.0m	12P	8000C	580T	A2	MT	9789233
9	CLEMENTINE	23986t	97	17.8k	162.5m	12P	630C	157T	A	BE	9125384
10	CYMBELINE	11866t	92	17.0k	147.4m	8P	350C	100T	A2	MT	9007462
11	DELPHINE	74273t	18	17.9k	235.0m	12P	8000C	580T	A2	MT	9789245
12	MAZARINE	25593t	09	18.5k	195.4m	12P	-	180T	A	MT	9376696
13	MELUSINE	23987t	99	17.8k	162.5m	12P	630C	157T	A	BE	9166637
14	OPALINE	33960t	10	18.5k	195.4m	12P	-	270T	A	MT	9424869
15	PALATINE	25593t	09	18.5k	195.4m	12P	-	180T	A	MT	9376701
16	PAULINE	49166t	06	21.7k	200.0m	12P	656C	258T	A	MT	9324473
17	PEREGRINE	25235t	10	18.5k	195.4m	12P	-	180T	A	MT	9376725
18	SEVERINE	16342t	12	16.0k	150.0m	12P	-	140T	A	NL	9539078

19	SOMERSET	21005t	00	18.0k	183.4m	12P	-	180T	A	MT	9188221
20	UNDINE	11854t	91	15.0k	147.4m	8P	350C	100T	A2	MT	9006112
21	VALENTINE	23987t	99	18.0k	162.5m	12P	630C	157T	A	BE	9166625
22	VESPERTINE	25235t	10	18.5k	195.4m	12P	-	180T	A	MT	9376713
23	VICTORINE	23987t	00	17.8k	162.5m	12P	630C	157T	A	BE	9184029
24	WILHELMINE	21020t	12	15.8k	150.0m	12P	-	170T	A	MT	9539080
25	YASMINE	49166t	07	21.7k	200.0m	12P	656C	258T	A	MT	9337353

ADELINE Built by the Kyokuyo Shipyard, Shimonoseki, Japan. After competition, a additional deck and sponsons were retro-fitted at the Chengxi Shipyard, Jiangyin, China.

AMANDINE Built by Flensburger Schiffbau-Gesellschaft, Flensburg, Germany. Operates mainly between Rotterdam and Killingholme and Rotterdam/Zeebrugge and Dublin.

ARX Container ship built as the LUPUS 1 by Detlef Hegemann Rolandwerft, Berne, Germany. In June 2005 chartered to *C2C Line* operating between Zeebrugge and Dublin and renamed the C2C LUPUS. In July 2007 renamed the C2C AUSTRALIS. In June 2010 purchased by an associated company of *CLdN* and renamed the ARX.

CAPUCINE, SEVERINE Built by the Kyokuyo Shipyard, Shimonoseki, Japan for *CLdN*. Initially operated on their Ipswich - Rotterdam service. This service was suspended in August 2012. In September, they were chartered to *Stena Line* and placed on the Harwich - Rotterdam service. Charter ended in January 2018. In February 2018 the CAPUCINE was chartered to the *Italian Ministry of Defence* for 12 months and in June 2018 the SEVERINE was chartered to *GNV* of Italy.

CATHERINE Built as the ROMIRA by Zhonghua Shipyard, Zhonghua, China for *Dag Engström Rederi* of Sweden. For six months engaged on a number of short-term charters, including *Cobelfret Ferries* who used her on both the Rotterdam - Immingham and Zeebrugge - Purfleet routes. In September 2002 purchased by *Cobelfret Ferries* and, in November 2002, renamed the CATHERINE and placed on the Rotterdam - Immingham service. In Spring 2003 chartered to the *US Defense Department* to convey materials to the Persian Gulf. Returned in late summer and operated thereafter on the Rotterdam - Immingham service. In January 2009 chartered to *CoTuNav* of Tunisia. In February 2010 returned to *Cobelfret* service and operated on the Rotterdam - Purfleet service. In March 2010 again chartered to *CoTuNav*. In March 2011 chartered to *RMR Shipping* to operate between Western Europe and Antwerpen, Eemshaven, Harwich and Dublin to Lagos (Nigeria). In May 2011 returned to *Cobelfret Ferries* and used on the Zeebrugge - Göteborg service until January 2013 when she began operating on the Purfleet route during the week and the Göteborg route at weekend (one round trip). From April 2013 operated full-time on the Purfleet service. In March 2014 transferred to the Rotterdam - Leixoes route.

CELANDINE, VALENTINE, VICTORINE Built by Kawasaki Heavy Industries, Sakaide, Japan for *Cobelfret*. The CELANDINE was originally to be called the CATHERINE and the VICTORINE the CELANDINE. The names were changed before delivery. Generally used on the Zeebrugge - Purfleet route. In May 2011 the CELANDINE was chartered to *RMR Shipping*. Returned in November 2013.

CELESTINE Built by Kawasaki Heavy Industries, Sakaide, Japan as the CELESTINE. In 1996 chartered to the *British MoD* and renamed the SEA CRUSADER. She was originally expected to return to *Cobelfret Ferries* in early 2003 and resume the name CELESTINE; however, the charter was extended because of the Iraq war. Returned in September 2003 and placed on the Zeebrugge - Immingham service. In November 2006 moved to the Zeebrugge - Purfleet route. In November 2008 moved to the Oostende - Dartford service. In April 2009 the route became Oostende - Purfleet. In April 2010 chartered to *RMR Shipping*. In May 2014 returned to *Cobelfret Ferries* and in May 2016 transferred to the Dagenham - Vlissingen service.

CELINE, DELPHINE Built by Hyundai Mipo Dockyard, Ulsan, South Korea. They are convertible to LPG propulsion and designed to be useable on deep sea ro-ro services as well as *CLdN's* current short sea routes.

SECTION 3 – FREIGHT ONLY FERRIES

Celine *(Nick Widdows)*

Clementine *(George Holland)*

CLEMENTINE Built by Kawasaki Heavy Industries, Sakaide, Japan for *Cobelfret Ferries*. Mainly used on the Zeebrugge - Immingham service. In 2007 moved to the Zeebrugge - Purfleet route. In March 2013 chartered to *RMR Shipping*. In July 2013 chartered to *DFDS Seaways* and placed on the Immingham - Cuxhaven service. In November 2014 returned to *Cobelfret Ferries*. In January 2015 she retuned to charter with *DFDS Seaways* for four weeks.

CYMBELINE, UNDINE Built by Dalian Shipyard, Dalian, China for *Cobelfret Ferries*. Currently mainly used on the Dagenham - Vlissingen route. They were occasionally used on a weekend Southampton - Vlissingen service but this ceased in 2012 following the closure of the Southampton Ford Transit factory. Occasional weekend trips are made to Middlesbrough (Teesport).

FADIQ Built as the BERING STRAIT by Odense Staalskibsværft A/S, Odense, Denmark for *Pacific Basin Shipping Ltd Hong Kong* of the UK. In September 2012 sold to *Atlantica Di Navigation (Grimaldi)* of Italy and, in October, renamed the EUROCARGO BRINDISI. In March 2015 sold to *CLdN* and chartered to *Ekol Logistik AS* of Turkey and renamed the FADIQ.

MASSIMO MURA Built as the BEACHY HEAD by Flensburger Schiffbau-Gesellschaft, Flensburg, Germany for *AWSR Shipping*. On delivery, chartered to *Transfennica* and operated between Hanko (Finland) and Lübeck (Germany). In July 2006 chartered to *Stora Enso* and placed on the Kotka - Göteborg route. In late August transferred to the Antwerpen - Göteborg service. In 2007 chartered to *Transfennica*. In January 2009 chartered to *Finnlines* and normally used on the Helsinki - Aarhus route. In January 2012 chartered to *North Sea RoRo*. In March 2013 the service ceased and she was chartered to *DFDS Seaways*. In April 2014 sold to *C Bulk NV* of Belgium, an associated company of *CLdN/Cobelfret Ferries* and renamed the WILLIAMSBORG. In July she was chartered to *Nordana Line A/S* of Denmark operating from Mediterranean ports to the USA and Latin America. In January 2016 chartered to *Grimaldi Lines* of Italy and renamed the MASSIMO MURA.

MAZARINE, PALATINE, PEREGRINE, VESPERTINE Built by Flensburger Schiffbau-Gesellschaft, Flensburg, Germany.

MELUSINE Built by Kawasaki Heavy Industries, Sakaide, Japan for *Cobelfret*. Similar to the CLEMENTINE.

OPALINE Built by Flensburger Schiffbau-Gesellschaft, Flensburg, Germany. Operates mainly between Rotterdam and Killingholme and Rotterdam and Dublin.

PAULINE, YASMINE Built by Flensburger Schiffbau-Gesellschaft, Flensburg, Germany to operate on the Zeebrugge - Killingholme route.

SOMERSET Built as the SPAARNEBORG by Flender Werft AG, Lübeck, Germany for *Wagenborg* of The Netherlands and time-chartered to *Stora-Enso* to operate between Zeebrugge and Göteborg in conjunction with *Cobelfret Ferries*. She also operated between Tilbury and Göteborg during 2010. In August 2011 chartered to the *Canadian MoD* to operate between Montreal and Cyprus in connection with the Libyan 'no fly zone'. On return in November she was laid up in Zeebrugge and in January 2012 moved to Göteborg. In August 2012 chartered to *LD Lines* to operate between Marseilles and Tunis. In March 2013 returned to the *Stora Enso/Cobelfret Ferries* Zeebrugge - Göteborg service. In November 2014 the arrangement between *Stora Enso* and *Cobelfret Ferries* ended and she was chartered to *SOL Continent Line* who took over the operation of the service, operating between Finland, Germany, Belgium and the UK. In January 2015 sold to *CLdN* and renamed the SOMERSET. Generally operates between Zeebrugge and Göteborg.

WILHELMINE Built by the Kyokuyo Shipyard, Shimonoseki, Japan for *CLdN*. After completion, a additional deck and sponsons were retro-fitted at the Chengxi Shipyard, Jiangyin, China. Initially used on the Zeebrugge - Purfleet service. In January 2013 chartered to *P&O Ferries* to operate between Tilbury and Zeebrugge. After three weeks moved to the Middlesbrough - Rotterdam service. In November 2014 the charter ended and she was placed on the Zeebrugge - Purfleet service. She returned to *P&O Ferries* for five weeks during the refit period in January and February 2015 and again operated Middlesbrough - Rotterdam.

SECTION 3 – FREIGHT ONLY FERRIES

Under construction

26	LAURALINE	50200t	18	18.0k	212.0m	12P	-	400T	A	-	-	-
27	NEWBUILDING 1	50200t	18	18.0k	212.0m	12P	-	400T	A	-	-	-
28	NEWBUILDING 2	50000t	18	17.6k	211.6m	12P	-	400T	A2	-	-	-
29	NEWBUILDING 3	50000t	18	17.6k	211.6m	12P	-	400T	A2	-	-	-
30	NEWBUILDING 4	50200t	19	18.0k	212.0m	12P	-	400T	A	-	-	-
31	NEWBUILDING 5	50200t	19	18.0k	212.0m	12P	-	400T	A	-	-	-

LAURALINE, NEWBUILDING 1, NEWBUILDING 4, NEWBUILDING 5 Under construction by Hyundai Mipo Dockyard, Ulsan, South Korea.

NEWBUILDING 2, NEWBUILDING 3 Under construction by Uljanik Shipyard, Pula, Croatia.

Note: Although the Uljanik vessels were ordered first it appears that the first Hyundai Mipo vessel will be delivered first. The order of subsequent deliveries is not known.

FINNLINES

THE COMPANY *Finnlines PLC* is a Finnish private sector company. Services to the UK are marketed by *Finnlines UK Ltd*, a British private sector company. From 1st January 2001, *Finncarriers* was merged into the parent company, trading as *Finnlines Cargo Service*.

MANAGEMENT President & CEO Emanuele Grimaldi, **Head of Group Marketing North Sea ro-ro** Staffan Herlin.

ADDRESS *Finland* PO Box 197, 00181 Helsinki, Finland, **UK** Finnlines UK Ltd, Finhumber House, Queen Elizabeth Dock, Hedon Road, HULL HU9 5PB.

TELEPHONE Administration & Reservations *Finland* +358 (0)10 343 50, **UK** +44 (0)1482 377 655.

FAX *Administration Finland* +358 (0)10 343 5200, **UK** +44 (0)1482 787 229.

INTERNET *Email Finland* info.fi@finnlines.com **UK** info.uk@finnlines.com **Website** www.finnlines.com *(English, Finnish, German, Polish, Swedish)*

ROUTES OPERATED Irregular service from St Petersburg, Helsinki, Rauma and Kotka to Hull, Immingham, Amsterdam, Antwerpen and Bilbao. For details see website. In view of the fact that ships are liable to be transferred between routes, the following is a list of all Finnlines Cargo Service ro-ro vessels, including those which currently do not serve the UK. Ro-pax vessels on Baltic services are listed in Section 6.

1	FINNBREEZE	28002t	11	20.0k	184.8m	12P	600C	200T	A	FI	9468889
2	FINNCARRIER	12251t	98	20.0k	154.5m	12P	-	124T	A2	FI	9132002
3	FINNHAWK	11530t	01	20.0k	162.2m	12P	-	140T	A	FI	9207895
4	FINNKRAFT	11530t	00	20.0k	162.2m	12P	-	140T	A	FI	9207883
5	FINNMASTER	12251t	98	20.0k	154.5m	12P	-	124T	A2	FI	9132014
6	FINNMERCHANT	23235t	03	21.0k	193.0m	12P	-	180T	A	FI	9234082
7	FINNMILL	25732t	02	20.0k	184.8m	12P	-	190T	A	FI	9212656
8	FINNPULP	25732t	02	20.0k	184.8m	12P	-	190T	A	FI	9212644
9	FINNSEA	28002t	11	21.0k	184.8m	12P	600C	320T	A	FI	9468891
10	FINNSKY	33816t	12	21.0k	217.8m	12P	600C	320T	A	FI	9468906
11	FINNSUN	33816t	12	21.0k	217.8m	12P	600C	320T	A	FI	9468918
12	FINNTIDE	33816t	12	21.0k	217.8m	12P	600C	320T	A	FI	9468920
13	FINNWAVE	33816t	12	21.0k	217.8m	12P	600C	320T	A	FI	9468932

FINNBREEZE, FINNSEA, FINNSKY, FINNSUN, FINNTIDE, FINNWAVE Built by Jinling Shipyard, Nanjing, China for *Finnlines*. The FINNSKY, FINNSUN, FINNTIDE, FINNWAVE were lengthened by approximately 30 metres at Remontowa Shipyard, Gdansk, Poland between November 2017 and May 2018. The FINNBREEZE and FINNSEA will be lengthened by December 2018.

FINNCARRIER Built as the UNITED CARRIER by Fosen Mekaniske Verksteder A/S, Rissa, Norway for *United Shipping* (a subsidiary of *Birka Shipping*) of Finland and chartered to

Transfennica. During 2000 she was used on their Kemi - Oulu - Antwerpen - Felixstowe service. In 2001 the route was transferred to *Finnlines* and the vessel used sub-chartered to them (charter later transferred to *Finnlines*). In 2002 *United Shipping* was renamed *Birka Cargo* and the ship was renamed the BIRKA CARRIER. In 2006 the service ceased. In 2008 the charter was extended a further four years. In January 2013 chartered to *Transfennica*. In June 2013 she was renamed the CARRIER. In January 2015 sold to *Finnlines* but not delivered until the end of the year, when the charter ended. In January 2016 renamed the FINNCARRIER. In July 2018 sold to *Color Line*. To enter service with them in January 2019.

FINNHAWK Built by Jinling Shipyard, Nanjing, China for the *Macoma Shipping Group* and chartered to *Finnlines*. In April 2008 purchased by *Finnlines*. Currently operates used on service between Finland and The Netherlands, Belgium, the UK and Spain.

FINNKRAFT Built by Jinling Shipyard, Nanjing, China for the *Macoma Shipping Group* and chartered to *Finncarriers*. In April 2008 purchased by *Finnlines*. Currently operates on services between Finland and Germany.

FINNMASTER Built as the UNITED TRADER by Fosen Mekaniske Verksteder A/S, Rissa, Norway for *United Shipping* (a subsidiary of *Birka Shipping*) of Finland and chartered to *Transfennica*. During 2000 used on their Kemi - Oulu - Antwerpen - Felixstowe service. In 2001 the route was transferred to *Finnlines* and the vessels used sub-chartered to them (charter later transferred to *Finnlines*). In 2002 *United Shipping* was renamed *Birka Cargo* and she was renamed the BIRKA TRADER. In 2006 the service ceased and she was transferred to other *Finnlines* routes. In 2008 the charter was extended a further four years. In January 2013 chartered to *Transfennica*. In July 2013 renamed the TRADER. In January 2015 sold to *Finnlines* but not delivered until the end of the year, when the charter ended. In January 2016 renamed the FINNMASTER. In November 2016 chartered to *DFDS Seaways*. Operated mainly between Immingham and Rotterdam. In July 2017 charter ended and she returned to *Finnlines*, operating on a new service between Oxelösund (Sweden) and Naantali (Finland).

FINNMERCHANT Built as the LONGSTONE by Flensburger Schiffbau-Gesellschaft, Flensburg, Germany for *AWSR Shipping* (later Foreland Shipping). Chartered to *Transfennica* and operated between Hanko (Finland) and Lübeck (Germany). In January 2009 chartered to *Finnlines* and placed on the Helsinki - Aarhus route. In January 2012 chartered to *North Sea RoRo*. In March 2013 the operation ceased and the charter was taken over by *DFDS Seaways* and she was placed on the Immingham - Cuxhaven route. In May took over the Zeebrugge - Rosyth route. In October 2013 sold to *C Bulk NV* of Belgium, an associated company of *CLdN/Cobelfret Ferries*. In April 2014 charter to *DFDS* ended and she was chartered to an Australian operator. In November 2014 renamed the DORSET. In December 2014 the charter ended and she returned to *CLdN*. In early January 2015 placed on the Zeebrugge - Purfleet service. Later in the month sold to *Finnlines* and renamed the FINNMERCHANT.

FINNMILL, FINNPULP Built by Jinling Shipyard, Nanjing, China for the *Macoma Shipping Group* and chartered to *Finnlines*. In 2008 purchased by *Finnlines*. During Winter 2008/09 extra ramps were added at STX Europe Helsinki shipyard to enable ro-ro traffic to be conveyed on the weather deck.

Under construction

14	NEWBUILDING 1	64000t	20	-	238.0m	12P	-	410T	A	FI	-
15	NEWBUILDING 2	64000t	21	-	238.0m	12P	-	410T	A	FI	-
16	NEWBUILDING 3	64000t	21	-	238.0m	12P	-	410T	A	FI	-

NEWBUILDING 1, NEWBUILDING 2, NEWBUILDING 3 Grimaldi Green 5th Generation (GG5G) Class hybrid vessels under construction by Jinling Shipyard, Nanjing, China. As well as the trailer deck capacity, there will be 5,600 square metres of car decks and space for 300 TEU of containers on the weather deck.

SECTION 3 – FREIGHT ONLY FERRIES

MANN LINES

THE COMPANY *Mann Lines* are owned by *Mann & Son (London) Ltd* of Great Britain. They replaced in 2001 *ArgoMann Ferry Service*, a joint venture between *Argo Reederei* of Germany and *Mann & Son*.

MANAGEMENT Managing Director Bill Binks, **Commercial Manager** David Brooks.

ADDRESS Mann & Son (London) Ltd, The Naval House, Kings Quay Street, Harwich CO12 3JJ.

TELEPHONE Administration & Reservations *UK* +44 (0)1255 245200, *Germany* +49 (0)40 25499070-0, *Finland* +358 (0)2 275 0000, *Estonia* +372 (0)679 1450.

FAX Administration & Reservations *UK* +44 (0)1255 245219, *Germany* + 49 (0)40 25499070-10, *Finland* +358 (0)2 253 5905, *Estonia* +372 (0)679 1455.

INTERNET Email enquiry@manngroup.co.uk **Website** www.mannlines.com *(English, Finnish, Estonian, German, Russian)*

ROUTES OPERATED Harwich (Navyard) - Cuxhaven (Germany) - Paldiski (Estonia) - Turku (Finland) - Bremerhaven (Germany) – Harwich (**ML FREYJA**; weekly).

1	ML FREYJA	23000t	17	19.0k	190.8m	12P	-	180T	A	IT	9799977

ML FREYJA Built by CN Visentini, Donada, Italy and chartered to *Mann Lines*. In June 2017 sub-chartered to *SOL Continent Line* for six months. In December 2017 entered service with *Mann Lines*.

SEA-CARGO

THE COMPANY *Sea-Cargo AS* of Norway is a subsidiary of *Seatrans AS* of Norway.

MANAGEMENT Managing Director Ole Saevild, **Director Business Development** Erik A Paulsen, **General Manager (Immingham)** Mark Brighton, **General Manager (Aberdeen)** Ian Shewan.

ADDRESS *Norway* Wernersholmvegen 5, 5232 Paradis, Norway, *Immingham* Sea-Cargo UK, West Riverside Road, Immingham Dock, Immingham DN40 2NT, *Aberdeen* Sea-Cargo Aberdeen Ltd, Matthews Quay, Aberdeen Harbour, Aberdeen, AB11 5PG.

TELEPHONE Administration & Bookings *Bergen* +47 55 10 84 84, *Immingham* +44 (0)1469 577119, *Aberdeen* +44 (0)1224 596481.

FAX Administration & Reservations *Bergen* +47 85 02 82 16, *Immingham* 44 (0)1469 577708, *Aberdeen* +44 (0)1224 582360.

INTERNET Email mail@sea-cargo.no **Website** www.sea-cargo.no *(English)*

ROUTES OPERATED *Sea-Cargo* operate a network of services from West Norway to Amsterdam, Aberdeen, Immingham and Esbjerg. The schedule varies from week to week and is shown on the company website. The *SC ASTREA* and *SC CONNECTOR* are generally used on the twice-weekly Immingham - Tanager, Haugesund, Bergen and Odda service and the *SEA-CARGO EXPRESS* on the weekly Aberdeen - Tanager, Haugesund, Bergen, Florø, Ålesund, Kristiansund, Trondheim and Molde service.

1	SC AHTELA	8610t	91	14.8k	139.5m	12P	-	92T	AS	MT	8911736
2	SC ASTREA	9528t	91	13.5k	129.1m	0p	-	58T	A	BS	8917895
3	SC CONNECTOR	12251t	97	15.0k	154.5m	12P	-	124T	AS	MT	9131993
4	SEA-CARGO EXPRESS	6693t	12	16.0k	117.4m	0P	-	35T	A	MT	9358060
5	TRANS CARRIER	9953t	94	14.5k	145.2m	0P	-	94T	AS	BS	9007879
6	TRANSFIGHTER	20851t	01	14.5k	178.6m	0P	-	100T	AS	MT	9216626

SC AHTELA Built as the AHTELA by Brodogradiliste "Sava", Macvanska Mitrovica, Yugoslavia, completed by Fosen Mekaniske Verksteder, Rissa, Norway for *Rederi AB Gustav Erikson* of Finland. Chartered to *Transfennica*. In 1995 chartered to *DFDS Tor Line*. In 1996 chartered to *Finncarriers Oy* of Finland and in 1997 renamed the FINNOAK. In 2007 sold to *Hollming Oy* of Finland and in 2008 the charter ended and she was renamed the AHTELA. Chartered to *Navirail* of Estonia to operate between Helsinki and Muuga (Estonia). Between February and May 2011 chartered to *Sea-Cargo* to operate between Esbjerg (Denmark) and Egersund (Norway). In October 2012 purchased by *Sea-Cargo* and renamed the SC AHTELA.

SC ASTREA Built as the ASTREA by Tangen Verft Kragerø A/S, Kragerø, Norway for *Finncarriers* of Finland. Operated between Finland and Spain - Portugal via Antwerpen. In 2006 chartered to *Danish MoD*. In 2007 chartered to *Sea-Cargo*. In August 2011 purchased by *Sea-Cargo* and renamed the SC ASTREA. Until early 2016 used primarily for moving windfarm equipment. In February placed on the Norway - Immingham service.

SC CONNECTOR Built as the UNITED EXPRESS by Fosen Mekaniske Verksteder A/S, Rissa, Norway for *United Shipping* (a subsidiary of *Birka Shipping*) of Finland and chartered to *Transfennica*. During 2000 used on their Kemi - Oulu - Antwerpen - Felixstowe service. In 2001 the route was transferred to *Finnlines* and the vessel used sub-chartered to them (charter later transferred to *Finnlines*). In 2002 *United Shipping* was renamed *Birka Cargo* and she was renamed the BIRKA EXPRESS. In 2008 the charter was extended a further four years. In June 2013 renamed the EXPRESS. In November 2013 chartered to *Transfennica*. In April 2014 sold to *Sea-Cargo* but initially continued to operate for *Transfennica*. During winter 2015 re-engined and modified to allow to side loading. In February 2015 renamed the SC CONNECTOR. Entered service in late April.

SEA-CARGO EXPRESS One of two vessels ordered in 2005 from Bharati Ratnagiri Ltd, Mumbai, India for *Sea-Cargo*. The order for the second ship was cancelled. Trailers are carried on the main deck only. Containers are carried on the weather deck and pallets on the lower decks. A crane is provided for the containers and a side door for pallets. She operates on the Aberdeen - Norway service.

TRANS CARRIER Built as the KORSNÄS LINK by Brodogradiliste Kraljevica, Kraljevica, Croatia for *SeaLink AB* of Sweden and due to be time-chartered to *Korsnäs AB*, a Swedish forest products company. However, due to the war in Croatia, delivery was seriously delayed and she was offered for sale. In 1994 sold to the *Swan Group* and renamed the SWAN HUNTER. She was placed on the charter market. In 1997 she was chartered to *Euroseabridge* and renamed the PARCHIM. In 1999 the charter ended and she resumed the name SWAN HUNTER. In 1999 she was sold to *SeaTrans* and renamed the TRANS CARRIER. She operated for *Sea-Cargo*. In 2005 chartered to *Finnlines* and used on the Finland to Spain/Portugal service. In 2006 returned to *Sea-Cargo*. In January and February 2009 lengthened by 18.9 metres in Poland.

TRANSFIGHTER Built as the FINNFIGHTER by Stocznia Gdynia, S.A. Gdynia, Poland for *B & N Nordsjöfrakt* of Sweden and chartered to F-Ships to operate between Finland and the USA. In 2004 Sold to *Gorthons Lines* of Sweden and in 2005 chartered to *Rederi AB Transatlantic* of Sweden. She continued to be operated between Scandinavia and North America. In 2006 extended by Blohm & Voss, Hamburg, Germany. In February 2009 she was renamed the TRANSFIGHTER. In November 2016 sold to *Seatrans AS* of Norway and chartered to *Sea-Cargo*. Operates between Norwegian ports, Rotterdam and Sheerness.

SEATRUCK FERRIES

THE COMPANY *Seatruck Ferries Ltd* is a British private sector company. It is part of the *Clipper Group*.

MANAGEMENT Chairman Flemming Steen, **CEO** Alistair Eagles.

ADDRESSES *Heysham (HQ)* North Quay, Heysham Port, Heysham, Morecambe, Lancs LA3 2UH, **Warrenpoint** Seatruck House, The Ferry Terminal, Warrenpoint, County Down BT34 3JR, **Liverpool:** Seatruck Ferry Terminal, Brocklebank Dock, Port of Liverpool, L20 1DB, **Dublin**: Seatruck Dublin, Terminal 5, Alexandra Road, Dublin 1 Irish Republic.

TELEPHONE Administration +44 (0)1524 855377, **Reservations *Heysham*** +44 (0)1524 853512. **Warrenpoint** +44 (0)28 754400, **Liverpool** + (0)151 9333660, **Dublin** + (0) 353 18230492.

FAX Administration +44 (0)28 4175 4545, **Reservations** *Warrenpoint* +44 (0)28 4177 3737, *Heysham* +44 (0)1524 853549.

INTERNET Email aje@seatruckgroup.co.uk **Websites** www.seatruckferries.com *(English)*

ROUTES OPERATED Heysham - Warrenpoint (9 hrs; *SEATRUCK PERFORMANCE*, *SEATRUCK PRECISION*; 2 per day), Heysham - Dublin (9 hrs; *CLIPPER POINT*; 1 per day), Liverpool - Dublin (9 hrs; *CLIPPER RANGER*, *SEATRUCK PACE*, *SEATRUCK POWER*, *SEATRUCK PROGRESS*; up to 4 per day).

1	CLIPPER PENNANT	14759t	09	22.0k	142.0m	12P	-	120T	A	CY	9372688
2	CLIPPER POINT	14759t	08	22.0k	142.0m	12P	-	120T	A	CY	9350666
3	CLIPPER RANGER	7606t	98	17.0k	122.3m	12P	-	84T	A	IM	9119402
4	SEATRUCK PACE	14759t	09	22.0k	142.0m	12P	-	120T	A	CY	9350678
5	SEATRUCK PANORAMA	14759t	09	22.0k	142.0m	12P	-	120T	A	CY	9372676
6	SEATRUCK PERFORMANCE	19722t	12	21.0k	142.0m	12P	-	151T	A	IM	9506227
7	SEATRUCK POWER	19722t	11	21.0k	142.0m	12P	-	151T	A	IM	9506215
8	SEATRUCK PRECISION	19722t	12	21.0k	142.0m	12P	-	151T	A	IM	9506239
9	SEATRUCK PROGRESS	19722t	11	21.0k	142.0m	12P	-	151T	A	IM	9506203

CLIPPER PENNANT Built by Astilleros Sevilla SA, Sevilla, Spain for *Seatruck Ferries*. In January 2013 chartered to *Stena RoRo*.

CLIPPER POINT Built by Astilleros de Huelva SA, Huelva, Spain for *Seatruck Ferries*. In May 2012 chartered to *DFDS Seaways* and placed on the Immingham-Cuxhaven route. In April 2013 chartered to the organisers of the 'SATA Rally Azores 2013' car rally to take cars from Portugal to the Azores. In May began operating for *DFDS Seaways* in the Baltic. In October transferred to the Immingham - Cuxhaven route. In June 2015 the charter ended. In July she was chartered to *InterShipping*, of Morocco to operate between Algeciras and Tangiers. In September 2016 the charter ended and she was placed on the Heysham - Dublin service.

CLIPPER RANGER Built as the LEMBITU by Astilleros de Huelva SA, Huelva, Spain for the *Estonian Shipping Company*. On completion chartered to *P&O European Ferries (Irish Sea)* and placed on their Liverpool - Dublin route. In Autumn 1998 she was chartered to *Dart Line* and placed on the Dartford - Vlissingen route. In 1999 she was renamed the DART 7. In Autumn 1999 the charter was ended and she was chartered to *Cetam* of France, resumed the name LEMBITU and was used on services between Marseilles and Tunis. In 2000 she was chartered to *P&O European Ferries (Irish Sea)* and renamed the CELTIC SUN; she operated between Liverpool and Dublin. In 2001 the charter ended; she then reverted to the name LEMBITU and was chartered to *NorseMerchant Ferries* and placed on the Heysham - Dublin service. In late 2001 the charter ended and she returned to *ESCO* service in the Baltic. In 2003 chartered to *Scandlines AG* and placed on their Rostock - Helsinki - Muuga service. This service finished in December 2004 and she was chartered to *Channel Freight Ferries* in January 2005. In March 2005 chartered to *NorseMerchant Ferries* again and operated between Heysham and Belfast. Later purchased by *Elmira Shipping* of Greece and renamed the RR CHALLENGE. In June 2005 chartered to *Seatruck Ferries*. In October 2007 sold to *Attica Group* of Greece and renamed the CHALLENGE. She continued to be chartered to *Seatruck Ferries*. In January 2008 she was transferred to the Liverpool - Dublin route and in April sold to *Seatruck Ferries*. In July renamed the CLIPPER RANGER. In June 2009 replaced the SHIELD (now the HILDASAY) until the new CLIPPER PENNANT took over in October. In May 2010 inaugurated a new Heysham - Larne service. In October 2013 chartered to *Caledonian MacBrayne* to replace the MUIRNEAG. The charter ended in May 2015. In November 2015 placed on the Liverpool - Dublin route as third ship. In March 2016 transferred to the Heysham - Dublin service. In September 2016 moved to the Liverpool - Dublin routes as fourth vessel.

Seatruck Ferries also own the ARROW currently on charter to *Isle of Man Steam Packet Company·* and the STENA PERFORMER and STENA PRECISION, currently on charter to *Stena Line*.

Finnsun *(Nick Widdows)*

Kraftca *(Nick Widdows)*

ML Freja *(John Bryant)*

Seatruck Power *(George Holland)*

Europe's leading guide to the UK & Northern European ferry industry

SEATRUCK PACE Built as the CLIPPER PACE by Astilleros Sevilla SA, Sevilla, Spain for *Seatruck Ferries*. In March 2012 renamed the SEATRUCK PACE. In January 2013 chartered to *Blue Water Shipping* of Denmark to carry wind turbine parts between Mostyn (Wales) and Esbjerg. Now operates on the Liverpool - Dublin route.

SEATRUCK PANORAMA Built by Astilleros de Huelva SA, Huelva Spain for *Seatruck Ferries*. Launched as the CLIPPER PENNANT and renamed the CLIPPER PANORAMA before delivery. In December 2011 renamed the SEATRUCK PANORAMA.

SEATRUCK PERFORMANCE Built as the SEATRUCK PERFORMANCE by Flensburger Schiffbau-Gesellschaft, Flensburg, Germany for *Seatruck Ferries*. In September 2012 chartered to *Stena Line* and renamed the STENA PERFORMER. She operated on both the Heysham - Belfast and Birkenhead - Belfast services. In August 2018 returned to *Seatruck Ferries*, renamed the SEATRUCK PERFORMANCE and placed on the Heysham - Warrenpoint service.

SEATRUCK POWER, SEATRUCK PROGRESS Built by Flensburger Schiffbau-Gesellschaft, Flensburg, Germany for *Seatruck Ferries*.

SEATRUCK PRECISION Built as the SEATRUCK PRECISION by Flensburger Schiffbau-Gesellschaft, Flensburg, Germany for *Seatruck Ferries*. In September 2012 chartered to *Stena Line* and renamed the STENA PRECISION. She operated on both the Heysham - Belfast and Birkenhead - Belfast services. In September 2015 moved to the Birkenhead - Belfast route. In August 2018 returned to *Seatruck Ferries*, renamed the SEATRUCK PRECISION and placed on the Heysham - Warrenpoint service.

SOL CONTINENT LINE

THE COMPANY *SOL Continent Line* is a division of *Swedish Orient Line*, a Swedish private sector company.

MANAGEMENT Managing Director Ragnar Johansson, **General Manager** Jonas Wåhlin, **Commercial Area Manager, North Sea** Pär Ekelöf

ADDRESSES Svenska Orient Linien AB, Klippan 1A, SE-414 51 Göteborg, Sweden.

TELEPHONE +46 (0)31-354 40 00.

FAX +46 (0)31-354 40 01.

INTERNET Email info@sollines.se **Website** www.sollines.se/en/content/sol-continent-line *(English)*

ROUTES OPERATED Göteborg - Zeebrugge (34 hrs; ***SCHIEBORG, SLINGEBORG, TAVASTLAND***; 8 per week), Oulu - Kemi - Husum - Lübeck - Göteborg - Zeebrugge - Tilbury - Zeebrugge - Oxelosund - Oulu (***THULELAND, TRANSTIMBER***; 1 per week), Kemi - Oulu - Antwerpen - Zeebrugge - Göteborg - Kemi (***BALTICA, VASALAND***; 1 per week).

1	BALTICA	21224t	90	19.0k	157.7m	0P	-	163T	A	FI	8813154
2	SCHIEBORG	21005t	00	18.0k	183.4m	12P	-	180T	A	NL	9188233
3	SLINGEBORG	21005t	00	18.0k	183.4m	12P	-	180T	A	NL	9188245
4	TAVASTLAND	23128t	06	16.0k	190.7m	12P	-	200T	A	SE	9334959
5	THULELAND	23128t	06	16.0k	190.7m	12P	-	200T	A	SE	9343261
6	TUNDRALAND	23128t	07	16.0k	190.7m	12P	-	200T	A	SE	9343273
7	VASALAND	20203t	84	19.5k	155.0m	12P	-	150T	A	UK	8222111

BALTICA Built by Hyundai Heavy Industries, Ulsan, South Korea as the AHLERS BALTIC for *Ahlers Line* and chartered to *Finncarriers*. In 1995 acquired by *Poseidon Schiffahrt AG* of Germany and renamed the TRANSBALTICA. She continued to be chartered to *Finncarriers* and was acquired by them when they purchased *Poseidon Schiffahrt AG* (now *Finnlines Deutschland AG*) in 1997. In 2003 sold to Norwegian interests and chartered back; She was renamed the BALTICA. In recent years she operated on the Helsinki - St Petersburg - Hamina - Helsinki - Zeebrugge - Tilbury – Amsterdam - Antwerpen - service with the MERCHANT. During 2007 she operated Helsinki - Turku - Antwerpen on a one-week cycle. In January 2008 moved to Baltic services. In April 2011 chartered to *Power Line* to operate

SECTION 3 – FREIGHT ONLY FERRIES

137

between Helsinki and Travemünde. In January 2013 returned to *Finnlines*. In October 2015 sold to *Godby Shipping* of Finland. In November chartered to *SOL Continent Line*.

ELISABETH RUSS Built by J J Sietas KG, Hamburg, Germany for *Ernst Russ* of Germany and chartered to *Transfennica*. In 2012 the charter ended and she was chartered to a number of operators. In November 2015 chartered to *SOL Continent Line*.

SCHIEBORG, SLINGEBORG, Built by Flender Werft AG, Lübeck, Germany for *Wagenborg* of The Netherlands and time-chartered to *Stora-Enso* to operate on the *Stora Enso/Cobelfret Ferries* service between Zeebrugge and Göteborg. In November 2014 the arrangement between *Stora Enso* and *Cobelfret Ferries* ended and they were chartered to *SOL Continent Line* who took over the operation of the service.

TAVASTLAND Built as the TRANSPAPER by Aker Finnyards, Rauma, Finland for *Baltic Container Shipping* of the UK and chartered to *Rederi AB Transatlantic* of Sweden. Operated on services operated for Stora Enso Paper Group, mainly in the Baltic. In December 2016 chartered to *SOL Continent Line* and used on their Baltic service; she was renamed the TAVASTLAND. In October 2017 transferred to the Oulu – Kemi – Lübeck – Antwerpen – Zeebrugge – Tilbury route.THULELAND Built as the TRANSPULP by Aker Finnyards, Rauma, Finland for *Baltic Container Shipping* of the UK and chartered to *Rederi AB Transatlantic* of Sweden. Operated on service operated for Stora Enso Paper Group, mainly in the Baltic. In early 2011 transferred to the Göteborg - Tilbury (once weekly) and Göteborg - Zeebrugge (CLdN service) (once weekly) services. In January 2013 began operating twice weekly to Tilbury, replacing the SELANDIA SEAWAYS of *DFDS Seaways*. In January 2015 chartered to *SOL Continent Line*. In December 2016 renamed the THULELAND.

TUNDRALAND Built as the TRANSTIMBER by Aker Finnyards, Rauma, Finland for *Baltic Container Shipping* of the UK and chartered to *Rederi AB Transatlantic* of Sweden. Operated on service operated for Stora Enso Paper Group, mainly in the Baltic. In January 2015 chartered to *SOL Continent Line*. In August 2017 she was renamed the TUNDRALAND.

VASALAND Built as the OIHONNA by Rauma Repola OY, Rauma, Finland for *Effoa-Finska Ångfartygs Ab*, of Finland. In December 1986 sold to *Fincarriers Ab* of Finland. In November 2003 sold to *Stena RoRo* of Sweden and renamed the VASALAND. Over the ensuing years, chartered to a number of companies including *Finnlines* and *Transfennica*. In September 2009 chartered to *SOL Continent Line*, initially operating purely in the Baltic but since 2016 used on their North Sea service.

FLOTA SUARDIAZ

THE COMPANY *Flota Suardiaz SL* is owned by *Grupo Suardiaz,* a Spanish private sector logistics company which operates divisions in ports, bunkering, warehousing, haulage, freight forwarding and shipping.

MANAGEMENT Presidente Don Juan Riva, **Director General** Alfredo Menendez Garcia.

ADDRESSES Spain Calle Ayala, 6 28001 Madrid, Spain, **UK** Suardiaz Shipping Ltd, Suardiaz House, 193 Shirley Road, Southampton SO15 3FG.

TELEPHONE Spain +34 914 31 66 40, **UK** +44 (0) 2380 211 981.

FAX Spain + 34 914 36 46 74, **UK** +44 (0) 2380 335309.

INTERNET Email infoweb@suardiaz.com, **Website** www.suardiaz.com *(English, Spanish).*

ROUTES OPERATED Northern Europe/Spain/Canaries/Med Lines Emden – Sheerness – Zeebrugge – Santander – Vigo - Las Palmas – Tenerife – Casablanca – Mostaganem – Barcelona (weekly with up to two sailings per week on some sections including Emden – Sheerness and Las Palmas – Tenerife – Barcelona). **Atlantic Line** Zeebrugge – St Nazaire – Vigo – Tanger Med (twice weekly with St Nazaire - Vigo four sailings per week). **Algeria Line** Barcelona – Marseille – Alger – Mostagenem (weekly).

Services listed carry unaccompanied ro-ro cargo together with large volumes of trade cars for vehicle manufacturers and distributors and interwork between routes. Occasional irregular calls are made at North Shields, Vlissingen, Le Havre and Southampton and sailings can sometimes omit scheduled ports. The Atlantic Line is operated with European Union funding from the TEN-T Programme and supported by a GEFCO car carrying contract between St Nazaire and Vigo. Vessels are regularly transferred between routes and are often chartered out for short periods to other operators and vehicle manufacturers. In view of this, the following is a list of all vessels in the *Flota Suardiaz* fleet including those not currently serving the UK.

1	BOUZAS	15224t	02	18.5k	149.4m	12P	1265C	105T	A	ES	9249996
2	GALICIA	16361t	03	15.0k	149.4m	12P	1390C	110T	A	PT	9268409
3	GRAN CANARIA CAR	9600t	01	18.0k	132.5m	0P	1150C	42T	AS	PT	9218014
4	IVAN	8191t	96	14.6k	102.5m	0P	853C	73T	A	PT	9112040
5	L'AUDACE	15222t	99	18.5k	149.4m	12P	1233C	105T	A	ES	9187318
6	LA SURPRISE	15222t	00	18.5k	149.4m	12P	1233C	105T	A	PT	9198719
7	SUAR VIGO	16361t	03	18.5k	149.4m	12P	1356C	110T	A	ES	9250000
8	TENERIFE CAR	13122t	02	20.0k	149.4m	12P	1354C	54T	AS	PT	9249984
9	VERONA	37237t	00	20.5k	176.7m	0P	3,919C	400T	QRS	NO	9190858

BOUZAS, GALICIA, L'AUDACE, LA SURPRISE, SUAR VIGO Built by Hijos de J. Barreras SA, Vigo, Portugal for *Flota Suardiaz* of Spain for use on services in the Mediterranean and to the Canaries, U.K. and Benelux. The vessels are highly flexible with a 12-driver capacity and three full height freight decks, each fitted with a mezzanine deck for cars, together with a further dedicated car deck. In addition to operating for *Flota Suardiaz* a number of vessels have spent periods on charter to *UECC*. The L'AUDACE was chartered to *P&O Ferries* to operate between Hull and Zeebrugge in early 2015. Since early 2017 she has been on charter to *Priority Ro-Ro Services* in the Caribbean sailing between Santo Domingo, Dominican Republic and San Juan, Puerto Rico.

GRAN CANARIA CAR Built as HARALD FLICK by Hijos de J. Barreras SA, Vigo, Portugal for *Naviera del Odiel*, one of the shareholders in Barreras and placed on 10 year charter to *Flota Suardiaz* of Spain for use on services in the Mediterranean and to the Canaries, U.K. and Benelux. Renamed GRAN CANARIA CAR before entering service. In 2008 ownership passed to *Navicar SA* a subsidiary of *Flota Suardiaz*. In addition to operating for *Flota Suardiaz* has been chartered to *UECC* on several occasions.

IVAN Built by Astilleros De Murueta, Vizcaya, Spain for *Adamastor - Sociedade de Navegação, Lda* a subsidiary of *Flota Suardiaz* for use on short sea services. For many years she operated a now ceased service from Sheerness and Grimsby to Calais.

TENERIFE CAR Built by Hijos de J. Barreras SA, Vigo, Portugal for *Navicar SA* a subsidiary of *Flota Suardiaz* for use on services in the Mediterranean and to the Canaries, UK and Benelux.

VERONA Built by Uljanik Shipbuilding Industries, Pula, Croatia for Montagu Bay Shipping, Monrovia, Liberia for charter to *Wallenius Wilhelmsen*. In 2002 sold to *Siem Car Carriers* of Panama. Of deep-sea ocean-going ro-ro design with a quarter ramp, she was chartered by *Suardiaz* from early 2016 onwards.

TRANSFENNICA

THE COMPANY *Transfennica Ltd* is a Finnish private sector company wholly owned by *Spliethoff Bevrachtingskantoor* of The Netherlands.

MANAGEMENT Managing Director Dirk P. Witteveen, **Sales Director (UK)** Andrew Clarke.

ADDRESSES *Finland* Eteläranta 12, 00130 Helsinki, Finland, **UK** Finland House, 47 Berth, Tilbury Port, Tilbury, Essex RM18 7EH.

TELEPHONE Administration & Reservations *Finland* +358 (0)9 13262, **UK** +44 (0)1375 363 900.

FAX Administration & Reservations *Finland* +358 (0)9 652377, **UK** +44 (0)1375 840 888.

SECTION 3 – FREIGHT ONLY FERRIES

Hafnia Sea *(Peter Therkildsen)*

Bore Bay *(Peter Therkildsen)*

INTERNET Email *Finland* info@transfennica.com *UK* info.uk@transfennica.com

Website www.transfennica.com *(English, Finnish, Russian)*

ROUTES OPERATED Tilbury (weekly) to various destinations in Finland and Russia. Please see the website. All *Transfennica* ships are listed below as ships are sometimes moved between routes.

1	BORE BANK	10585t	96	20.0k	138.8m	12P	-	105T	A2	FI	9160774
3	BORE SEA	25586t	11	18.5k	195.0m	12P	-	210T	A2	NL	9443554
4	CORONA SEA	25609t	08	20.0k	184.8m	12P	-	250T	AS	UK	9357597
5	GENCA	28301t	07	22.0k	205.0m	12P	-	200T	A2	NL	9307372
6	HAFNIA SEA	25609t	08	20.0k	184.8m	12P	-	250T	AS	UK	9357602
7	KRAFTCA	28301t	06	22.0k	205.0m	12P	-	200T	A2	NL	9307360
8	PLYCA	28301t	09	22.0k	205.0m	12P	-	200T	A2	NL	9345398
9	PULPCA	28301t	08	22.0k	205.0m	12P	-	200T	A2	NL	9345386
10	SEAGARD	10488t	99	21.0k	153.5m	12P	-	134T	A2	FI	9198977
11	TIMCA	28301t	06	22.0k	205.0m	12P	-	200T	A2	NL	9307358
12	TRICA	28301t	07	22.0k	205.0m	12P	-	200T	A2	NL	9307384

BORE BANK Built as the SERENADEN by Umoe Sterkoder AS, Kristiansund, Norway for *Rederi AB Engship* of Finland and chartered to *Transfennica*. In 2006 *Rederi AB Engship* was taken over by *Rettig Group Bore*. In 2007 converted at COSCO Shipyard, Nantong, China to add a garage on top of the weather deck, renamed AUTO BANK and placed on long-term charter to *UECC*. Generally used on the Baltic or Iberian services. In December 2016 converted back to a conventional ro-ro freighter by Öresundwerft, Landskrona, Sweden and renamed the BORE BANK. Chartered to *Transfennica*.

BORE SEA Built by Flensburger Schiffbau-Gesellschaft, Flensburg, Germany for *Bore Shipowners (Rettig Group Bore)* of Finland. In May 2011 chartered to *Transfennica* and operated between Zeebrugge and Bilbao. In January 2013 chartered for three years to *Fret Cetam* of France and used for the conveyance of parts for Airbus aircraft. In September 2016 chartered to *CLdN/Cobelfret Ferries*. Initially used mainly on the Zeebrugge - Purfleet service but later also used on the Iberian routes. In January 2018 chartered to *Transfennica*.

CORONA SEA Built as the TOR CORONA by Jinling Shipyard, Nanjing, China for *Macoma Shipping Ltd* of the UK and time-chartered to *DFDS Tor Line* for ten years. Used on the Fredericia – København - Klaipėda service. In April 2012 renamed the CORONA SEAWAYS. In January 2018 chartered to *Transfennica* and, in February, renamed the CORONA SEA.

GENCA, KRAFTCA, PLYCA, PULPCA, TIMCA, TRICA Built by New Szczecin Shipyard (SSN), Szczecin, Poland for *Spliethoff Bevrachtingskantoor*, owners of *Transfennica*.

HAFNIA SEA Built as the TOR HAFNIA by Jinling Shipyard, Nanjing, China for *Macoma Shipping Ltd* of the UK and time-chartered to *DFDS Tor Line* for ten years. Until 2013, mainly operated on the Immingham - Esbjerg route. In March 2011 renamed the HAFNIA SEAWAYS. In January 2015 chartered to *Cobelfret Ferries* for four weeks. In January 2018 chartered to *Transfennica* and in March 2018 renamed the HAFNIA SEA.

SEAGARD Built by J J Sietas KG, Hamburg, Germany for *Bror Husell Chartering* of Finland (later acquired by *Bore Shipowning* of Finland) and chartered to *Transfennica*.

UECC

THE COMPANY *United European Car Carriers AS* is a Norwegian private sector company jointly owned in equal shares by *Nippon Yusen Kabushiki Kaisha (NYK)* of Japan and *Wallenius Lines* of Sweden. *UECC* consists of companies in Norway, Germany, Spain, France, Portugal and the UK. The fleet technical and ship management department is based in Grimsby (UK).

MANAGEMENT Chief Executive Officer Glenn Edvardsen **Sales Manager UK** Nick Clark.

ADDRESSES Norway Karenlyst Allè 57, 0277 Oslo, **UK** 17 St. Helen's Place, London EC3A 6DG and Units 5B & 5C Appian Way, Europa Park, Grimsby, DN31 2UT.

TELEPHONE Norway +47 21 00 98 00, **UK** +44 (0)207 628 2855 and +44 (0)1472 269429.

FAX Norway +47 21 00 98 01, **UK** +44 (0)207 628 2858.

INTERNET Email companymail@uecc.com, **Website** www.uecc.com *(English).*

ROUTES OPERATED Atlantic Service Vigo – Le Havre – Zeebrugge – Sheerness – Vigo (*RCC PASSION*; weekly), Vigo – Zeebrugge – Bremerhaven – Drammen – Wallhamn – Cuxhaven – Southampton – Vigo (*BALTIC BREEZE, ARABIAN BREEZE*; weekly), **Baltic Service** Southampton – Zeebrugge – Bremerhaven – Malmo – Hanko – St Petersburg – Gdynia – Southampton (*AUTO ECO, AUTO ENERGY*; weekly), **Bristol Service** Portbury - Pasajes (*AUTOSUN*; weekly), **Biscay Services** Santander – Pasajes – Zeebrugge – Southampton – Santander (*AUTOSTAR*; weekly), Santander – Pasajes – Rotterdam - Zeebrugge – Santander (*AUTOSKY*, weekly), Pasajes – Zeebrugge – Southampton – Le Havre – Pasajes (*AUTOPROGRESS; AUTOPRESTIGE, VIKING CONSTANZA* weekly with extra sailings as required), **Norway Service** Bremerhaven – Oslo – Drammen – Walhamn – Oslo – Drammen – Bremerhaven (*AUTOPRIDE*; weekly), **North Sea Service** Cuxhaven – Immingham (*AUTOPRESTIGE*, twice weekly), **North – South Service** Bremerhaven – Zeebrugge – Portbury – Vigo – Sagunto – Tarragona – Livorno – Pireaus – Autoport – Yenikoy – Borusan – Vigo – Southampton – Bremerhaven (*CORAL LEADER, EMERALD LEADER, OPAL LEADER, VEGA LEADER, VIKING LEADER*; weekly).

Services listed carry unaccompanied ro-ro cargo together with large volumes of trade cars and often call at additional ports for an inducement and these have included Cork, Dublin, Immingham, Liverpool, Tilbury, and Newcastle. In addition, ad-hoc short-sea contract sailings for vehicle manufacturers and distributors are also operated throughout Northern Europe. Vessels are regularly transferred between routes and contracts and the following is a list of all owned and long term chartered vessels currently in the *UECC* fleet including those not presently serving the UK. The fleet is regularly supplemented by occasional voyages made by vessels of *Flota Suardiaz* and *LDA Seaplane* (the *Louis Dreyfus Armateurs* Airbus ro-ro operation) and by deep sea ocean-going ro-ro vessels long term chartered from parent companies *NYK Line* and *Wallenius Lines* and Eukor (which is 40% owned by Wallenius). Long term chartered vessels at the time of preparation and considered out of the scope of this book were the CORAL LEADER, EMERALD LEADER, OPAL LEADER, VEGA LEADER AND VICTORY LEADER all of which belong to parent *NYK Line* and the RCC PASSION.

1	AEGEAN BREEZE	27876t	83	18.0k	164.0m	0P	3242C	260T	QRS	SG	8202367
2	ARABIAN BREEZE	27876t	83	18.0k	164.0m	0P	3242C	260T	QRS	SG	8202355
3	ASIAN BREEZE	27876t	83	18.0k	164.0m	0P	3242C	260T	QRS	SG	8202381
4	AUTO ECO	43424t	16	18.6k	181.0m	0P	3800C	-	QRS	PT	9736365
5	AUTO ENERGY	43424t	16	18.6k	181.0m	0P	3800C	-	QRS	PT	9736377
6	AUTOPREMIER	11591t	97	20.0k	128.8m	0P	1220C	-	AS	PT	9131943
7	AUTOPRESTIGE	11596t	99	20.0k	128.8m	0P	1220C	-	AS	PT	9190157
8	AUTOPRIDE	11591t	97	20.0k	128.8m	0P	1220C	-	AS	PT	9131955
9	AUTOPROGRESS	11591t	98	20.0k	128.8m	0P	1220C	-	AS	PT	9131967
10	AUTOSKY	21010t	00	20.9k	140.0m	0P	2080C	-	AS	PT	9206774
11	AUTOSTAR	21010t	00	20.9k	140.0m	0P	2080C	-	AS	PT	9206786

12	AUTOSUN	21094t	00	20.9k	140.0m	0P	1220C	-	AS	PT	9227053
13	BALTIC BREEZE	29979t	83	17.5K	164.0m	0P	3242C	260T	QRS	SG	8312590
14	VIKING CONSTANZA	20216t	09	18.0k	139.9m	0P	2000C	65T	AQR	SG	9407689

AEGEAN BREEZE, ARABIAN BREEZE, ASIAN BREEZE Built by Kurushima Dockyard, Onishi, Japan for *Fuji Shipping* of Tokyo. Sold in 1988 to *Amon Shipping*. In 1990 sold to *Wallenius Lines*, Singapore and later chartered to *UECC*. Designated Breeze Class and of deep-sea ocean-going ro-ro design with quarter ramps, each was re-engined and heavily rebuilt in 2008 at COSCO Dalian Shipyard, China to extend lifespan and improve suitability for short sea service.

AUTO ECO, AUTO ENERGY Designated as E-Class both are Dual fuel LNG Ice Class 1A pure car and truck carriers with side and quarter ramps built by Kawasaki Heavy Industries at NACKS shipyard, Nantong, China for *UECC*. Used on Baltic services, the vessels are refuelled by a specialist barge in Zeebrugge. Both vessels are used on the Baltic service.

AUTOPREMIER, AUTOPRESTIGE, AUTOPROGRESS, AUTOPRIDE Built by Frisian Shipyard, Harlingen, the Netherlands for *UECC*. Designated P-class, they are an enlarged version of the now scrapped R-class and built to a 'Grimsby-Max' specification with greater capacity for ro-ro cargo. Generally used on scheduled sailings between Iberia and the Benelux and UK or between Germany and Norway.

AUTOSKY, AUTOSTAR, AUTOSUN Built by Tsuneishi Zosen, Tadotsu, Japan for *UECC* Designated S-class, they are a further enlargement of the P-class and R-class designs and are normally used on Biscay routes.

BALTIC BREEZE Built by Kurushima Dockyard, Onishi, Japan for *Fuji Shipping Co* of Tokyo. Sold in 1988 to *Amon Shipping*. Sold to *Wallenius Lines*, Singapore in 1990. Chartered to *Eukor* then to *UECC*. Of deep-sea ocean-going ro-ro design with quarter ramps, she was re-engined and heavily rebuilt in 2008 at COSCO Dalian Shipyard, China along with her sister Breeze Class vessels.

VIKING CONSTANZA Built by Kyokuyo Shipyard Corporation, Japan for *Gram Car Carriers*, Norway for operation on the charter market as part of a series of four vessels. Of short sea PTCC design the vessels have both stern and quarter ramps. In 2015 chartered by *UECC*. In 2017 chartered by *Suardiaz*. In 2018 charted by *UECC* to replace sister vessel *VIKING ODESSA*.

SECTION 4 - RO-RO OPERATORS CONVEYING PRIVATE TRAFFIC

The following operators employ ro-ro freight ships for the conveyance of their own traffic or traffic for a limited number of customers and do not normally solicit general traffic from hauliers or shippers.

FORELAND SHIPPING

THE COMPANY *Foreland Shipping Limited* (formerly *AWSR Shipping Limited*) is a UK private sector company. The principal shareholder in *Foreland Shipping* is *Hadley Shipping Group*.

MANAGEMENT Chairman Peter Morton, **Managing Director** Paul Trudgeon, **Operations Director** Stuart Williams.

ADDRESS 117-119 Houndsditch, London EC3A 7BT.

TELEPHONE +44 (0)20 7480 4140.

FAX +44 (0)20 7280 8790.

INTERNET Website www.foreland-shipping.co.uk *(English)*

ROUTES OPERATED No routes are operated. Ships are for charter to the *UK Ministry of Defence* for their 'Strategic Sealift Capability'.

1	ANVIL POINT	23235t	03	17.1k	193.0m	12P	-	180T	A	UK	9248540
2	EDDYSTONE	23235t	02	17.1k	193.0m	12P	-	180T	A	UK	9234070
3	HARTLAND POINT	23235t	03	17.1k	193.0m	12P	-	180T	A	UK	9248538
4	HURST POINT	23235t	02	17.1k	193.0m	12P	-	180T	A	UK	9234068

ANVIL POINT, HARTLAND POINT Built by Harland & Wolff, Belfast, UK for *AWSR Shipping*.

EDDYSTONE, HURST POINT Built by Flensburger Schiffbau-Gesellschaft, Flensburg, Germany for *AWSR Shipping*.

HOLMEN CARRIER

THE COMPANY *Holmen Carrier* is the branding of ships operated for *Holmen Paper AB*, an international company based in Sweden.

MANAGEMENT President and CEO Henrik Sjölund.

ADDRESS Holmen AB, P.O. Box 5407, SE-114 84 Stockholm, Sweden.

TELEPHONE +46 8 666 21 00

INTERNET Website www.holmen.com/en **Email** info@holmen.com *(English, Swedish)*

ROUTES OPERATED Norrköping (Sweden) - Travemünde - Sheerness - Hull - Norrköping (2 weeks; **EXPORTER, SHIPPER**; 1 per week).

1	EXPORTER	6620t	91	16.5k	122.0m	0P	-	90T	A	FI	8820860
2	SHIPPER	6620t	91	16.5k	122.0m	0P	-	90T	A	FI	8911748

EXPORTER Built as the GRANÖ by Brodogradiliste "Sava", Macvanska Mitrovica, Yugoslavia (fitted out by Fosen Mekaniske Verksteder of Rissa, Norway) for *Rederi AB Gustav Erikson* of Finland and chartered to *Transfennica* for service between Finland and Germany. In 1995 the owning company became *United Shipping* and in 2002 *Birka Cargo AB*. In 2000 she was chartered to the *Korsnäs Paper Group* to carry their traffic from Gävle (Sweden) to Chatham and Terneuzen (The Netherlands). In 2002 she was renamed the BIRKA EXPORTER. In 2005 the charter and operation of the services were taken over by *DFDS Tor Line*. The northbound Terneuzen - Gävle section became a ferry route marketed as part of the *DFDS Tor Line* network. This arrangement ceased in 2006. In 2008 chartered to *Finnlines*. In January 2010 chartered to *Holmen Paper AB*. In June 2013 renamed the EXPORTER.

SHIPPER Built as the STYRSÖ and renamed the BIRKA SHIPPER in 2002 and the SHIPPER in June 2013. Otherwise all details as the EXPORTER.

LD SEAPLANE

THE COMPANY LD Seaplane (formerly Fret-CETAM) is a French private sector company, 100% owned by Louis Dreyfus Armateurs SAS.

MANAGEMENT General Manager Jean-Louis Cadoret.

ADDRESS LD Seaplane, 21 Quai Gallieni - 92158, Suresnes Cedex, France.

TELEPHONE +33 (0)1 7038 6000.

INTERNET Website www.lda.fr/ld-seaplane-145 (English)

ROUTES OPERATED Mostyn (Wales) - Bordeaux (France) **CIUDAD DE CADIZ**, Tunis – Tangiers Med – Cadiz (Spain) – Bordeaux **VILLE DE BORDEAUX**, Hamburg - St Nazaire – Bordeaux **CITY OF HAMBURG**. Vessels are used for conveying Airbus materials under contract. Spare capacity and light ship sailings are regularly used for conveying trailers, heavy rolling cargo and trade cars and calls are often made at other ports for such cargos and regularly include Pasajes, Santander, Portbury, Sheerness and Zeebrugge. In addition vessels are regularly chartered out for short periods when idle.

1	CITY OF HAMBURG	15643t	08	180k	126.5m	4P	853C	31T	A	FR	9383558
2	CIUDAD DE CADIZ	15643t	09	180k	126.5m	4P	853C	31T	A	FR	9383560
3	VILLE DE BORDEAUX	21528t	04	210k	154.3m	12P	658C	123T	A	FR	9270842

CITY OF HAMBURG, CIUDAD DE CADIZ Built by Singapore Technologies Marine Ltd, Singapore for Louis Dreyfus Armateurs of France. Able to operate as a conventional ro-ro or as a car carrier using portable mezzanine decks and a dedicated car deck.

VILLE DE BORDEAUX Built by JinLing Shipyard, Nanjing, China for Louis Dreyfus Armateurs of France. Able to operate as a conventional ro-ro or as a car carrier using portable mezzanine decks. Short periods have been previously been spent on charter to Trasmediterranea, UECC, Cobelfret, LD Lines and P&O North Sea Ferries. In 2009 laid up for a year in St Nazaire when Airbus production was temporarily reduced.

SCA TRANSFOREST

THE COMPANY SCA Transforest is a Swedish company.

MANAGEMENT Managing Director (UK) Hugo Heij.

ADDRESS Sweden Box 805, 851 23, Sundsvall, Sweden, **UK** Interforest Terminal London Ltd, 44 Berth, Tilbury Dock, Essex RM18 7HP.

TELEPHONE Administration & Reservations Sweden +46 (0)60 19 35 00, **UK** +44 (0)1375 488500.

FAX Administration & Reservations Sweden +46 (0)60-19 35 65, **UK** +44 (0)1375 488503.

INTERNET Email Sweden info@transforest.sca.com **UK** interforest.london@sca.com

Website www.sca.com/transforest (English)

ROUTE OPERATED Umeå - Sundsvall - Sheerness - Rotterdam (Eemhaven) - Helsingborg - Oxelösund - Umeå (8/9 day round trip; **SCA OBBOLA, SCA ORTVIKEN, SCA ÖSTRAND**; 1 per week).

1	SCA OBBOLA	20168t	96	16.0k	170.6m	0P	-	-	A	SE	9087350
2	SCA ORTVIKEN	20154t	97	16.0k	170.4m	0P	-	-	A	SE	9087374
3	SCA ÖSTRAND	20171t	96	16.0k	170.6m	0P	-	-	A	SE	9087362

SCA OBBOLA, SCA ORTVIKEN, SCA ÖSTRAND Built as the OBBOLA, ORTVIKEN and ÖSTRAND by Astilleros Españoles, Sevilla, Spain for Gorthon Lines and chartered to SCA Transforest.

They are designed for the handling of forest products in non-wheeled 'cassettes' but can also accommodate trailers. The ORTVIKEN was lengthened during Autumn 2000 and the others during 2001. In June 2001 purchased by *SCA Transforest*. In spring 2016 renamed the SCA OBBOLA, SCA ORTVIKEN and SCA ÖSTRAND.

SMURFIT KAPPA GROUP

THE COMPANY *Smurfit Kappa Group* is an international company registered in the Irish Republic.

MANAGEMENT Group CEO Tony Smurfit.

ADDRESS Beech Hill, Clonskeagh, Dublin 4, Irish Republic.

TELEPHONE +353 (0)1 202 7000.

INTERNET Website www.smurfitkappa.com *(English)*

ROUTE OPERATED Södertälje (Sweden) - Harraholmen (Sweden) - Bremen (Germany)- Sheerness - Terneuzen (Netherlands) - Cuxhaven (Germany) - - Sodertalje (12 days; *BALTICBORG, BOTHNIABORG*; 1 per week).

1	BALTICBORG	12460t	04	16.5 k	153.1m	0P	-	104T	A	NL	9267716
2	BOTHNIABORG	12460t	04	16.5 k	153.1m	0P	-	104T	A	NL	9267728

BALTICBORG, BOTHNIABORG Built by Bodewes Volharding, Volharding, The Netherlands (hull built by Daewoo Mangalia Heavy Industries SA, Mangalia, Romania) for *Wagenborg Shipping* of The Netherlands. Time-chartered to *Kappa Packaging* (now *Smurfit Kappa Group)*. Placed on service between Piteå and Northern Europe. Northbound journeys (Terneuzen - Piteå) marketed as *RORO2 Stockholm*, with a call at Södertälje (Sweden (near Stockholm)) and, from 2005, the section Bremen - Sheerness - Terneuzen marketed as *RORO2 London*. In 2007 these arrangements ceased and *Mann Lines* took over the marketing of northbound traffic, a northbound call at Harwich (Navyard) being introduced and the Södertälje call being replaced by a call at Paldiski in Estonia. This arrangement ceased in 2013 and they reverted to their previous schedules.

SECTION 5 - GB & IRELAND - CHAIN, CABLE ETC FERRIES

CUMBRIA COUNTY COUNCIL

Address Resources Directorate, Highways Transportation and Fleet, County Offices, Kendal, Cumbria LA9 4RQ **Tel** +44 (0)1539 713040, **Fax** +44 (0)1539 713035.

Internet Email peter.hosking@cumbria.gov.uk *(English)*

Website www.cumbria.gov.uk/roads-transport/highways-pavements/windmereferry.asp *(English)*

Route Bowness-on-Windermere - Far Sawrey.

1	MALLARD		-	90	-	25.9m	140P	18C	-	BA

MALLARD Chain ferry built by F L Steelcraft, Borth, Dyfed for *Cumbria County Council*.

DARTMOUTH – KINGSWEAR FLOATING BRIDGE CO LTD

Address Dart Marina, Sandquay Road, Dartmouth, Devon TQ6 9PH. **Tel** +44 (0)7866 531687.

Internet Website www.dartmouthhigherferry.com *(English)*

Route Dartmouth - Kingswear (Devon) across River Dart (higher route) (forms part of A379).

1	HIGHER FERRY		540t	09	-	52.7m	240P	32C	-	BA

HIGHER FERRY Built by Ravestein BV, Deest, The Netherlands under contract to Pendennis Shipyard, Falmouth, who fitted the vessel out between January and June 2009.

ISLE OF WIGHT COUNCIL (COWES FLOATING BRIDGE)

Address Ferry Office, Medina Road, Cowes, Isle of Wight PO31 7BX. **Tel** +44 (0)1983 293041. **Internet Website** www.iwfloatingbridge.co.uk/timetable **Route** Cowes - East Cowes. **Note** the service is unable to operate at times of very low tide; a passenger service by launch is operated. Details are shown on the website.

| 1 | FLOATING BRIDGE NO 6 | - | 17 | - | 38.0m | - | 20C | - | BA | | |
| 2• | NO 5 | - | 76 | - | 33.5m | - | 15C | - | BA | | |

FLOATING BRIDGE NO 6 Chain ferry built by Mainstay Marine Solutions Ltd, Pembroke Dock, UK.

NO 5 Chain ferry built by Fairey Marine, East Cowes, UK for *Isle of Wight County Council*, now *Isle of Wight Council*. In January 2017 withdrawn for sale.

KING HARRY FERRY AND CORNWALL FERRIES

Address 2 Ferry Cottages, Feock, Truro, Cornwall TR3 6QJ. **Tel** +44 (0)1326 741194.

Internet Email beverley@kingharry.net **Website** www.falriver.co.uk *(English)*

Route Philliegh - Feock (Cornwall) (across River Fal)

| 1 | KING HARRY FERRY | 500t | 06 | - | 55.2m | 150P | 34C | - | BA | UK | 9364370 |

KING HARRY FERRY Chain ferry built by Pendennis Shipyard, Falmouth (hull constructed at Ravestein Shipyard, Deest, The Netherlands) to replace the previous ferry.

LUSTY BEG ISLAND FERRY

Address Lusty Beg, Boa Island, Kesh, County Fermanagh BT93 8AD.

Tel +44 (0)28 686 33300 **Fax** +44 (0)28 686 32033 E-mail:

Internet Email info@lustybegisland.com **Website** www.lustybegisland.com *(English)*

Route Boa Island, County Fermanagh - Lusty Beg Island (Lower Lough Erne)

| 1 | CORLOUGHAROO | - | - | - | 10.0m | 30P | 2C | - | BA | | |

CORLOUGHAROO Cable ferry, built for *Lusty Beg Island*.

REEDHAM FERRY

Address Reedham Ferry, Ferry Inn, Reedham, Norwich NR13 3HA. **Tel** +44 (0)1493 700429.

Internet Email info@reedhamferry.co.uk **Website** www.reedhamferry.co.uk *(English)*

Route Acle - Reedham - Norton (across River Yare, Norfolk).

| 1 | REEDHAM FERRY | - | 84 | - | 11.3m | 20P | 3C | - | BA | | |

REEDHAM FERRY Chain ferry built by Newsons, Oulton Broad, Lowestoft, UK for *Reedham Ferry*. Maximum vehicle weight: 12 tons.

SANDBANKS FERRY

Address *Company* Bournemouth-Swanage Motor Road and Ferry Company, Shell Bay, Studland, Swanage, Dorset BH19 3BA. **Tel** +44 (0)1929 450203, *Ferry* Floating Bridge, Ferry Way, Sandbanks, Poole, Dorset BH13 7QN. **Tel** +44 (0)1929 450203.

Internet Email email@sandbanksferry.co.uk **Website** www.sandbanksferry.co.uk *(English)*

Route Sandbanks - Shell Bay (Dorset).

| 1 | BRAMBLE BUSH BAY | 625t | 93 | - | 74.4m | 400P | 48C | - | BA | UK | 9072070 |

BRAMBLE BUSH BAY Chain ferry, built by Richard Dunston (Hessle) Ltd, Hessle, UK for the *Bournemouth-Swanage Motor Road and Ferry Company.*

SOUTH HAMS DISTRICT COUNCIL

Address Lower Ferry Office, The Square, Kingswear, Dartmouth, Devon TQ6 0AA. **Tel** +44 (0)1803 861234.

Internet Website www.southhams.gov.uk/DartmouthLowerFerry *(English)*

Route Dartmouth - Kingswear (Devon) across River Dart (lower route).

| 1 | THE TOM AVIS | - | 94 | - | 33.5m | 50P | 8C | - | BA |
| 2 | THE TOM CASEY | - | 89 | - | 33.5m | 50P | 8C | - | BA |

THE TOM AVIS Float (propelled by tugs) built by C Toms & Sons, Fowey, UK for *South Hams District Council.*

THE TOM CASEY Float (propelled by tugs) built by Cosens, Portland, UK for *South Hams District Council.*

TORPOINT FERRY

Address 2 Ferry Street, Torpoint, Cornwall PL11 2AX. **Tel** +44 (0)1752 812233.

Internet Website www.tamarcrossings.org.uk *(English)*

Route Devonport (Plymouth) - Torpoint (Cornwall) across the Tamar. The three ferries operate in parallel, each on her own 'track'. Pre-booking is not possible and the above number cannot be used for that purpose.

1	LYNHER II	748t	06	-	73.0m	350P	73C	-	BA	-	9310941
2	PLYM II	748t	04	-	73.0m	350P	73C	-	BA	-	9310927
3	TAMAR II	748t	05	-	73.0m	350P	73C	-	BA	-	9310939

LYNHER II, PLYM II, TAMAR II Chain ferries built by Ferguson Shipbuilders Ltd, Port Glasgow, UK to replace 1960s-built ships. Number is Lloyds number, not IMO.

WATERFORD CASTLE HOTEL

Address The Island, Waterford, Irish Republic. **Tel** +353 (0)51 878203, Fax: + 353 (0)51 879 316.

Internet Email info@waterfordcastleresort.com **Website** www.waterfordcastleresort.com *(English)*

Route Grantstown - Little Island (in River Suir, County Waterford).

| 1 | MARY FITZGERALD | 122t | 72 | 10.0k | 35.0m | 100P | 14C | - | BA | IR | 8985531 |

MARY FITZGERALD Built as the STEDINGEN by Abeking & Rasmussen, Lemwerder, Germany for *Schnellastfähre Berne-Farge GmbH* (from 1993 *Fähren Bremen-Stedingen GmbH*) to operate across the River Weser (Vegesack - Lemwerder and Berne - Farge). In 2004 sold to the *Lough Foyle Ferry Company Ltd* and renamed the FOYLE RAMBLER. Generally used on the Buncrana - Rathmullan (Lough Swilly) service, which did not resume in summer 2014. In 2014 sold to *Waterford Castle Hotel* and renamed the MARY FITZGERALD. Modified to be cable guided.

Mary Fitzgerald *(Brain Maxted)*

Floating Bridge No 6 *(Nick Widdows)*

SECTION 6 - GB & IRELAND - MAJOR PASSENGER-ONLY FERRIES

There are a surprisingly large number of passenger-only ferries operating in the British Isles, mainly operated by launches and small motor boats. There are, however, a few 'major' operators who operate only passenger vessels (of rather larger dimensions) and have not therefore been mentioned previously.

Aran Island Ferries BANRÍON NA FARRAIGE (117t, 27.4m, 1984, 188 passengers, IMO 8407709) (ex ARAN EXPRESS 2007), CEOL NA FARRAIGE (234t, 2001, 37.4m, 294 passengers, IMO 9246750), DRAÍOCHT NA FARRAIGE (318t, 1999, 35.4m, 294 passengers, IMO 9200897), GLÓR NA FARRAIGE (170t, 1985, 33.5m, 244 passenger, IMO 8522391) (ex ARAN FLYER 2007). **Routes operated** Rossaveal (Co Galway) – Inishmor, Rossaveal - Inis Meáin, Rossaveal - Inisheer. **Tel** +353 (0)91 568903 (572050 after 19.00), **Fax** +353 (0)91 568538, **Email** info@aranislandferries.com **Website** www.aranislandferries.com *(English)*

Blue Funnel Cruises HYTHE SCENE (66t, 1992, 21.3m, 162 passengers - catamaran) (ex GREAT EXPECTATIONS 2017), JENNY ANN (1979, 11.6m, 50 passengers) ex JENNY ANN 1998, ex FALDORE III 2015, ex PUFFIN BELLE 2017), JENNY BLUE (ex OSSIAN OF STAFFA 2017) (1993, 13.7m, 65 passengers), JENNY R* (12t, 1984, 13.7m, 75 passengers), OCEAN SCENE (279t, 1994, 29.0m, 350 passengers - catamaran, IMO 8633865), OLIVER B* (21t, 1988, 12.2m, 62 passengers - catamaran). Note: The HYTHE SCENE is the regular ferry. Other vessels in the fleet (which are used for charters and excursions) can cover as necessary. **Route Operated** Southampton - Hythe, **Tel** +44 (0)2380 239800 **Email** office@bluefunnel.co.uk **Website** www.bluefunnel.co.uk *(English)*. *The JENNY R is owned by Blue Funnel* but operated by *Solent and Wightline Cruises Ltd*, the OLIVER B is owned by *Solent and Wightline Cruises Ltd* but operated by *Blue Funnel Cruises*.

Clyde Cruises (Clyde Marine Services Ltd) CHIEFTAIN (54t, 2007, 19.5m, 100 passengers) (ex SEABUS, 2014), **Route operated** Gourock - Kilcreggan (operated on behalf of *Strathclyde Partnership for Transport*), CLYDE CLIPPER (125t, 2009, 27m, 250 passengers), CRUISER (119t, 1974, 24.4m, 245 passengers) (ex POOLE SCENE, 2001, HYTHE HOTSPUR, 1995, SOUTHSEA QUEEN, 1978), FENCER (18t, 1976, 11.0m, 33 passengers), ROVER (48t, 1964, 19.8m, 120 passengers). **Routes operated** Glasgow city cruise, Caledonian Canal sailings, Oban from Dunstaffnage Marina, Aberdeen Harbour tours and cruises and private charters around the Clyde area. **Tel** +44 (0)1475 721281, **Email** info@clydecruises.com **Website** www.clydecruises.com www.clyde-marine.co.uk *(English)*.

Clydelink ISLAND TRADER (12 passengers), SILVER SWAN (12 passengers) **Route operated** Renfrew - Yoker (operated on behalf of *Strathclyde Partnership for Transport*). **Tel** 0871 705 0888, **Websites** www.clydelink.co.uk www.spt.co.uk/kilcreggan-ferry *(English)*.

Cremyll Ferry (Plymouth Boat Trips) EDGCUMB BELLE (35t, 1957, 17.6m, 128 passengers) (ex HUMPHREY GILBERT 1978) **Route operated** Stonehouse, Plymouth, Devon - Cremyll, Cornwall. **Note:** River craft owned by this operator are also used for the ferry service on some occasions. **Tel** +44 (0)1752 253153 or +44 (0)7971 208381 **Email** info@plymouthboattrips.co.uk **Website** www.plymouthboattrips.co.uk/ferries/cremyll-ferry *(English)*

Dartmouth Steam Railway & Riverboat Company DARTMOUTH PRINCESS (ex DEVON BELLE II 2000) (22t, 1990, 18.3m, 156 passengers), KINGSWEAR PRINCESS (27t, 1978, 19.1m, 150 passengers) (ex TWIN STAR II 2010). **Route operated** Dartmouth - Kingswear. **Note:** River craft owned by this operator are also used for the ferry service on some occasions. **Tel** +44 (0)1803 555872, **Email** bookings@dsrrb.co.uk **Website** www.dartmouthrailriver.co.uk *(English)*

Doolin2Aran Ferries DOOLIN DISCOVERY (2009, 15.2m, 72 passengers), HAPPY HOOKER (77t, 1989, 19.8m, 96 passengers), JACK B (2005, 15.2m, 67 passengers), ROSE OF ARAN (113t, 1976, 20.1m, 96 passengers. IMO 7527916), STAR OF DOOLIN (2018, 24.0m, 200 passengers). **Routes operated** Doolin - Inisheer, Doolin - Inishmore, Doolin - Inishmaan.

Also Cliffs of Moher Cruise. **Tel** +353 (0)65 707 5949, **Email** info@doolin2aranferries.ie **Website** www.doolin2aranferries.com *(English)*

Doolin Ferry (O'Brien Line) CAILIN OIR (1999, 15.2m, 72 passengers), DOOLIN EXPRESS, (2010, 24.5m, 250 passengers), (ex BLANCHE HERMINE 2016, ex SAINT VINCENT DE PAUL 2014), TRANQUILITY (62t, 1988, 15.8m, 100 passengers). **Routes operated** Doolin - Inisheer, Doolin - Inishmaan, Doolin - Inishmore. Also cruises to Cliffs of Mohr. **Tel** +353 (0)65 707 5555, +353 (0)65 707 5618, **Email** info@doolinferry.com **Website** www.doolinferry.com *(English)*

Exe2Sea Cruises MY QUEEN (1929, 37t, 18m, 127 passengers) (ex GONDOLIER QUEEN) (laid up), ORCOMBE (1954, 14.3m, 90 passengers), PRINCESS MARINA (1936, 15.8m, 60 passengers). **Route operated** Exmouth - Starcross. **Tel** +44 (0)7974 022536 / +44 (0)7779 157280. **Email** info@exe2sea.co.uk **Website** www.exe2sea.co.uk (diverts to Facebook page) *(English)*

Fleetwood – Knott End Ferry (operated by *Wyre Marine Services Ltd*) WYRE ROSE (2005, 32 passengers). **Route operated** Fleetwood - Knott End. **Tel** +44 (0)1253 871113, **Ferry mobile** +44 (0) 7793 270934, **Email** info@wyremarine.co.uk **Website** www.wyre.gov.uk (search for ferry) *(English)*

Gosport Ferry HARBOUR SPIRIT (293t, 2015, 32.8m, 297 passengers, IMO 9741669), SPIRIT OF GOSPORT (300t, 2001, 32.6m, 300 passengers, IMO 8972089), SPIRIT OF PORTSMOUTH (377t, 2005, 32.6m, 300 passengers, IMO 9319894). **Route operated** Gosport - Portsmouth. **Tel** +44 (0)23 9252 4551, **Fax:** +44(0)23 9252 4802, **Email** admin@gosportferry.co.uk **Website** www.gosportferry.co.uk *(English)*

Gravesend – Tilbury Ferry (operated by the *JetStream Tours*) THAMES SWIFT (25.6t, 1995, 18.3m, 50 passengers (tri-maran)), (ex MARTIN CHUZZLEWIT 2001), JACOB MARLEY (29t, 1985, 15.5m, 98 passengers) (ex SOUTHERN BAY ROSE 2016, ex SEAWAYS EXPRESS 2006, ex CONDOR KESTREL). **Note** the THAMES SWIFT is the regular ferry; the JACOB MARLEY may substitute on occasions. **Route operated** Gravesend (Kent) - Tilbury (Essex), **Tel** +44 (0)1634 525202, **Email** bookings@jetstreamtours.com **Website** www.jetstreamtours.com *(English)*

Hamble – Warsash Ferry CLAIRE (2.1t, 1985, 7.3m, 12 passengers), EMILY (3.7t, 1990, 8.5m, 12 passengers. **Route operated** Hamble - Warsash (across Hamble River). **Tel** +44 (0)23 8045 4512, **Mobile** +44 (0) 7720 438402 Duty Ferryman +44 (0) 07827 157154. **Email** mike@hambleferry.co.uk, **Website** www.hambleferry.co.uk *(English)*

Harwich Harbour Foot & Bicycle Ferry HARBOUR FERRY (8t, 1969, 11.4m, 58 passengers) (ex lifeboat from the liner CANBERRA, ex TAURUS 2012, ex PUFFIN BILLI, 2016). **Routes operated** Harwich (Ha'penny Pier) - Shotley (Marina), Harwich - Felixstowe (Landguard Point) (Easter to end of September). **Tel** +44 (0) 7919 911440, **Email** chris@harwichharbourferry.com **Website** www.harwichharbourferry.com *(English)*

Hayling Ferry (operated by **Baker Trayte Marine Ltd**). PRIDE OF HAYLING (1989, 11.9m, 63 passengers), **Route operated** Eastney – Hayling Island. **Tel/Fax:** +44(0)23 9229 4800, +44(0)23 9266 2942, **Mobile** +44(0)7500 194854, **Website** www.haylingferry.net *(English)*

Hovertravel ISLAND FLYER (161t, 2016, 22.4m, 80 passengers, IMO 9737797, Griffon Hovercraft 12000TD/AP), SOLENT FLYER (161t, 2016, 40.0k, 22.4m, 80 passengers, IMO 9737785, Griffon Hovercraft 12000TD/AP), FREEDOM 90 (1990, 25.4m, 95 passengers, BHC AP1-88/100S hovercraft, converted from AP1-88/100 in 1999), ISLAND EXPRESS (1985, 25.4m, 95 passengers, BHC AP1-88/100S hovercraft, converted from BHC AP1-88/100 in 2001) (ex FREJA VIKING, 2002). **Route operated** Southsea - Ryde. **Tel** +44 1983 717700, **Email** info@hovertravel.com **Website** www.hovertravel.co.uk *(English)*

Isle of Sark Shipping Company BON MARIN DE SERK (118t, 1983, 20.7m, 131 passengers, IMO 8303056), SARK BELLE (50t, 1979, 26.2m, 180 passengers) (ex BOURNEMOUTH BELLE 2011), SARK VENTURE (133t, 1986, 21.3m, 122 passengers, IMO 8891986), SARK VIKING (Cargo Vessel) (104t, 2007, 21.2m, 12 passengers, IMO 8648858). **Route operated** St Peter

Port (Guernsey) - Sark. **Tel** +44 (0) 1481 724059, **Fax** +44 (0) 1481 713999, **Email** info@sarkshipping.gg **Website** www.sarkshippingcompany.com *(English)*

John O'Groats Ferries PENTLAND VENTURE (186t, 1987, 29.6m, 250 passengers, IMO 8834122). **Route operated** John O'Groats – Burwick (Orkney). **Tel** +44 (0)1955 611353, **Email** Office@jogferry.co.uk **Website** www.jogferry.co.uk *(English)*

Kintyre Express KINTYRE EXPRESS V (2012, 12.5m, 12 passengers), **Routes operated** Campbeltown - Ballycastle, Port Ellen (Islay) - Ballycastle. **Tel** +44 (0) 1586 555895, **Email** info@kintyreexpress.com **Website** www.kintyreexpress.com *(English)*

Lundy Company OLDENBURG (294t, 1958, 43.6m, 267 passengers, IMO 5262146). **Routes operated** Bideford - Lundy Island, Ilfracombe - Lundy Island. Also North Devon coastal cruises and River Torridge cruises. **Tel** +44 (0)1237 470074, **Fax** +44 (0)1237 477779, **Email** info@lundyisland.co.uk **Website** www.lundyisland.co.uk *(English)*

Manche Iles Express (trading name of Société Morbihannaise de Navigation) GRANVILLE (325t, 2006, 41.0m, 245 passengers, IMO 9356476 - catamaran) (ex BORNHOLM EXPRESS 2014), VICTOR HUGO (387t, 1997, 35.0m, 195 passengers, IMO 9157806 - catamaran) (ex SALTEN 2003). **Routes operated** Jersey - Guernsey, Granville – Jersey - Sark - Guernsey, Portbail or Carteret – Jersey, Guernsey and Sark, Diélette - Alderney - Guernsey. **Tel *Jersey*** +44 (0)1534 880756, ***France*** +33 0825 131 050, **Fax** +33 02 33 90 03 49, **Website** www.manche-iles-express.com *(French, English)*

MBNA Thames Clippers (trading name of Collins River Enterprises Ltd) AURORA CLIPPER (181t, 2007, 37.8m, 27.5k, 220 passengers, IMO 9451824), CYCLONE CLIPPER (181t, 2007, 37.8m, 27.5k, 220 passengers, IMO 9451880), GALAXY CLIPPER (155t, 2015, 34.0m, 155 passengers, IMO 9783784), HURRICANE CLIPPER (181t, 2002, 37.8m, 27.5k, 220 passengers, IMO 9249702), JUPITER CLIPPER (155t, 2017, 35.0 m, 28.0k, 170 passengers, IMO 9223796), MERCURY CLIPPER (155t, 2017, 35.0 m, 28.0k, 170 passengers, IMO 9223801),METEOR CLIPPER (181t, 2007, 37.8m, 27.5k, 220 passengers, IMO 9451812), MONSOON CLIPPER (181t, 2007, 37.8m, 27.5k, 220 passengers, IMO 9451795), MOON CLIPPER (98t, 2001, 32.0m, 25.0k, 138 passengers, IMO 9245586) (ex DOWN RUNNER 2005), NEPTUNE CLIPPER (155t, 2015, 34.0m, 155 passengers, IMO 9783796), SKY CLIPPER (60t, 1992, 25.0m, 62 passengers) (ex VERITATUM 1995, SD10 2000),STAR CLIPPER (60t, 1992, 25.0m, 62 passengers) (ex CONRAD CHELSEA HARBOUR 1995, SD9 2000), STORM CLIPPER (60t, 1992, 25.0m, 62 passengers) (ex DHL WORLDWIDE EXPRESS 1995, SD11 2000), SUN CLIPPER (98t, 2001, 32.0m, 25.0k, 138 passengers, IMO 9232292) (ex ANTRIM RUNNER 2005), TORNADO CLIPPER (181t, 2007, 37.8m, 27.5k, 220 passengers, IMO 9451783), TWIN STAR (45t, 1974, 19.2m, 120 passengers), TYPHOON CLIPPER (181t, 2007, 37.8m, 27.5k, 220 passengers, IMO 9451771, (2015, 34.0m, 154 seats). The 'Typhoon', 'Tornado', 'Cyclone' and 'Monsoon', 'Aurora' and 'Meteor' Clippers were designed by AIMTEK and built by Brisbane Ship Constructions in Australia in 2007. 'Galaxy' and 'Neptune' were designed by One2three Naval Architects and built by Incat Tasmania, Hobart, Australia. **Routes operated** Embankment - Waterloo - Blackfriars – Bankside - London Bridge - Tower - Canary Wharf – Greenland - Masthouse Terrace - Greenwich - North Greenwich - Woolwich, Bankside – Millbank - St George (Tate to Tate Service), Putney - Wandsworth - Chelsea Harbour - Cardogan - Embankment - Blackfriars, Canary Wharf - Rotherhithe Hilton Docklands Hotel (TWIN STAR). +44 (0)870 781 5049, **Fax** +44 (0)20 7001 2222, **Email** web@thamesclippers.com **Website** www.thamesclippers.com *(English)*

Mersey Ferries ROYAL DAFFODIL (751t, 1962, 46.6m, 860 passengers, IMO 4900868) (ex OVERCHURCH 1999) (laid up), ROYAL IRIS OF THE MERSEY (464t, 1960, 46.3m, 650 passengers, IMO 8633712) (ex MOUNTWOOD 2002), SNOWDROP (670t, 1960, 46.6m, 650 passengers, IMO 8633724) (ex WOODCHURCH 2004). **Routes operated** Liverpool (Pier Head) - Birkenhead (Woodside), Liverpool - Wallasey (Seacombe) with regular cruises from Liverpool and Seacombe to Salford along the Manchester Ship Canal. **Tel *Admin*** +44 (0)151 639 0609, ***Reservations*** +44 (0)151 330 10003, **Twitter** @merseyferries, **Facebook** Mersey Ferries **Website** www.merseyferries.co.uk *(English)*

Lynher II *(Brian Maxted)*

Jenack *('Brian Maxted)*

Solent Flyer (Andrew Cooke)

Pride of Hayling (Nick Widdows)

Mudeford Ferry (Derham Marine) FERRY DAME (4t, 1989, 9.1m, 48 passengers), JOSEPHINE (10.5t, 1997, 10.7m, 70 passengers - catamaran), JOSEPHINE II (10.5t, 2013, 11.0m, 86 passengers - catamaran). **Route operated** Mudeford Quay - Mudeford Sandbank. **Tel** +44 (0)7968 334441 **Email** information@mudefordferry.co.uk **Website** www.mudefordferry.co.uk *(English)*

Nexus (trading name of Tyne & Wear Integrated Transport Authority) PRIDE OF THE TYNE (222t, 1993, 24.0m, 240 passengers, IMO 9062166), SPIRIT OF THE TYNE (174t, 2006, 25.0m, 200 passengers). **Route operated** North Shields - South Shields. Also cruises South Shields - Newcastle. **Tel** +44 (0)191 2020747, **Email** customerservices@nexus.org **Website** www.nexus.org.uk/ferry *(English)*

The Little Ferry Company SPIKE ISLANDER (13.0m, 12 passengers), **Route Operated** St Peter Port (Guernsey) - Alderney (11 week trail). **Tel** +44 (0)1481 822828 **Website** www.thelittleferrycompany.com *(English)*

Travel Trident HERM TRIDENT V (79t, 1989, 25.9m, 250 passengers), TRIDENT VI (79t, 1992, 22.3m, 250 passengers). **Route operated** St Peter Port (Guernsey) - Herm. **Tel** +44 (0)1481 721379, **Fax** +44 (0)1481 700226, **Email** peterwilcox@cwgsy.net **Website** www.traveltrident.com *(English)*

Waverley Excursions WAVERLEY (693t, 1946, 73.13m, 860 passengers, IMO 5386954). **Routes operated** Excursions all round British Isles. However, regular cruises in the Clyde, Bristol Channel, South Coast and Thames provide a service which can be used for transport purposes and therefore she is in a sense a ferry. She is the only seagoing paddle steamer in the world. **Tel** +44 (0)845 130 4647, **Fax** +44 (0)141 243 2224, **Email** info@waverleyexcursions.co.uk **Website** www.waverleyexcursions.co.uk *(English)*

Western Isles Cruises Ltd LARVEN (14.0m, 2017, 42 passengers (catamaran)), WESTERN ISLES (45t, 1960, 18.0m, 82 passengers). **Route Operated** Mallaig - Inverie (Knoydart) - Tarbet. **Tel** +44 (0)1687 462233, **Email** info@westernislescruises.co.uk, **Website** www.westernislescruises.co.uk *(English)*

Western Lady Ferry Service WESTERN LADY VI (ex TORBAY PRINCESS ex DEVON PRINCESS II) (50t, 1981, 19.2m, 173 passengers), WESTERN LADY VII (ex TORBAY PRINCESS II, ex BRIXHAM BELLE II, ex DEVON PRINCESS III) (46t, 1984, 19.8m, 177 passengers). **Route Operated** Torquay - Brixham. **Tel** +44 (0)1803 293797, **Website** www.westernladyferry.com *(English)* Note: The service is now part of *Dartmouth Steam Railway & Riverboat Company* but is marketed separately.

White Funnel BALMORAL (735t, 1949, 62.2m, 800 passengers, IMO 5034927) Excursions in Bristol Channel, North West, South Coast, Thames and Clyde. However, no services operated in 2018. Services may resume in 2019. **Email** balmoral@whitefunnel.co.uk **Website** www.whitefunnel.co.uk *(English)*

SECTION 6 – MAJOR PASSENGER ONLY FERRIES

Mecklenburg-Vorpommern *(Richard Kirkman)*

SCANDINAVIAN & NORTHERN EUROPE REVIEW 2017-18

The following geographical review again takes the form of a voyage along the coast of the Netherlands and Germany, round the southern tip of Norway, down the Kattegat, through the Great Belt and into the Baltic, then up to the Gulf of Finland and Gulf of Bothnia.

FRISIAN ISLANDS & ELBE

TESO's new *Texelstroom* had entered service between Den Helder and the island of Texel in September 2016. However, problems with *Texelstroom* necessitated the retention of the *Schulpengat* throughout 2017 and this continued into 2018.

The Elb-Link service between Cuxhaven and Brunsbüttel had suffered from poor loadings ever since its inauguration in August 2015 and by autumn 2016 was in financial difficulties. Despite a refinancing by German banks which saw Saaremaa Laevakompanii (SLK) withdraw from the operation, instead chartering their two vessels to Elb-Link, the company went into administration on 1 March 2017. A 'new' Elb-Link started operation in late May 2017 with their former operations director Bernd Baessman having reformed the company. The service became a one-ship operation, retaining the *Muhumaa* which was formally renamed *Grete*. The *Saaremaa* had been returned to her owners when the company went bankrupt. However, in October 2017 the service again ran into financial difficulties and the service ceased; in November the 'new' company filed for bankruptcy. All three ex-Saaremaa Laevakompanii vessels are now laid up and owned by German company Conmar Shipping.

Reederei Norden-Frisia ordered a new vessel from Pella Sietas Werft, Hamburg to operate on the Norddeich-Norderney service. A sister vessel of the *Frisia III*, she is due to be delivered in 2020 and will probably be called the *Frisia IV*.

Wyker Dampfschiffs-Reederei's new vessel, the 3,250t *Norderaue*, entered service in Spring 2018. The company operates to a number of islands on the North Sea coast, just south of the Danish frontier.

NORWEGIAN DOMESTIC

The first new vessel ordered by Hurtigruten in 2016 - the *Roald Amundsen*, due to enter service in late 2018 and undertake Antarctic, Greenland and Spitsbergen cruises was delayed and will not now arrive until 2019. Her sister, the *Fridtjof Nansen*, was due to arrive in 2019 but may also be delayed. In June 2018, Hurtigruten took over the Kleven Verft, Ulsteinvik yard in which the ships were being built.

As part of the Norwegian government's policy of putting the services on the *Kystruten* (Coastal Express) out to tender, about 33% of the service will, from 1st January 2021, be operated by *Havila Shipping ASA* of Norway, trading as *Havila Kystruten*. Four new cruise ferries have been ordered from Norwegian and Spanish yards to operate the service. Hurtigruten have said some of their vessels will be transferred to a cruise role with fewer calls.

The *Bastø VI*, Bastø-Fosen's first new ship arrived from her Turkish builder in mid December 2016, entering service in early 2017. The other two vessels in the class, the *Bastø IV* and *Bastø V*, arrived in Norway in March, entering service the following month.

SKAGERRAK & KATTEGAT

Color Line's new hybrid ferry for the Sandefjord - Strömstad service will enter service on the route in 2019, replacing the *Bohus*. The following year, once the new roster comes into effect, the new ship will be the sole Color Line vessel on the route with the withdrawal of *Color Viking*, whilst Fjord Line will operate two vessels. However, Fjord Line have not yet ordered a second vessel

The Port of Varberg has announced redevelopment plans which will require Stena to find a new port for their operation to Grenå from Autumn 2019. The service will switch to Halmstad, approximately 70 kilometres south of Varberg.

Berlin *(Scandlines)*

Prins Richard *(Scandlines)*

Gotlandia II *(Destination Gotland)*

Cracovia *(John Bryantl)*

In early 2017 HH Ferries converted two of their Helsingør – Helsingborg double-enders to battery power. The *Tycho Brahe* and *Aurora af Helsingborg* were refitted in early 2017 in a €26 million project, part funded by the European Union.

DANISH DOMESTIC

In preparation for their new contract for the Bornholm services from September 2018, Mols-Linien adopted a new branding for their operations: Molslinjen for the Kattegat services and Bornholmslinjen for the new service. The *KatExpress 1* and *KatExpress 2* were renamed simply as *Express 1* and *Express 2* and the new *Express 3* (ordered as *KatExpress 3*) entered service between Sjællands Odde and Århus on 1st June 2017. The new catamaran, *Express 4*, under construction at Henderson is expected to enter service on the Kattegat route with *Express 1* being deployed to the new Bornholm contract. The company also purchased the *Povl Anker* from Færgen to act as a support vessel. A new ro-pax vessel, the *Hammerhus*, to operate the services from Rønne to Køge and Rønne to Sassnitz was delivered from Rauma in July. The Sassnitz service, previously summer only, will operate all year round.

Færgen's *Hammerodde*, was sold to Stena RoRo in 2017 and chartered back until the service ceases; in September she will be renamed and switched to Stena's Gothenburg - Frederikshavn route . Færgen sold the *Leonora Cristina* to Lineas Fred. Olsen for delivery in September 2018 and the *Villum Clausen* to an unidentified buyer in the Mediterranean.

SOUTH BALTIC

Polferries have invested in additional tonnage for the Świnoujście – Ystad route, purchasing the *Drujba* from Bulgaria. She was brought to Szczecin in June for refitting and entered service as the *Cracovia* in September 2017, taking the roster of the *Baltivia*, although the latter remained in service on a reduced timetable. In September 2018, capacity on the Gdansk - Nynäshamn route will be doubled with the introduction of the *Nova Star*. This Singapore built vessel which was rejected by LD Lines for their Portsmouth - Le Havre service and failed commercially in North America, will hopefully have a better future in the Baltic.

Polferries have also ordered a new ferry from Morska Stocznia Remontowa Grufia shipyard at Szczecin. The new vessel will be 228 metres long and powered by Liquified Natural Gas (LNG). She is expected to be delivered in 2019.

Euroafrica Shipping in December 2017 purchased the 50 passenger ro-pax *Puglia* from Moby Line of Italy, taking delivery in spring 2018. Renamed the *Copernicus*, she arrived at Szczecin in January 2018 but did not enter service on the Unity Line Świnoujście - Trelleborg route until August.

Both Polferries and TT-Line started operations between Swinoujscie and Bornholm during 2017, using the *Cracovia* and the *Nils Dacke* respectively. In June 2018 TT-Line started a weekly service between Trelleborg and Klaipėda in Lithuania.

In February TT-Line signed a letter of intent with the Jinling shipyard in China for two new ro-pax vessels. The vessels will be a similar size to the DFDS newbuildings with 4,600 lane metres for freight and capacity for 650 passengers. It is likely that the new vessels will replace the *Huckleberry Finn* and *Tom Sawyer*. TT-Line's *Peter Pan* was lengthened by about 30 metres at Bremerhaven in Spring 2018. She returned to service at the end of May.

Stena expanded their Baltic operations, with the *Gute* joining the Karlskrona – Gdynia route as fourth ship from Autumn 2017. The *Stena Nordica*, back from her charter to GNV, partners the *Urd* on the Travemünde - Liepaja service. A freight-only service between Gdynia - Nynäshamn was introduced in October 2017, using the chartered *Elisabeth Russ*. She was replaced by the smaller *Bore Bay* in February 2018.

In February 2018 DFDS Seaways ordered two 600 passenger ro-pax vessels from Guangzhou Shipyard International, China. They will operate on Baltic routes from Klaipėda to Kiel and Karlshamn from 2021.

Destination Gotland's new ferries under construction in China were somewhat delayed and the first vessel, the *Visborg* is now expected to enter service in September 2018. The second, the *Thjelvar*, will follow in 2019.

NORTH BALTIC

Tallink's new LNG-powered *Megastar* entered service on 29th January 2017, making an immediate impression on the Tallinn – Helsinki 'Shuttle' with her array of onboard facilities and cutting edge design. The *Megastar* replaced the *Superstar* which was sold to Corsica Ferries, refitted and entered service as the *Pascal Lota* in June 2017. Meanwhile the *Star*, Tallink's other vessel on the service, was converted to double-deck loading during her refit in March 2017.

The company has also redeployed certain units in its fleet during the early part of the year, with *Baltic Queen* being withdrawn from the Tallinn – Helsinki cruise circuit, leaving a comprehensively refitted *Silja Europa* to operate the service alone. The *Baltic Queen* was switched to the Stockholm – Tallinn service, replacing the *Romantika* which was sent to partner the *Isabelle* on the Stockholm – Riga route.

A new Viking Line ship is being built at Xiamen Shipbuilding in China. She will measure 218 metres in length, 63,000 gross tons and will be powered by LNG. The new ship is anticipated to enter service in Spring 2020, partnering the *Viking Grace*. The new ship will feature two Flettner rotors which will provide additional power and a single rotor was fitted to *Viking Grace* during its annual refit in March 2018.

Viking Line also chartered *Express*, operated for Gotlandsbåten in 2016, to provide additional capacity between Tallinn and Helsinki during the summer season of 2017. Marketed as "Viking FSTR", she partnered *Viking XPRS*. However, the project was not successful and has not been repeated in 2018.

In October 2017 Finnlines sold the *Finneagle* to parent company Grimaldi Line of Italy, who had chartered her since July 2016. She was renamed the *Euroferry Corfu*. In April 2018 the *Europalink* returned to the Malmö - Travemünde service after five years in the Mediterranean. She replaced *Nordlink* which, renamed *Finnswan*, was transferred to the FinnLink Kapellskär - Naantali route replacing the *Finnclipper* , which was chartered to Baleària of Spain and renamed the *Rosalind Franklin*.

St Peter Line and Moby Line announced a new strategic partnership for 2017 with the Italian company refinancing the operation. The *Princess Anastasia* was placed on a new five-day circuit incorporating St Petersburg – Helsinki – Tallinn – Stockholm – Helsinki – St Petersburg. The ship was re-liveried, with Moby funnel colours to starboard and St Peter Line to port. The other vessel on the service, the *Princess Maria*, was transferred to Moby Line as part of the deal and renamed *Moby Dada* for further service to Corsica.

Praamid's were finally able to maintain the service which they took over from Saaremaa Laevakompanii from their own resources when their third and fourth new vessels - the *Piret* and the *Tiiu* - entered service in April 2017. The charter of the *Hiiumaa* ended but the 1971 former Öresund vessel *Regula* has been retained to act as a back-up vessel. SLK's *St Ola* was meanwhile sold to Medmar of Italy and renamed *Medmar Giulia*.

Matthew Punter

Megastar *(Richard Kirkman)*

Ærøskøbing *(Peter Therkildsen)*

Color Magic *(Color Line)*

SECTION 7 - NORTHERN EUROPE
ÆRØFÆRGERNE

THE COMPANY *Ærøfærgerne* is a Danish company, owned by the municipality of Ærø.

MANAGEMENT Managing Director Kelda Møller, **Marketing Coordinator** Jeanette Erikson.

ADDRESS Vestergade 1, 5970 Ærøskøbing, Denmark.

TELEPHONE Administration & Reservations +45 62 52 40 00.

FAX Administration & Reservations +45 62 52 20 88.

INTERNET Email info@aeroe-ferry.dk **Website** www.aeroe-ferry.dk *(Danish, English, German)*

ROUTE OPERATED Ærøskøbing (Ærø) - Svendborg (Funen) (1hr 15mins; **ÆRØSKØBING**, **MARSTAL**; every 1/2 hours), Søby (Ærø) - Faaborg (Funen) (1hr; **SKJOLDNÆS**; 3 per day), Søby (Ærø) - Funenshav (Als) (1hr 10mins; **SKJOLDNÆS**; 3 per day).

1	ÆRØSKØBING	1617t	99	12.0k	49.0m	395P	42C	-	BA	DK	9199086
2	MARSTAL	1617t	99	12.0k	49.0m	395P	42C	-	BA	DK	9199074
3	SKJOLDNÆS	986t	79	11.0k	47.1m	245P	31C	-	BA	DK	7925649

ÆRØSKØBING, MARSTAL Built by EOS, Esbjerg, Denmark for *Ærøfærgerne*.

SKJOLDNÆS Built as the SAM-SINE by Søren Larsen & Sønner Skibsværft A/S, Nykøbing Mors, Denmark for *Hou-Sælvig Ruten Aps* of Denmark. Operated between Hou (Jylland) and Sælvig (Samsø). In 1995 she was taken over by *Samsø Linien*. In 2001 she was lengthened by Ørskov Christensen's Staalskibsværft, Frederikshavn, Denmark. In 2009 sold to *Ærøfærgerne* and renamed the SKJOLDNÆS. To be replaced by the ELLEN

Under Construction

| 4 | ELLEN | 1000t | 18 | 13.0k | 59.4m | 198P | 31C | | BA | DK | 9805374 |

ELLEN Under construction by Søby Vaerft, Søby, Ærø, Denmark for *Ærøfærgerne*. Hybrid electric powered. Expected to enter service Autumn 2019.

BASTØ FOSEN

THE COMPANY *Bastø Fosen* is a Norwegian private sector company, a subsidiary of *Torghatten ASA - Brønnøysund*.

MANAGEMENT Managing Director May Kristin Salberg.

ADDRESS PO Box 94, 3191 Horten, Norway.

TELEPHONE Administration +47 33 03 17 40, **Reservations** +47 33 03 17 40 (buses only).

FAX Administration +47 33 03 17 49, **Reservations** +47 33 03 17 49 (buses only).

INTERNET Email bastohorten@fosen.no **Website** www.basto-fosen.no *(Norwegian, English)*

ROUTE OPERATED Moss - Horten (across Oslofjord, Norway) (30 mins; **BASTØ I, BASTØ II, BASTØ III, BASTØ IV, BASTØ V, BASTØ VI**; up to every 15 mins).

1	BASTØ I	5505t	97	14.0k	109.0m	550P	200C	18L	BA	NO	9144081
2	BASTØ II	5505t	97	14.0k	109.0m	550P	200C	18L	BA	NO	9144093
3	BASTØ III	7310t	05	18.0k	116.2m	540P	212C	18L	BA	NO	9299408
4	BASTØ IV	7700t	16	16.0k	142.9m	600P	200C	30L	BA	NO	9771420
5	BASTØ V	7700t	17	16.0k	142.9m	600P	200C	30L	BA	NO	9771432
6	BASTØ VI	7870t	16	16.0k	142.9m	600P	200C	30L	BA	NO	9769219

BASTØ I, BASTØ II Built by Fosen Mekaniske Verksteder, Frengen, Norway.

BASTØ III Built by Stocznia Remontowa, Gdańsk, Poland.

BASTØ IV, BASTØ V Built by Sefine Shipyard, Yalova, Turkey.

BASTØ VI Built by Cemre Shipyard, Yalova, Turkey.

COLOR LINE

THE COMPANY Color Line ASA is a Norwegian private sector stock-listed limited company. The company merged with Larvik Scandi Line of Norway (which owned Larvik Line and Scandi Line) in 1996. In 1997 the operations of Larvik Line were incorporated into Color Line; Scandi Line continued as a separate subsidiary until 1999, when it was also incorporated into Color Line. The marketing name Color Scandi Line was dropped at the end of 2000.

MANAGEMENT Managing Director Trond Kleivdal.

ADDRESS Commercial Postboks 1422 Vika, 0115 Oslo, Norway, **Technical Management** Color Line Marine AS, PO Box 2090, 3210 Sandefjord, Norway.

TELEPHONE Administration +47 22 94 44 00, **Reservations Germany** +49 04 31/73 00 - 100, **Denmark** +45 99 56 10 00, **Norway** 810 00 811.

INTERNET Email kundeservice@colorline.no **Website** www.colorline.com (English, Danish, German, Norwegian, Swedish)

ROUTES OPERATED Conventional Ferries Oslo (Norway) - Kiel (Germany) (19 hrs 30 mins; **COLOR FANTASY**, **COLOR MAGIC**; 1 per day), Kristiansand (Norway) - Hirtshals (3 hrs 15 mins; **SUPERSPEED 1**; 4 per day), Larvik (Norway) - Hirtshals (Denmark) (3 hrs 45 mins; **SUPERSPEED 2**; up to 2 per day), Sandefjord (Norway) - Strömstad (Sweden) (2 hrs 30 mins; **BOHUS**, **COLOR VIKING**; up to 4 per day).

Color Line is to launch a freight service between Oslo and Kiel in January 2019. The vessel to be used is the FINNCARRIER of Finnlines which will be renamed.

1	BOHUS	9149t	71	20.5k	123.4m	1165P	240C	34T	BA	NO	7037806
2	COLOR FANTASY	75027t	04	22.3k	224.0m	2750P	750C	90T	BA	NO	9278234
3	COLOR MAGIC	75100t	07	22.3k	223.7m	2750P	550C	90T	BA	NO	9349863
4	COLOR VIKING	19763t	85	16.4k	134.0m	2000P	320C	40T	BA2	NO	8317942
5	SUPERSPEED 1	36822t	08	27.0k	211.3m	2250P	525C	121T	BA2	NO	9374519
6	SUPERSPEED 2	34231t	08	27.0k	211.3m	1800P	525C	121T	BA2	NO	9378682

BOHUS Built as the PRINSESSAN DESIREE by Aalborg Værft A/S, Aalborg, Denmark for Rederi AB Göteborg-Frederikshavn Linjen of Sweden (trading as Sessan Linjen) for their service between Göteborg and Frederikshavn. In 1981 the company was taken over by Stena Line and she became surplus to requirements. During 1981 she had a number of charters including B&I Line of Ireland and Sealink UK. In 1982 she was chartered to Sally Line to operate as second vessel on the Ramsgate - Dunkerque service between June and September. She bore the name 'VIKING 2' in large letters on her hull although she was never officially renamed. In September 1982 she returned to Stena Line and in 1983 she was transferred to subsidiary company Varberg-Grenaa Line for their service between Varberg (Sweden) and Grenaa (Denmark), renamed the EUROPAFÄRJAN. In 1985 she was renamed the EUROPAFÄRJAN II. In 1986, following a reorganisation within Stena Line, ownership was transferred to subsidiary company Lion Ferry AB and she was named the LION PRINCESS. In 1993 she was sold to Scandi Line and renamed the BOHUS. In 1999 Scandi Line operations were integrated into Color Line.

COLOR FANTASY Built by Kværner Masa-Yards, Turku, Finland for Color Line to replace the PRINSESSE RAGNHILD on the Oslo – Kiel service.

COLOR MAGIC Built by Aker Yards, Turku, Finland (hull construction) and Rauma, Finland (fitting out), for the Oslo - Kiel route.

COLOR VIKING Built as the PEDER PAARS by Nakskov Skibsværft A/S, Nakskov, Denmark for DSB (Danish State Railways) for their service between Kalundborg (Sjælland) and Århus

Bohus *(John Bryant)*

Gotland *(Destination Gotland)*

Ferries 2019

(Jylland). In 1990 purchased by *Stena Line* of Sweden for delivery in 1991. In that year renamed the STENA INVICTA and entered service on the *Sealink Stena Line* Dover - Calais service. She was withdrawn from the route in February 1998, before the formation of *P&O Stena Line*, but ownership was transferred to that company. In Summer 1998, she was chartered to *Silja Line* to operate between Vaasa and Umeå under the marketing name 'WASA JUBILEE'. In Autumn 1998 she was laid up at Zeebrugge. She remained there until Autumn 1999 when she was chartered to *Stena Line* to operate between Holyhead and Dublin. In 2000 she was chartered to *Color Line*, renamed the COLOR VIKING and in April entered service on the Sandefjord - Strömstad service. In 2002 purchased by *Color Line*.

SUPERSPEED 1, SUPERSPEED 2 Built by Aker Yards, Rauma, Finland for the Kristiansand - Hirtshals and Larvik - Hirtshals routes. In January 2011, the SUPERSPEED 1 was modified to provide additional facilities and increase passenger capacity.

Under construction

| 7 | NEWBUILDING | 18000t | 19 | - | 160.0m | 2000P | 500C | - | BA | NO |

NEWBUILDING Under construction by Ulstein Verft A/S, Ulsteinvik, Norway, to replace the BOHUS on the Sandefjord - Strömstad route. She will be a hybrid vessel, operating in both battery and diesel-electric mode.

DESTINATION GOTLAND

THE COMPANY *Destination Gotland AB* is a Swedish private sector company owned by *Rederi AB Gotland*.

MANAGEMENT Managing Director Christer Bruzelius, **Marketing Manager** Per-Erling Evensen.

ADDRESS PO Box 1234, 621 23 Visby, Gotland, Sweden.

TELEPHONE Administration +46 (0)498-20 18 00, **Reservations** +46 (0)771-22 33 00.

FAX Administration +46 498 20 18 90 **Reservations** +46 (0)498-20 13 90.

INTERNET Email info@destinationgotland.se **Website** www.destinationgotland.se *(Swedish, English, German)*

ROUTES OPERATED Fast Conventional Ferries Visby (Gotland) - Nynäshamn (Swedish mainland) (3 hrs 15 mins; *GOTLAND*, *VISBY*; 1/2 per day), Visby - Oskarshamn (Swedish mainland) (2 hrs 55 mins; *GOTLAND*, *VISBY*; 1/4 per day). **Fast Ferries (Summer only)** Visby - Nynäshamn (2 hrs 55 mins; *GOTLANDIA II*; up to 3 per day), Visby - Oskarshamn (Swedish mainland) (2 hrs 55 mins; *GOTLANDIA*; 1 per day), Visby - Vastervik (2 hrs 10 mins; *GOTLANDIA*; 1 per day)

1	GOTLAND	29746t	03	28.5k	195.8m	1500P	500C	118T	BAS2	SE	9223796
2»	GOTLANDIA	5632t	99	35.0k	112.5m	700P	140C	-	A	SE	9171163
3»	GOTLANDIA II	6554t	06	36.0k	122.0m	780P	160C	-	A	SE	9328015
4	VISBORG	32000t	18	28.5k	200.0m	1650P	-	110L	BAS2	SE	9763655
5	VISBY	29746t	03	28.5k	195.8m	1500P	500C	118T	BAS2	SE	9223784

GOTLAND, VISBY Built by Guangzhou Shipyard International, Guangzhou, China for *Rederi AB Gotland* for use on *Destination Gotland* services.

GOTLANDIA Alstom Leroux Corsair 11500 monohull vessel built as the GOTLAND at Lorient, France for *Rederi AB Gotland* and chartered to *Destination Gotland*. In 2003 renamed the GOTLANDIA. In 2006 laid up. In 2007 inaugurated a new route between Visby and Grankullavik (Öland).

GOTLANDIA II Fincantieri SF700 monohull fast ferry built at Riva Trigoso, Italy for *Rederi AB Gotland* for use by *Destination Gotland*.

VISBORG Built by Guangzhou Shipyard International, Guangzhou, China for *Rederi AB Gotland* for use on *Destination Gotland* services. LNG powered. Expected to enter service in September 2018.

Under Construction

6	THJELVAR	32000t	19	28.5k	200.0m	1650P	-	110L	BAS2	SE	9783071

THJELVAR Under construction by Guangzhou Shipyard International, Guangzhou, China for *Rederi AB Gotland* for use on *Destination Gotland* services. To be LNG powered.

DFDS SEAWAYS

THE COMPANY *DFDS Seaways* is a division of *DFDS A/S*, a Danish private sector company.

MANAGEMENT CEO DFDS A/S Niels Smedegaard, **Executive Vice-President Shipping Division** Peder Gellert Pedersen, **Head of Baltic Sea Business Area** Anders Refsgaard.

ADDRESS *København* Sundkrogsgade 11, 2100 København Ø, Denmark.

TELEPHONE Administration +45 33 42 33 42, **Reservations *Denmark*** +45 78 79 55 36, **Germany** +49 (0)40-389030, **Lithuania** +370 46 393616, **Sweden** +46 454 33680

FAX Administration +45 33 42 33 41. **INTERNET Administration** incoming@dfdsseaways.dk, **Reservations *Denmark*** incoming@dfdsseaways.dk **Germany** service.de@dfds.com **Lithuania** booking.lt@dfds.com, **Sweden** pax@dfds.com

Website www.dfdsseaways.com *(English, Danish, Dutch, German, Italian, Japanese, Norwegian, Polish, Swedish)*

ROUTES OPERATED *Passenger services* København - Oslo (Norway) (16 hrs 30 mins; *CROWN SEAWAYS*, *PEARL SEAWAYS*; 1 per day), Klaipėda (Lithuania) - Kiel (Germany) (21 hrs; *REGINA SEAWAYS*, *VICTORIA SEAWAYS*; 7 per week), Klaipėda - Karlshamn (Sweden) (14 hrs; *ATHENA SEAWAYS*, *OPTIMA SEAWAYS*, *PATRIA SEAWAYS*,; 10 per week), Paldiski (Estonia) - Kapellskär (Sweden) (10 hrs; *LIVERPOOL SEAWAYS*; 6 per week), Paldiski - Hanko (Finland) (3 hrs; *SAILOR*; 2 per day). *Freight only service* Fredericia - København - Klaipėda (*ARK FUTURA*; 2 per week).

See Section 1 for services operating to Britain.

1F	ARK FUTURA	18725t	96	19.7k	183.3m	12P	-	164T	AS	DK	9129598
2	ATHENA SEAWAYS	24950t	07	23.0k	199.1m	500P	-	190T	A	LT	9350680
3F	BOTNIA SEAWAYS	11530t	00	20.0k	162.2m	12P	-	140T	A	LT	9192129
4	CROWN SEAWAYS	35498t	94	22.0k	169.4m	1940P	450C	50T	BA	DK	8917613
5	LIVERPOOL SEAWAYS	21856t	97	20.0k	186.0m	320P	100C	135T	A	LT	9136034
6	OPTIMA SEAWAYS	25206t	99	21.5k	186.3m	327P	164C	150T	A	LT	9188427
7	PATRIA SEAWAYS	18332t	92	17.0k	154.0m	242P	-	114T	BA2	LT	8917390
8	PEARL SEAWAYS	40039t	89	21.0k	178.4m	2090P	350C	70T	BA	DK	8701674
9	REGINA SEAWAYS	25518t	10	24.0k	199.1m	600P	-	190T	A	LT	9458535
10	SAILOR	20921t	87	19.0k	157.6m	119P	50C	82L	A2	EE	8401444
11	VICTORIA SEAWAYS	24950t	09	23.0k	199.1m	600P	-	190T	A	LT	9350721

ARK FUTURA Built as the DANA FUTURA by C N Visentini di Visentini Francesco & C, Donada, Italy for *DFDS*. In 2001 she was renamed the TOR FUTURA. Initially operated mainly between Esbjerg and Harwich, but latterly operated mainly between Esbjerg and Immingham. In 2004 chartered to *Toll Shipping* of Australia. Later time-chartered to the *Danish MoD* for 5.5 years. However, when not required for military service she has been chartered to other operators such as *P&O Ferries*, *Cobelfret Ferries* and *Van Uden Ro-Ro* and used on *DFDS Tor Line* services. In 2006 sold to *DFDS Lys Line Rederi A/S* of Norway, a *DFDS* subsidiary and chartered back. In April 2011 renamed the ARK FUTURA. Currently operating on the Fredericia - København - Klaipėda service.

ATHENA SEAWAYS Built as the CORAGGIO by Nuovi Cantieri Apuani, Marina di Carrara, Italy. First of an order of eight vessels for *Grimaldi Holdings* of Italy. Used on *Grimaldi Lines*

SECTION 7 – NORTHERN EUROPE

Mediterranean services. In September 2010, bare-boat chartered to *Stena Line* to operate between Hoek van Holland and Killingholme. In November 2011 replaced by the new STENA TRANSIT and returned to Mediterranean service. In December 2013 renamed the ATHENA SEAWAYS, chartered to *DFDS* and replaced the LIVERPOOL SEAWAYS on the Klaipėda - Kiel service. In May 2016 purchased by *DFDS*.

BOTNIA SEAWAYS Built as the FINNMASTER by Jinling Shipyard, Nanjing, China for the *Macoma Shipping Group* and chartered to *Finncarriers*. In 2008 sold to *DFDS Lisco* and in January 2009 delivered, chartered to *DFDS Tor Line* and renamed the TOR BOTNIA. Operated on the Immingham - Rotterdam route until December 2010. In January 2011 moved to the Kiel - St Petersburg route. In January 2013 renamed the BOTNIA SEAWAYS. Currently operating on the Marseilles - Tunis service.

CROWN SEAWAYS Launched as the THOMAS MANN by Brodogradevna Industrija, Split, Croatia for *Euroway AB* for their Lübeck - Travemünde - Malmö service. However, political problems led to serious delays and, before delivery, the service had ceased. She was purchased by *DFDS*, renamed the CROWN OF SCANDINAVIA and introduced onto the København - Oslo service. In January 2013 renamed the CROWN SEAWAYS.

LIVERPOOL SEAWAYS Built as the LAGAN VIKING by CN Visentini, Donada, Italy for *Levantina Trasporti* of Italy and chartered to *Norse Irish Ferries*, operating between Liverpool and Belfast. In 1999 the charter was taken over by *Merchant Ferries*. Purchased by *NorseMerchant Ferries* in 2001. In 2002 the service transferred to Twelve Quays River Terminal, Birkenhead. In January 2005 renamed the LIVERPOOL VIKING and in December moved to the Birkenhead – Dublin route. In August 2010 renamed the LIVERPOOL SEAWAYS. In February 2011 moved to the Klaipėda - Karlshamn service. In January 2014 chartered to *NaviRail*. In January 2015 returned to *DFDS* and placed on the Paldiski - Kapellskär service.

OPTIMA SEAWAYS Ro-pax vessel built as the ALYSSA by C N Visentini di Visentini Francesco & C Donada, Italy for *Levantina Trasporti* of Italy for charter. Initially chartered to *CoTuNav* of Tunisia for service between Marseilles, Génova and Tunis and in 2000 to *Trasmediterranea* of Spain for service between Barcelona and Palma de Mallorca. In 2001 chartered to *Stena Line Scandinavia AB*, renamed the SVEALAND and placed as second vessel on the *Scandlines AB* freight-only Trelleborg - Travemünde service. In 2003 sub-chartered to *Scandlines AG* and placed on the Kiel - Klaipėda route, replacing the ASK and PETERSBURG. In 2004 sold to *Rederia AB Hornet*, a *Stena* company. In late 2005 the *Scandlines* Kiel - Klaipėda service ended. In early 2006 she was chartered to *TT-Line* to cover for the rebuilding of the engines of their four newest vessels. Later sold to *DFDS*, renamed the LISCO OPTIMA. In April 2012 renamed the OPTIMA SEAWAYS. Currently operates on the Karlshamn - Klaipėda route.

PATRIA SEAWAYS Ro-pax vessel built as the STENA TRAVELLER by Fosen Mekaniske Verksteder, Trondheim, Norway for *Stena RoRo*. After a short period with *Stena Line* on the Hoek van Holland - Harwich service, she was chartered to *Sealink Stena Line* for their Southampton - Cherbourg route, initially for 28 weeks. At the end of the 1992 summer season she was chartered to *TT-Line* to operate between Travemünde and Trelleborg and was renamed the TT-TRAVELLER. In late 1995, she returned to *Stena Line*, resumed the name STENA TRAVELLER and inaugurated a new service between Holyhead and Dublin. In Autumn 1996 she was replaced by the STENA CHALLENGER (18523t, 1991). In early 1997 she was again chartered to *TT-Line* and renamed the TT-TRAVELLER. She operated on the Rostock - Trelleborg route. During Winter 1999/2000 her passenger capacity was increased to 250 and passenger facilities renovated. In early 2002 the charter ended and she was renamed the STENA TRAVELLER, chartered to *Stena Line* and placed on their Karlskrona - Gdynia service. This charter ended in May 2003 and she was sold to *Lisco Baltic Service* and renamed the LISCO PATRIA. Placed on the Klaipėda - Karlshamn service. In January 2006 transferred to the Klaipėda - Kiel service to replace the *Scandlines* vessel SVEALAND following that company's withdrawal from the joint route. In Spring 2006 returned to the Klaipėda – Karlshamn route. In May 2011 chartered to *Baltic Scandinavia Lines* and placed on their Paldiski - Kapellskär service. In September 2011 a controlling interest in this service was acquired by *DFDS Seaways*. In January 2012 renamed the PATRIA SEAWAYS. In September 2014 replaced by the *Sirena Seaways* and became a relief vessel. In April 2015 chartered as

Pearl Seaways *(DFDS)*

Botnia Seaways *(Darren Holdaway)*

SECTION 7 – NORTHERN EUROPE

171

Athena Seaways *(DFDS)*

Finlandia *(Richard Kirkman)*

a windfarm accommodation vessel off Esbjerg. In January 2016 chartered to *P&O Ferries* to cover for refits on the Hull routes. In April 2016 became third vessel on the Klaipėda – Karlshamn route.

PEARL SEAWAYS Built as the ATHENA by Wärtsilä Marine, Turku, Finland for *Rederi AB Slite* of Sweden (part of *Viking Line*) and used on 24-hour cruises from Stockholm to Mariehamn (Åland). In 1993 the company went into liquidation and she was sold to *Star Cruises* of Malaysia for cruises in the Far East. She was renamed the STAR AQUARIUS. Later that year she was renamed the LANGKAPURI STAR AQUARIUS. In February 2001 sold to *DFDS* and renamed the AQUARIUS. After rebuilding, she was renamed the PEARL OF SCANDINAVIA and introduced onto the København - Oslo service. In January 2011 renamed the PEARL SEAWAYS.

REGINA SEAWAYS Built as the ENERGIA by Nuovi Cantieri Apuani, Marina di Carrara, Italy for *Grimaldi Holdings* of Italy. In August 2011 chartered to DFDS Seaways and moved to Klaipėda for modifications. In September 2011 renamed the REGINA SEAWAYS and placed on the Klaipėda - Kiel service.

SAILOR Built as the FINNSAILOR by Gdańsk Shipyard, Gdańsk, Poland for *Finnlines* of Finland for freight service between Finland and Germany. In 1996 converted to ro-pax format to inaugurate a new passenger/freight service between Helsinki and Norrköping (Sweden) for subsidiary *FinnLink*. In 1997 this service was transferred to the Kapellskär - Naantali route and passengers (other than lorry drivers) ceased to be conveyed. In 2000 she was chartered to *Nordö-Link* to operate between Travemünde and Malmö. In 2002 she returned to *FinnLink*. In 2004 transferred to *Nordö-Link*. In 2007 returned to *FinnLink* as fourth ship. In early 2009 transferred to *Finnlines'* freight service operating between Helsinki, Turku and Travemünde but in April transferred back. In March 2011 moved back to *Finnlines Nordö-Link*. In November 2013 chartered to *Navirail* of Estonia to operate between Paldiski and Hanko. In January 2014 returned to *Finnlines* and placed on the Naantali - Kapellskär route. In January 2015 time chartered again to *Navirail*. In February 2015 demise chartered to *Navirail* and renamed the SAILOR. In October 2016 time chartered to *DFDS Seaways*, following their take over of the Hanko and Paldiski route.

VICTORIA SEAWAYS Built by Nuovi Cantieri Apuani, Marina di Carrara, Italy. Launched as the FORZA. Fifth of an order of eight vessels for *Grimaldi Holdings* of Italy. Whilst under construction, sold to *DFDS Tor Line*. On delivery renamed the LISCO MAXIMA. In March/April 2012 renamed the VICTORIA SEAWAYS. Operates between Kiel and Klaipėda.

Under construction

| 12 | NEWBUILDING 1 | 54900t | 21 | 23.0k | 230.0m | 600P | - | 270L | A2 | - |
| 13 | NEWBUILDING 2 | 54900t | 21 | 23.0k | 230.0m | 600P | - | 270L | A2 | - |

NEWBUILDING 1, NEWBUILDING 2 Under construction by Guangzhou Shipyard International, China. They will operate on Baltic routes from Klaipėda to Kiel and Karlshamn.

REDERIJ DOEKSEN

THE COMPANY *BV Rederij G. Doeksen en Zn BV* is a Dutch private sector company. Ferries are operated by subsidiary *Terschellinger Stoomboot Maatschappij*, trading as *Rederij Doeksen*.

MANAGEMENT Managing Director P J M Melles, **Manager Operations** R. de Vries, **Controller** R. Herrema, **Manager Hospitality, FO & CC** D Spoor, **Manager Marketing & Communications** A. van Brummelen.

ADDRESS Waddenpromenade 5, 8861 NT Harlingen, The Netherlands.

TELEPHONE *In The Netherlands* 088 - 9000 888, *From abroad* +31 562 442 002.

FAX +31 (0)517 413303.

SECTION 7 – NORTHERN EUROPE

INTERNET Email info@rederij-doeksen.nl **Website** www.rederij-doeksen.nl *(Dutch, English, German))* **Facebook** www.facebook.com/rederijdoeksen **Twitter** www.twitter.com/rederijdoeksen

ROUTES OPERATED Conventional Ferries Harlingen (The Netherlands) - Terschelling (Frisian Islands) (2 hrs; *FRIESLAND, MIDSLAND*; up to 6 per day), Harlingen - Vlieland (Frisian Islands) (1 hr 45 mins; *VLIELAND*; 3 per day). **Fast Passenger Ferries** Harlingen - Terschelling (45 mins; *KOEGELWIECK, TIGER*; 3 to 6 per day), Harlingen - Vlieland (45 mins; *KOEGELWIECK, TIGER*; 2 per day), Vlieland - Terschelling (30 mins; *KOEGELWIECK, TIGER*; 2 per day). **Freight Ferry** Harlingen - Terschelling (2 hrs; *NOORD-NEDERLAND*), Harlingen - Vlieland (1hr 45 mins; *NOORD-NEDERLAND*).

1	FRIESLAND	3583t	89	14.0k	69.0m	1100P	122C	12L	BA	NL	8801058
2»p	KOEGELWIECK	439t	92	33.0k	35.5m	315P	0C	0L	-	NL	9035527
3	MIDSLAND	1812t	74	15.5k	77.9m	700P	55C	6L	BA	NL	7393066
4F	NOORD-NEDERLAND	361t	02	14.0k	68.0m	12P	-	-	BA	NL	9269611
5»p	TIGER	660t	02	37.0k	52.0m	414P	0C	0L	BA	NL	9179191
6	VLIELAND	2726t	05	15.0k	64.1m	1950P	58C	4L	BA	NL	9303716

FRIESLAND Built by Van der Giessen-de Noord, Krimpen aan den IJssel, Rotterdam, The Netherlands for *Rederij Doeksen*. Used on the Harlingen - Terschelling route.

KOEGELWIECK Harding 35m catamaran built at Rosendal, Norway for *Rederij Doeksen* to operate between Harlingen and Terschelling, Harlingen and Vlieland and Terschelling and Vlieland.

MIDSLAND Built as the RHEINLAND by Werftunion GmbH & Co, Cassens-Werft, Emden, Germany for *AG Ems* of Germany. In 1993 purchased by *Rederij Doeksen* and renamed the MIDSLAND. Used mainly on the Harlingen - Terschelling route but also used on the Harlingen - Vlieland service. She is now a reserve vessel.

NOORD-NEDERLAND Catamaran built by ASB, Harwood, New South Wales, Australia for *Rederij Doeksen*. Used on freight services from Harlingen to Terschelling and Vlieland. In spring 2017 lengthened by 20 metres.

TIGER Catamaran built as the SUPERCAT 2002 by FBMA Babcock Marine, Cebu, Philippines for *SuperCat* of the Philippines. In 2007 purchased by *Rederij Doeksen* and renamed the TIGER. Operates from Harlingen to Terschelling and Vlieland.

VLIELAND Catamaran built by FBMA Babcock Marine, Cebu, Philippines for *Rederij Doeksen* to operate between Harlingen and Vlieland.

Under Construction

7	WILLEM BARENTSZ	-	19	14.0k	70.0m	600P	64C	-	BA	NL	-
8	WILLEM DE VLAMINGH	-	19	14.0k	70.0m	600P	64C	-	BA	NL	-

WILLEM BARENTSZ, WILLEM DE VLAMINGH Under construction by Strategic Marine, Vung Tau, Vietnam. They will be aluminium catamarans and LNG powered. They will replace the MIDSLAND.

REDERI AB ECKERÖ

THE COMPANY *Rederi AB Eckerö* is an Åland Islands company. It operates two ferry companies, a cruise operation from Stockholm (*Birka Cruises*), a ro-ro time chartering company (*Eckerö Shipping*) and a bus company on Åland (*Williams*).

ADDRESS PO Box 158, AX-22101 Mariehamn, Åland, Finland.

TELEPHONE Administration +358 (0)18 28 030.

FAX Administration +358 (0)18 12 011.

INTERNET Email info@rederiabeckero.ax **Website** www.rederiabeckero.ax *(English, Swedish)*

ECKERÖ LINE

THE COMPANY *Eckerö Line Ab Oy* is a Finnish company, 100% owned by *Rederi Ab Eckerö* of Åland, Finland. Until January 1998, the company was called *Eestin-Linjat*.

MANAGEMENT Managing Director Taru Keronen, **Marketing Director** Ida Toikka-Everi.

ADDRESS PO Box 307, 00181 Helsinki, Finland.

TELEPHONE Administration & Reservations +358 9 (0) 6000 4300.

INTERNET Email info@eckeroline.fi **Website** www.eckeroline.fi *(Swedish, Finnish, English)*

ROUTE OPERATED Passenger Service Helsinki (Länsisatama) - Tallinn (Estonia) (2 hrs 30 mins; *FINLANDIA*; up to 2 per day).

1	FINLANDIA	36093t	01	27.0k	175.0m	1880P	665C	116T	BA	FI	9214379

FINLANDIA Built as the MOBY FREEDOM by Daewoo Shipbuilding & Heavy Machinery Ltd, Okpo, South Korea for *Moby SpA (Moby Line)* of Italy. Operated on their Génova/Civitavecchia/Livorno - Olbia routes. In March 2012 sold to *Eckerö Line*, and renamed the FREEDOM. Refitted at Landskrona and, in June, renamed the FINLANDIA. She entered service on 31st December 2012.

ECKERÖ LINJEN

THE COMPANY *Eckerö Linjen* is an Åland Islands company 100% owned by *Rederi AB Eckerö*.

MANAGEMENT Managing Director Tomas Karlsson, **Marketing Director** Maria Hellman.

ADDRESS Torggatan 2, Box 158, AX-22100 Mariehamn, Åland.

TELEPHONE Administration +358 (0)18 28 000, **Reservations** +358 (0)18 28 300.

FAX Administration +358 (0)18 28 380. **Reservations** +358 (0)18 28 230.

INTERNET Email info@eckerolinjen.ax **Website** www.eckerolinjen.se *(Swedish, Finnish, English)*

ROUTE OPERATED Eckerö (Åland) - Grisslehamn (Sweden) (2 hrs; *ECKERÖ*; 3 per day).

1	ECKERÖ	12358t	79	19.5k	121.1m	1500P	265C	34T	BA	SE	7633155

ECKERÖ Built as the JENS KOFOED by Aalborg Værft A/S, Aalborg, Denmark for *Bornholmstrafikken*. Used on the Rønne - København, Rønne - Ystad and (until December 2002) Rønne - Sassnitz services. Rønne - København service became Rønne – Køge in September 2004. In October 2004 sold to *Eckerö Linjen* for delivery in May 2005. Renamed the ECKERÖ and substantially rebuilt before entering service in early 2006. In January 2009 transferred from the Finnish to the Swedish flag.

AG EMS

THE COMPANY *AG Ems* is a German public sector company.

MANAGEMENT Managing Director & Chief Executive Dr Bernhard Brons, **Marine Superintendent** Knut Gerdes, **Operations Manager** Hans-Jörg Oltmanns.

ADDRESS Am Aussenhafen, Postfach 1154, 26691 Emden, Germany.

TELEPHONE Administration & Reservations +49 (0)1805-180182.

FAX Administration & Reservations +49 (0)4921-890740.

INTERNET Email info@ag-ems.de **Website** www.ag-ems.de *(German)* www.borkumlijn.nl *(Dutch)* www.helgolandlinie.de *(German)*

ROUTES OPERATED Conventional Ferries Emden (Germany) - Borkum (German Frisian Islands) (2 hrs; *GRONINGERLAND*, *MÜNSTERLAND*, *OSTFRIESLAND*, *WESTFALEN*; up to

SECTION 7 – NORTHERN EUROPE

4 per day), Eemshaven (The Netherlands) - Borkum (55 mins; **GRONINGERLAND**, **MÜNSTERLAND**, **OSTFRIESLAND**, **WESTFALEN**; up to 4 per day). **Fast Ferry** Emden - Borkum (1 hr; **NORDLICH**; up to 4 per day), Eemshaven - Borkum (30 mins; **NORDLICHT**; 1 per week in summer).

1	GRONINGERLAND	1070t	91	12.0k	44.4m	621P	30C	-	BA	DE	9002465
2	MÜNSTERLAND	1859t	86	15.5k	78.7m	1200P	70C	10L	BA	DE	8601989
3p»	NORDLICHT	435t	89	33.0k	38.8m	272P	0C	0L	-	DE	8816015
4	OSTFRIESLAND	1859t	85	16.0k	78.7m	1200P	70C	10L	BA	DE	8324622
5p	WAPPEN VON BORKUM	287t	76	11.5k	42.8m	358P	0C	0L	-	DE	7525918
6	WESTFALEN	1812t	72	15.5k	77.9m	1200P	65C	10L	BA	DE	7217004

GRONINGERLAND Built by Husumer Schiffswerft, Husum, Germany as the HILLIGENLEI for *Wyker Dampfschiffs-Reederei Föhr-Amrum GmbH* of Germany. Operated Schlüttsiel - Halligen – Wittdün (North Frisian Islands). In 2004 laid up. In late 2005 sold to *AG Ems*. In 2006 renamed the GRONINGERLAND.

MÜNSTERLAND Built by Martin Jansen GmbH & Co KG Schiffswerft, Leer, Germany for *AG Ems*.

NORDLICHT Fjellstrand 38m passenger-only catamaran built at Mandal, Norway for *AG Ems*.

OSTFRIESLAND Built by Martin Jansen GmbH & Co KG Schiffswerft, Leer, Germany for *AG Ems*. In 2015 lengthened by 15.4 m by BVT Brenn-und Verformtechnik GmbH, Bremen, Germany.

WAPPEN VON BORKUM Built as the HANNOVER by Schiffswerft Schlömer GmbH & Co KG, Oldersum, Germany for *Friesland Fahrlinie* of Germany. In 1979 sold to *AG Ems* and renamed the STADT BORKUM. In 1988 sold to *ST-Line* of Finland, operating day trips from Rauma and renamed the PRINCESS ISABELLA. In 1994 returned to *AG Ems* and renamed the WAPPEN VON BORKUM.

WESTFALEN Built by as the WESTFALEN by C Cassens Schiffswerft, Emden, Germany for *AG Ems*. Rebuilt in 1994. In 2006 renamed the HELGOLAND and inaugurated a new Wilhelmshaven - Helgoland service for subsidiary *Helgoland Linie*. In January 2016 reverted to the name WESTFALEN and used on service from Borkum.

FÆRGEN

THE COMPANIES *Danske Færger A/S* trading as *Færgen (previously Nordic Ferry Services A/S)* is a Danish mixed public and private sector company.

MANAGEMENT CEO John Steen-Mikkelsen.

ADDRESSES Dampskibskajen 3, 3700 Rønne, Denmark.

TELEPHONE Administration & Reservations +45 70 23 15 15. (Reservations not possible on FanøFærgen).

INTERNET Website www.faergen.com *(Danish, German, English)*

ROUTES OPERATED

AlsFærgen Fynshav (Als) - Bøjden (Funen) (50 mins; **FRIGG SYDFYEN**, **FYNSHAV**; hourly (summer) two-hourly (winter)), **FanøFærgen** Esbjerg (Jylland) - Nordby (Fanø) (12 mins; **FENJA**, **MENJA**, **SØNDERHO**; every 20-40 mins), **LangelandsFærgen** Spodsbjerg (Langeland) - Tårs (Lolland) (45 mins; **LANGELAND**, **LOLLAND**; hourly), **SamsøFærgen** Kalundborg - Ballen (Samsø) (1 hr 15 min; **SAMSØ**; up to 4 per day).

1	FENJA	751t	98	11.5k	49.9m	396P	34C	4L	BA	DK	9189378
2	FRIGG SYDFYEN	1676t	84	13.5k	70.1m	338P	50C	8L	BA	DK	8222824
3	FYNSHAV	3380t	98	14.5k	69.2m	450P	96C	8L	BA	DK	9183025
4	LANGELAND	4500t	12	16.0k	99.9m	600P	122C	36L	BA	DK	9596428
5	LOLLAND	4500t	12	16.0k	99.9m	600P	122C	36L	BA	DK	9594690
6	MENJA	751t	98	11.5k	49.9m	396P	34C	4L	BA	DK	9189380

7	SAMSØ	4250t	08	16.0k	91.4m	600P	122C	30L	BA	DK	9548562
8p	SØNDERHO	93t	62	10.0k	26.3m	163P	0C	0L	-	DK	

FENJA Built by Morsø Værft A/S, Nykøbing Mors, Denmark for *Scandlines Sydfyenske A/S* for the Esbjerg - Nordby service.

FRIGG SYDFYEN Built by Svendborg Skibsværft A/S, Svendborg, Denmark for *Sydfyenske Dampskibsselskab (SFDS)* of Denmark for the service between Spodsbjerg and Tårs. In June 2012 moved to the Fynshav - Bøjden service.

FYNSHAV Built as the KYHOLM by Ørskov Staalskibsværft, Frederikshavn, Denmark for *Samsø Linien* of Denmark. In October 2008 chartered to *Nordic Ferry Services* and in July 2009 sold to them. Used on the Kalundborg - Koby Kås service. In March 2015 renamed the FYNSHAV and moved to the Fynshav - Bøjden service.

LANGELAND Built by Sietas Werft, Hamburg, Germany for the Spodsbjerg - Tårs route.

LOLLAND Built by Sietas Werft, Hamburg, Germany. She was launched as the SAMSØ and it was intended that she would be operated on the Hou - Sælvig service, being owned by *Samsø Linien* and operated by *Færgen*. However, these plans were dropped and in February 2012 she was renamed the LOLLAND. After delivery in March 2012 she was, in April, placed on the Spodsbjerg - Tårs route.

MENJA Built by Morsø Værft A/S, Nykøbing Mors, Denmark for *Scandlines Sydfyenske A/S* for the Esbjerg - Nordby service.

SAMSØ Built as the KANHAVE by Frantzis Shipyard, Perama, Greece. Used on the Hou - Sælvig route. In January 2015 transferred to the Kalundborg - Koby Kås (Samsø) service. Later in January 2015 the Samsø terminal was moved to Ballen. In August 2015 renamed the SAMSØ.

SØNDERHO Passenger-only ferry built by Esbjerg Jernstøberi & Maskinfabrik A/S, Esbjerg, Denmark for *Post & Telegrafvæsenet* (Danish Post Office). In 1977 taken over by *DSB*. Used on extra peak sailings and late night and early morning sailings between Esbjerg and Nordby.

FINNLINES

THE COMPANY *Finnlines plc* is a Finnish private sector company. The Italian company *Grimaldi Compagnia de Navigazione SpA* has a controlling interest. It operates four passenger brands: *Finnlines HansaLink*, *Finnlines NordöLink* and *FinnLink* and *TransRussiaExpress*.

MANAGEMENT President and CEO Emanuele Grimaldi, **Head of Passenger Services and Line Manager HansaLink & Hanko–Rostock** Kielo Vesikko, **Line Manager NordöLink, Finnlink and Russia** Antonio Raimo.

ADDRESS PO Box 197, 00181 Helsinki, Finland.

TELEPHONE Administration +358 (0)10 343 50, **Passenger Reservations** +358 (0)9 231 43 100.

INTERNET *Finnlines* **Email** info.fi@finnlines.com **Website** *Finnlines* www.finnlines.com *(English, Finnish, German, Polish, Swedish)*

ROUTES OPERATED *Finnlines Hansalink branded routes* Helsinki (Vuosaari) - Travemünde (27 hrs; **FINNLADY**, **FINNMAID**, **FINNSTAR**; 7 per week).

Finnlines NordöLink branded route Malmö - Travemünde (9 hrs; **EUROPALINK**, **FINNPARTNER**, **FINNTRADER**; up to 3 per day).

FinnLink branded route Naantali (Finland) - Långnäs - Kapellskär (Sweden) (6 hrs; **FINNFELLOW**, **FINNSWAN**; 2 per day).

1	EUROPALINK	45923t	07	25.0k	216.0m	500P	-	300T	BA2	SE	9319454
2	FINNFELLOW	33769t	00	22.0k	188.3m	452P	-	220T	BA	FI	9145164
3	FINNLADY	45923t	07	25.0k	216.0m	500P	-	300T	BA2	FI	9336268

177

4	FINNMAID	45923t	06	25.0k	216.0m	500P	-	300T	BA2	FI	9319466
5	FINNPARTNER	32534t	94	21.3k	183.0m	270P	-	236T	A2	SE	9010163
6	FINNSTAR	45923t	06	25.0k	216.0m	500P	-	300T	BA2	FI	9319442
7	FINNSWAN	45923t	07	25.0k	216.0m	500P	-	300T	BA2	SE	9336256
8	FINNTRADER	32534t	95	21.3k	183.0m	270P	-	220T	BA2	SE	9017769
9	ROSALIND FRANKLIN	29841t	99	22.0k	188.3m	440P	-	210T	BA2	SE	9137997

EUROPALINK Built by Fincantieri-Cantieri Navali Italiani SpA, Castellamare, Italy for *Finnlines* to operate for *Finnlines NordöLink* between Travemünde and Malmö. Launched as the FINNLADY but name changed before delivery. In April 2009 transferred to *Finnlines HansaLink*. In October 2012 sold to *Atlantica Navigazione* of Italy, another company within the *Grimaldi Group*, for Mediterranean service. In January 2018 repurchased by *NordöLink* (a subsidiary of *Finnlines*) and returned to the Travemünde and Malmö service.

FINNFELLOW 'Ro-pax' ferry built as the STENA BRITANNICA by Astilleros Españoles, Cadiz, Spain for *Stena RoRo* and chartered to *Stena Line BV* to operate between Hoek van Holland and Harwich. In 2003 replaced by a new STENA BRITANNICA, sold to *Finnlines*, renamed the FINNFELLOW and placed on the Helsinki – Travemünde route. In 2004 transferred to *FinnLink*.

FINNLADY, FINNMAID Built by Fincantieri-Cantieri Navali Italiani SpA, Ancona, Italy to operate between Helsinki and Travemünde.

FINNPARTNER 'Ro-pax' vessel built by Stocznia Gdańska SA, Gdańsk, Poland for *Finnlines Oy* of Finland to provide a daily service conveying both freight and a limited number of cars and passengers on the previously freight-only route between Helsinki and Travemünde. In February 2007 replaced by the FINNLADY and placed on the Turku - Travemünde freight service; in May sent to the Remontowa Shipyard in Gdańsk for rebuilding to increase passenger capacity and allow for two-deck through loading. Currently operating on the Travemünde - Malmö and Lübeck - St Petersburg services.

FINNSTAR Built by Fincantieri-Cantieri Navali Italiani SpA, Castellamare, Italy to operate between Helsinki and Travemünde.

FINNSWAN Built by Fincantieri-Cantieri Navali Italiani SpA, Castellamare, Italy as the NORDLINK for *Finnlines* to operate for *Finnlines NordöLink* between Travemünde and Malmö. In February 2018 renamed the FINNSWAN and in May moved to the Naantali - Långnäs - Kapellskär route.

FINNTRADER 'Ro-pax' vessel built by Stocznia Gdańska SA, Gdańsk, Poland for *Finnlines Oy* of Finland to provide a daily service conveying both freight and a limited number of cars and passengers on the previously freight-only route between Helsinki and Travemünde. In 2006/07 rebuilt to increase passenger capacity and allow for two-deck through loading. In 2007 transferred to the Malmö - Travemünde route.

ROSALIND FRANKLIN 'Ro-pax' ferry built by Astilleros Españoles, Cadiz, Spain. Ordered by *Stena RoRo* of Sweden and launched as the STENA SEAPACER 1. In 1998 sold, before delivery, to *Finnlines* and renamed the FINNCLIPPER. Entered service on the Helsinki - Travemünde route in 1999. During Winter 1999/2000 she was converted to double-deck loading. In 2003 transferred to *FinnLink*. In 2007 an additional freight deck was added. In May 2018 chartered to *Baleària* of Spain and renamed the ROSALIND FRANKLIN.

FJORD LINE

THE COMPANY *Fjord Line* is a Norwegian company. During 2007 most of the shares of the company were purchased by *Frode and Ole Teigen*. The company bought and merged with *Master Ferries* during December 2007 and all operations are branded as *Fjord Line*.

MANAGEMENT CEO Rickard Ternblom, **Communications Director** Eva Sørås Mellgren.

ADDRESS PO Box 513, 4379 Egersund, Norway.

TELEPHONE Administration & Reservations +47 51 46 40 99.

INTERNET Email info@fjordline.com **Website** www.fjordline.com *(English, Danish, German, Dutch, Polish, Norwegian,)*

ROUTES OPERATED Conventional Ferry Bergen (Norway) – Stavanger - Hirtshals (Denmark) (17 hrs; **BERGENSFJORD, STAVANGERFJORD**; daily), Langesund (Norway) - Hirtshals (4 hrs 30 mins; **BERGENSFJORD, STAVANGERFJORD**; daily), Sandefjord (Norway) - Strömstad (Sweden) (2 hrs 30 mins; **OSLOFJORD**; 2 per day), **Fast Ferry May-August** Kristiansand (Norway) – Hirtshals (Denmark) (2 hrs 15 min); **FJORD CAT**; up to 3 per day).

1	BERGENSFJORD	31678t	13	21.5k	170.0m	1500P	600C	90T	BA	DK	9586617
2»	FJORD CAT	5619t	98	43.0k	91.3m	663P	220C	-	A	DK	9176060
3	OSLOFJORD	16794t	93	19.0k	134.4m	882P	350C	44T	BA	DK	9058995
4	STAVANGERFJORD	31678t	13	21.5k	170.0m	1500P	600C	90T	BA	DK	9586605

BERGENSFJORD, STAVANGERFJORD Built by Bergen Group Fosen AS, Rissa, Norway for *Fjord Line*. They operate on LNG.

FJORD CAT Incat 91-metre catamaran, built speculatively at Hobart, Tasmania, Australia. In Spring 1998, following *Incat's* acquisition of a 50% share in *Scandlines Cat-Link A/S*, she was chartered by *Nordic Catamaran Ferries K/S* to that company, operating between Århus and Kalundborg and named the CAT-LINK V. She is the current holder of the Hales Trophy for fastest crossing of the Atlantic during her delivery voyage between the USA and Falmouth, UK (although this claim is disputed because it was not a genuine commercial service). In 1999 the charter was transferred to *Mols-Linien*, she was renamed the MADS MOLS and operated between Århus and Odden. Charter ended in July 2005. Laid up and renamed the INCAT 049. In 2006 sold to *Gabriel Scott Rederi (Master Ferries)* and renamed the MASTER CAT. In December 2008 purchased by *Fjord Line* renamed the FJORD CAT. Did not operate in 2009 but service resumed in 2010.

OSLOFJORD Built by Fosen Mekaniske Verksteder, Rissa, Norway for *Rutelaget Askøy-Bergen* as the BERGEN and used on the *Fjord Line* Bergen - Egersund - Hanstholm service. In April 2003 chartered to *DFDS Seaways*, renamed the DUCHESS OF SCANDINAVIA and, after modifications, introduced onto the Harwich - Cuxhaven service. In 2004 sold to *Bergensfjord KS* of Norway and chartered to *DFDS Seaways*. In 2005 sub-chartered to *Fjord Line* for 5 months (with *DFDS* officers and deck-crew) and renamed the ATLANTIC TRAVELLER. In 2006 chartered directly to *Fjord Line*. In March 2008 purchased by *Fjord Line* and renamed the BERGENSFJORD. In January 2014 renamed the OSLOFJORD, rebuilt as a day ferry by STX Finland, Rauma, Finland and, in June 2014, inaugurated a new service between Sandefjord and Strömstad.

Under Construction

5»	NEWBUILDING	-	20	40.0k	109.0m	1200P	410C	30L	A	DK	-

NEWBUILDING Austal 109m catamaran under construction by Austal Ships, Fremantle, Australia to replace the FJORD CAT.

HAVILA KYSTRUTEN

THE COMPANY *Havila Kystruten* is a trading name of *Havila Shipping ASA*, a Norwegian private sector company, In March 2018 it won a ten-year concession to operate, with *Hurtigruten*, the 'Kystruten' (coastal route) between Bergen and Kirkenes from 1st January 2021.

MANAGEMENT CEO Njål Sævik.

ADDRESS P.O.Box 215, N-6099 Fosnavaag, Norway.

TELEPHONE +47 70 08 09 00.

FAX +47 70 08 09 01.

INTERNET Email office@havila.no **Website** www.havila.no

ROUTE OPERATED Bergen - Kirknes (from 1st January 2021).

Under Construction

1	NEWBUILDING 1	-	20	18.0k	125.0m	700P	-	0L	S	NO	-
2	NEWBUILDING 2	-	20	18.0k	125.0m	700P	-	0L	S	NO	-
3	NEWBUILDING 3	-	20	18.0k	125.0m	700P	-	0L	S	NO	-
4	NEWBUILDING 4	-	20	18.0k	125.0m	700P	-	0L	S	NO	-

NEWBUILDING 1, NEWBUILDING 2 Hybrid vessel under construction by Havyard, Leirvik, Norway. To run on LPG and they will be fitted with large battery packs.

NEWBUILDING 3, NEWBUILDING 4 Under construction by Barreras Shipyard, Vigo, Spain. Construction of one of the vessels will be sub-contracted to another shipyard in the wider Vigo area. To run on LPG and they will be fitted with large battery packs.

HURTIGRUTEN

THE COMPANY Hurtigruten AS is a Norwegian private sector company. The service was originally provided by a consortium of companies. By 2006, through mergers and withdrawal from the operation, there were just two companies - *Troms Fylkes D/S* and *Ofotens og Vesteraalens D/S* and in that year *Hurtigruten ASA* was formed. In September 2015 it was taken over by *Silk Bidco AS* of Norway and the company changed its name to *Hurtigruten AS*.

MANAGEMENT Chairman Trygve Hegnar, **Chief Executive Officer** Daniel Skjeldam.

ADDRESS Hurtigruten ASA, Fredrik Lamges gate 14, Postboks 6144, 9291 Tromsø, Norway.

TELEPHONE Administration +47 970 57 030, **Reservations Norway** +47 810 03 030,

UK +44 (0)203 603711, **Ireland** +353 (0)1607 4420

INTERNET Email firmapost@hurtigruten.com uk.sales@hurtigruten.com

Websites www.hurtigruten.co.uk *(English)* www.hurtigruten.no *(Norwegian)* www.hurtigruten.de *(German)* www.hurtigruten.fr *(French)* www.hurtigruten.us *(US English)*

ROUTE OPERATED 'Hurtigruten' sail every day throughout the year from Bergen and calls at 34 ports up to Kirkenes and takes you along one of the world's most exciting coast lines, where you will find yourself close to nature, people and traditions. Daily departures throughout the year. The round trip takes just under 11 days.

1	FINNMARKEN	15539t	02	18.0k	138.5m	1000P	47C	0L	S	NO	9231951
2p	FRAM	11647t	07	18.0k	110.0m	500P	0C	0L	-	NO	9370018
3	KONG HARALD	11204t	93	18.0k	121.8m	691P	45C	0L	S	NO	9039119
4	LOFOTEN	2621t	64	16.0k	87.4m	410P	0C	0L	C	NO	5424562
5	MIDNATSOL	16151t	03	18.0k	135.7m	1000P	45C	0L	S	NO	9247728
6	NORDKAPP	11386t	96	18.0k	123.3m	691P	45C	0L	S	NO	9107772
7	NORDLYS	11204t	94	18.0k	121.8m	691P	45C	0L	S	NO	9048914
8	NORDNORGE	11384t	97	18.0k	123.3m	691P	45C	0L	S	NO	9107784
9	POLARLYS	11341t	96	18.0k	123.0m	737P	35C	0L	S	NO	9107796
10	RICHARD WITH	11205t	93	18.0k	121.8m	691P	45C	0L	S	NO	9040429
11p	SPITSBERGEN	7344t	09	16.0k	100.5m	335P	0C	0L	-	NO	9434060
12	TROLLFJORD	16140t	02	18.0k	135.7m	822P	45C	0L	S	NO	9233258
13	VESTERÅLEN	6262t	83	18.0k	108.6m	560P	35C	0L	S	NO	8019368

FINNMARKEN Built by Kværner Kleven Skeppsvarv, Ulsteinvik, Norway for *Ofotens og Vesteraalens D/S*. In October 2009 chartered as a support vessel for the Gorgon Project (natural gas) in Western Australia. In November 2011 returned to *Hurtigruten* and, in February 2012, returned to service.

FRAM Built by Fincantieri-Cantieri Navali Italiani SpA at Trieste for *Hurtigruten Group ASA* (ordered by *OVDS*). Since 2007 she has operated cruises around Greenland and Svalbad during the summer period and in South America during the winter and this has been the

Spitsbergen *(John Bryant)*

Nordkapp *(John Bryant)*

pattern since. She is named after Fridtjof Nansen's expedition ship FRAM and has ice class 1A/1B.

KONG HARALD Built by Volkswerft, Stralsund, Germany for *Troms Fylkes D/S*.

LOFOTEN Built by A/S Aker Mekaniske Verksted, Oslo, Norway for *Vesteraalens D/S*. In 1988 she was sold to *Finnmark Fylkesrederi og Ruteselskap*. In 1996 she was sold to *Ofotens og Vesteraalens D/S*. In 2002 she was replaced by the FINNMARKEN but she then operated summer cruises and in the winter months substituted for the NORDNORGE when that vessel was sailing in the Chilean Fjords and Antarctica. Since 2008 she has operated on the main Hurtigruten roster.

MIDNATSOL Built by Fosen Mekaniske Verksteder, Rissa, Norway for *Troms Fylkes D/S*. From 2016 also used as an expedition ship in the Antarctic.

NORDKAPP Built by Kværner Kleven Skeppsvarv, Ulsteinvik, Norway for *Ofotens og Vesteraalens D/S*. During the winters of 2005/06 and 2006/07 she operated cruises in South America but following the delivery of the FRAM she now remains on the Hurtigruten throughout the year.

NORDLYS Built by Volkswerft, Stralsund, Germany for *Troms Fylkes D/S*. In 2002 sold to *Kilberg Shipping KS* of Norway and leased back on 15 year bareboat charter with options to repurchase. She was laid up during winter 2008/09 until required to replace the damaged RICHARD WITH from the end of January. She now operates full-time on the Hurtigruten roster.

NORDNORGE Built by Kværner Kleven, Ulsteinvik, Norway for *Ofotens og Vesteraalens D/S*. During winters 2002/03 - 2007/08 she operated cruises in South America. During most of Winter 2008/09 she was used as an accommodation vessel for a liquefied natural gas field. Laid up at Bremerhaven during winter 2009/10.

POLARLYS Built by Ulstein Verft A/S, Ulsteinvik, Norway for *Troms Fylkes D/S*.

RICHARD WITH Built by Volkswerft, Stralsund, Norway for *Ofotens og Vesteraalens D/S*. In 2002 sold to *Kystruten KS*, of Norway and leased back on 15 year bareboat charter with options to re-purchase.

SPITSBERGEN Built as the ATLANTIDA by Estaleiros Navais de Viana do Castelo, Viana do Castelo, Portugal for *Atlanticoline* of Portugal as a ro-ro ferry to operate in the Azores. Although completed in 2009, she was never delivered because she did not meet the required specification. In June 2015 purchased by *Hurtigruten* and renamed the NORWAY EXPLORER. Taken to the Öresund Drydocks shipyard, Landskrona, Sweden for rebuilding to make her suitable for *Hurtigruten* service and cruising in polar waters. In May 2016 renamed the SPITSBERGEN and entered service on the *Hurtigruten*, running along-side the LOFOTEN. Unlike most other *Hurtigruten* vessels, no cars can be conveyed.

TROLLFJORD Built by Fosen Mekaniske Verksteder, Rissa, Norway for *Troms Fylkes D/S*.

VESTERÅLEN Built by Kaarbös Mekaniske Verksted A/S, Harstad, Norway for *Vesteraalens D/S*. From 1987 owned by *Ofotens og Vesteraalens D/S* and from 2006 by *Hurtigruten Group ASA*.

Under Construction

| 14p | ROALD AMUNDSEN | 20889t | 19 | 15k | 140.0m | 530P | 0C | 0L | S | NO | 9813072 |
| 15p | FRIDTJOF NANSEN | 20889t | 20 | 15k | 140.0m | 530P | 0C | 0L | S | NO | - |

ROALD AMUNDSEN, FRIDTJOF NANSEN Under construction by Kleven Verft, Ulsteinvik, Norway. They are designed to cope with both polar waters (for cruising) and service on the regular routes along the Norwegian coastline. There is an option for two more.

FÆRGESELSKABET LÆSØ

THE COMPANY *Færgeselskabet Læsø K/S* is a Danish public sector company, 50% owned by the county of North Jylland and 50% by the municipality of Læsø.

MANAGEMENT Managing Director Lars Ricks, **Marketing Manager** Bente Faurholt.

ADDRESS Havnepladsen 1, Vesterø Havn, 9940 Læsø, Denmark.

TELEPHONE Administration & Reservations +45 98 49 90 22

INTERNET Email info@laesoe-line.dk **Website** www.laesoe-line.dk *(Danish, German)*

ROUTE OPERATED Læsø - Frederikshavn (Jylland) (1 hr 30 mins; *ANE LÆSØ, MARGRETE LÆSØ*; up 7 per day).

1	ANE LÆSØ	2208t	95	12.0k	53.8m	440P	72C	-	BA	DK	9107370
2	MARGRETE LÆSØ	3668t	97	13.5k	68.5m	586P	76C	12L	BA	DK	9139438t

ANE LÆSØ Built as the VESBORG by Ørskov Stålskibsværft, Ørskov, Denmark for *Samsø Linien*. In March2012 sold to *Læsø Færgen*. Rebuilt by Soby Yard, Aerø, Denmark and renamed the ANE LÆSØ. Between September 2014 and February 2015 she operated on the Hou - Sælvig (Samsø) service which had been taken over by *Samsø Rederi* before their new SAMSØ (now PRINSESSE ISABELLA) was delivered. She will continue to act as reserve vessel on this route.

MARGRETE LÆSØ Built as the LÆSØ FÆRGEN by A/S Norsdsøværftet, Ringkøbing, Denmark for *Andelsfærgeselskabet Læsø* of Denmark. In June 1997 renamed the MARGRETE LÆSØ. In July 1999 transferred to *Færgeselskabet Læsø*.

MOBY SPL

THE COMPANY *Moby SPL* is a joint venture between *Moby Lines* of Italy and *St. Peter Line*, a EU registered private sector company.

MANAGEMENT CEO Sergey Kotenev.

18/2 South Street, Valetta, VLT 1102, Malta; Representative office in St. Petersburg Russia – 199106, St. Petersburg, Martime Glory Plaza, 1.

TELEPHONE *Russia* +7 (812) 702 0777, *Finland* +358 (0)9 6187 2000

INTERNET Email sales@stpeterline.com **Website** www.stpeterline.com *(Russian, English, Estonian, Finnish, Swedish)*

ROUTES OPERATED St Petersburg - Helsinki - Tallinn - Stockholm - Helsinki - St Petersburg *SPL PRINCESS ANASTASIA*; 1 per week), St Petersburg - Helsinki - St Petersburg. *SPL PRINCESS ANASTASIA*; 1 per week).

1	SPL PRINCESS ANASTASIA	37583t	86	22.988k	176.8 m	2500P	318C	63L	BA2	IT	8414582

SPL PRINCESS ANASTASIA Built as the OLYMPIA by Oy Wärtsilä Ab, Turku, Finland for *Rederi AB Slite* of Sweden for *Viking Line* service between Stockholm and Helsinki. In 1993 she was chartered to *P&O European Ferries* to inaugurate a new service between Portsmouth and Bilbao. Renamed the PRIDE OF BILBAO. During the summer period she also operated, at weekends, a round trip between Portsmouth and Cherbourg. In 1994 she was purchased by the *Irish Continental Group* and re-registered in the Bahamas. In 2002 her charter was extended for a further five years and again for a further three years from October 2007. The Cherbourg service ended at the end of 2004. In September 2010 redelivered to *Irish Continental Group*. In October 2010 renamed the BILBAO. In November 2010 chartered to *St. Peter Line*, in February 2011 renamed the SPL PRINCESS ANASTASIA and in April 2011 inaugurated a new Stockholm - St Petersburg service. In February 2011 purchased by an associated company of *St. Peter Line*. During January and February 2014 she served as a floating hotel at the Winter Olympics in Sochi, Russia. In November 2016 sold to *Moby Lines* of Italy and chartered to *Moby SPL*.

MOLSLINJEN/BORNHOLMSLINJEN

THE COMPANY Molslinjen and Bornholmslinjen are trading names of Mols-Linien A/S, a Danish private sector company. In March 2017 the trading name was changed to Molslinjen. From 1st September 2018 the company took over the BornholmerFærgen services operated by Danske Færger A/S. They are branded as Bornholmslinjen.

MANAGEMENT CEO Søren Jespersen, **Communications Manager** Jesper Maack **Marketing Manager** Mikkel Hybel.

ADDRESS Hveensgade 4, 8000 Aarhus C, Denmark.

TELEPHONE Administration +45 89 52 52 00, **Reservations** +45 70 10 14 18 (press 1).

FAX Administration +45 89 52 53 93.

INTERNET Email molslinjen@molslinjen.dk **Websites** www.molslinjen.dk www.bornholmslinjen.com (Danish)

ROUTES OPERATED Molslinjen (all service fast ferry) All year Århus (Jylland) - Odden (Sjælland) (1 hr 5 mins; **EXPRESS 2**, **EXPRESS 3**, **MAX MOLS**; up to 12 per day), **April - October- weekends only** Ebeltoft (Jylland) - Odden (45 mins; **MAX MOLS**; 1 per day). **Bornholmslinjen** Rønne (Bornholm, Denmark) – Køge (5 hrs 30 mins; **HAMMERSHUS**; 1 per day, Rønne – Sassnitz (Germany) (3 hrs 20 mins; **HAMMERSHUS**; 1 per day). **Fast Ferry** Rønne - Ystad (Sweden) (1 hr 20 mins; **EXPRESS 1**; 4 per day).

1»	EXPRESS 1	10504t	09	40.0k	112.6m	1200P	417C	34L	A	DK	9501590
2»	EXPRESS 2	10500t	13	40.0k	112.6m	1000P	417C	34L	A	DK	9561356
3»	EXPRESS 3	10842t	17	40.0k	109.4m	1000P	411C	34L	A	DK	9793064
4	HAMMERSHUS	18500	18	17.7k	158.0m	720P	-	90L	BA	DK	9812107
5»	MAX MOLS	5617t	98	43.0k	91.3m	800P	220C	-	A	DK	9176058
6	POVL ANKER	12131t	78	19.5k	121.0m	1500P	262C	26T	BA	DK	7633143

EXPRESS 1 Incat 112m catamaran built by Incat Tasmania Pty Ltd for MGC Chartering of the Irish Republic. Launched as the INCAT 066. On completion, sold to for MGC Chartering of the Irish Republic and renamed the MGC 66. In April 2009 chartered to LD Lines, renamed the NORMAN ARROW and, in June, placed on the Dover - Boulogne route. In November 2009 withdrawn and laid up for the winter. In April 2010 began operating on the Portsmouth Le Havre - route. In March 2012 chartered to Mols-Linien and renamed the KATEXPRESS 1 (Note: in upper and lower case spelt 'KatExpress 1'). Entered service in May 2012. In January 2017 renamed the EXPRESS 1. In September 2018 moved to Bornholmslinjen service.

EXPRESS 2 Incat 112m catamaran built by Incat Tasmania Pty Ltd. Launched as INCAT 067. In March 2013 chartered to Mols-Linien and renamed the KATEXPRESS 2 for ten years with a purchase option. (Note: in upper and lower case spelt 'KatExpress 2'). Entered service in May 2013. In March 2017 renamed the EXPRESS 2.

EXPRESS 3 Incat 109m catamaran built by Incat Tasmania Pty Ltd, Hobart, Australia.

HAMMERSHUS Built by Rauma Marine Constructions Oy, Rauma, Finland. Delivered in July 2018. She will operate between Rønne and Køge (Bornholm) and Rønne and Sassnitz from 1st September 2018.

MAX MOLS Incat 91-metre catamaran, built speculatively at Hobart, Tasmania, Australia. In Spring 1998, following Incat's acquisition of a 50% share in Scandlines Cat-Link A/S, she was sold to that company and named the CAT-LINK IV. In 1999 purchased by Mols-Linien and renamed the MAX MOLS. In 2000 chartered to Marine Atlantic of Canada to operate between Port aux Basques (Newfoundland) and North Sydney (Nova Scotia). Returned to Mols-Linien in Autumn 2000. In Summer 2002 chartered to Riga Sea Lines to operate between Riga and Nynäshamn. Returned to Mols-Linien in Autumn 2002. In 2004 chartered to P&O Ferries to operate between Portsmouth and Caen. Operated under the marketing name 'Caen Express'. In November 2004 returned to Mols-Linien and placed on the Århus – Odden route to enhance the service. In June 2017 transferred to the Ebeltoft - Odden route.

Povl Anker *(John Bryant)*

Prins Richard *(Scandlines)*

POVL ANKER Built by Aalborg Værft A/S, Denmark for *Bornholmstrafikken*. Used on the Rønne - København (until September 2004), Rønne - Køge (October 2004-date), Rønne - Ystad and Rønne - Sassnitz services. In recent years she has operated between Rønne and Sassnitz and Rønne and Ystad in the peak summer period. In July 2016 sold to *Mols-Linien A/S* and chartered back. Delivered to *Mols-Linien* at the end of August 2018.

Under Construction

7»	EXPRESS 4		-	18	37.0k	109.0m	1006P	425C	36L	A	DK	-

EXPRESS 4 Austal 109m catamaran under construction by from Austal Ships, Fremantle, Australia.

REEDEREI NORDEN-FRISIA

THE COMPANY *Aktiengesellschaft Reederei Norden-Frisia* is a German public sector company.

MANAGEMENT President/CEO C U Stegmann, **Managing Director/CFO** Prok. Graw, **Technical Manager** Prok. H Stolle.

ADDRESS Postfach 1262, 26534 Norderney, Germany.

TELEPHONE *Administration* +49 (0)4931 987 0.

FAX *Administration* +49 (0)4931 987 1131.

INTERNET *Email* info@reederei-frisia.de **Website** www.reederei-frisia.de *(German)*

ROUTES OPERATED Car Ferries & Passenger Ferries Norddeich (Germany) - Norderney (German Frisian Islands) (1 hr; ***FRISIA I, FRISIA III, FRISIA IV, FRISIA VI***; up to 15 per day), Norddeich - Juist (German Frisian Islands) (1 hr 20 mins; ***FRISIA II, FRISIA VII***; up to 15 per day). **Excursion Vessels (*FRISIA IX, FRISIA X, RÜM HART, WAPPEN VON NORDENEY***; varies).

1	FRISIA I	1020t	70	12.3k	63.7m	1500P	53C	-	BA	DE	7018604
2	FRISIA II	1125t	78	12.0k	63.3m	1340P	53C	-	BA	DE	7723974
3	FRISIA III	1786t	15	12.0k	74.3m	1342P	58C	-	BA	DE	9732450
4	FRISIA IV	1574t	02	12.0k	71.7m	1342P	58C	-	BA	DE	9246839
5	FRISIA VI	768t	68	12.0k	54.9m	1096P	35C	-	BA	DE	8827179
6F	FRISIA VII	363t	84	12.0k	53.0m	12P	30C	-	BA	DE	8891807
7p	FRISIA IX	571t	80	11.0k	57.0m	785P	0C	-	-	DE	7924310
8p	FRISIA X	187t	72	12.0k	36.3m	290P	0C	-	-	DE	7222308
9p	FRISIA XI	105t	69	12.0k	35.4m	940P	0C	-	-	DE	8137237
10p	WAPPEN VON NORDENEY	154t	67	14.0k	31.1m	200P	0C	-	-	DE	7935395

FRISIA I, FRISIA II, FRISIA VI Built by Jos L Meyer Werft, Papenburg, Germany for *Reederei Norden-Frisia*. Passenger capacities relate to the summer season. Capacity is reduced during the winter.

FRISIA III Built by Cassen-Werft, Emden, Germany.

FRISIA IV Built by Schiffswerft und Maschinenfabrik Cassens GmbH, Emden, Germany for *Reederei Norden-Frisia* to replace the FRISIA VIII.

FRISIA VII Built by Schlömer Werft, Oldersum, Germany for *Reederei Norden-Frisia*. Conveys ro-ro freight to Norderney and Juist.

FRISIA IX, FRISIA X Built by Schiffswerft Julius Diedrich GmbH & Co. KG, Oldersum, Germany for *Reederei Norden-Frisia*. The FRISIA IX was built to convey 9 cars at the bow end but is now used in passenger-only mode. These ships are generally used for excursions.

FRISIA XI Built by Julius Diedrich Schiffswerft, Odersum, Germany as the BALTRUM IV for *Baltrum-Linie* of Germany. In November 1982 sold to *Wyker Dampfschiffs-Reederei* and renamed the RÜM HART. In March 2014 sold to *Reederei Norden-Frisia*. In October renamed the FRISIA XI.

WAPPEN VON NORDENEY Built by Cassens-Werft, Emden, Germany for *Reederei Norden-Frisia*. Used for excursions.

Under Construction

| 11 | NEWBUILDING | 1786t | 20 | 12.0k | 74.3m | 1338P | 58C | - | BA | DE | - |

NEWBUILDING Under construction by Pella Sietas Werft, Hamburg. To operate on the Norddeich-Norderney service. A sister vessel of the FRISIA III.

POLFERRIES

THE COMPANY *Polferries* is the trading name of *Polska Zegluga Baltycka SA (Polish Baltic Shipping Company)*, a Polish state-owned company.

MANAGEMENT President Piotr Redmerski.

ADDRESS ul Portowa 41, 78-100 Kolobrzeg, Poland.

TELEPHONE Administration & Reservations *Poland* +48 94 35 52 100, *Sweden* +46 (0)8 520 686 60.

INTERNET Email info@polferries.pl **Website** www.polferries.pl *(Polish, Danish, English, German, Swedish)*

ROUTES OPERATED Świnoujście - Ystad (7 hrs; *BALTIVIA*, *CRACOVIA*, *MAZOVIA*; up to 3 per day), Gdańsk - Nynäshamn (Sweden) (18 hrs; *NOVA STAR*, *WAWEL*; up to 6 per week.

1	BALTIVIA	17790t	81	19.0k	146.9m	250P	30C	80L	BA	BS	7931997
2	CRACOVIA	25028t	02	22.8k	180.0m	550P	-	150T	BA	BS	9237242
3	MAZOVIA	25996t	96	21.0k	168.0m	200P	-	154T	BA2	BS	9010814
4	NOVA STAR	27744t	11	19.0k	162.0m	1215P	400C	90L	A	BS	9462067
5	WAWEL	25318t	80	19.0k	163.9m	900P	550C	75L	A2	BS	7814462

BALTIVIA Built as the SAGA STAR by Fartygsentreprenader AB, Kalmar, Sweden for *TT-Saga-Line* and, from 1982, used on freight services between Travemünde and Trelleborg/Malmö. (Originally ordered by *Rederi AB Svea* as the SAGALAND). In 1989 sold to *Cie Meridionale* of France, renamed the GIROLATA and used on *SNCM* (later *CMR*) services in the Mediterranean. In 1993 she was chartered back to *TT-Line*, resumed her original name and was used on the Travemünde - Trelleborg service. Following delivery of the ROBIN HOOD and the NILS DACKE in 1995, she was transferred to the Rostock - Trelleborg route. In July 1997 she was purchased by *TT-Line* and in 1998 passenger facilities were completely renovated to full ro-pax format; following the delivery of the TOM SAWYER she was transferred back to the Travemünde - Trelleborg route, operating additional freight sailings. Briefly transferred back to Rostock - Trelleborg when the charter of the TT-TRAVELLER ended. Withdrawn in 2002, sold to *Transmanche Ferries* and renamed the DIEPPE. In 2006 replaced by the SEVEN SISTERS, sold to *Polferries*, renamed the BALTIVIA and, in 2007, placed on the Gdańsk - Nynäshamn route. In February 2013 transferred to the Świnoujście – Ystad service.

CRACOVIA Built as the MURILLO by Astilleros Españoles SA, Seville, Spain for *Trasmediterranea* of Spain. Used mainly on the service between Cadiz and Canary Islands. In June 2014 sold to *Bulgaria West Port* of Bulgaria and renamed the DRUJBA. She operated between Bourgas, Bulgaria, Batumi (Georgia) and Novorossiysk (Russia). In March 2017 sold to *Polferries* and, in June 2017, renamed the CRACOVIA. In September 2017 introduced onto the Świnoujście - Ystad route.

MAZOVIA Built as the GOTLAND by Pt Dok Kodja Bahri, Kodja, Indonesia for *Rederi AB Gotland* for charter. In 1997 briefly chartered to *Tor Line* and then to *Nordic Trucker Line*, to operate between Oxelösund and St Petersburg (a ro-ro freight service). In June 1997 she was chartered to *SeaWind Line*, enabling a twice-daily passenger service to be operated. In late 1997 she was sold to *Finnlines* and renamed the FINNARROW. She started operating twice weekly between Helsinki and Travemünde. During Summer 1998 she was transferred to

SECTION 7 – NORTHERN EUROPE

Ferries 2019

FinnLink; a bow door was fitted and she was modified to allow for two-level loading. In 2003 transferred to *Nordö Link*. In 2005 returned to *FinnLink*. In 2006 transferred to *Finnlines Nordö Link* again. In 2007 chartered to *Stena Line* to operate between Karlskrona and Gdynia. In December 2011 transferred to the Hoek van Holland - Killingholme route. In March 2011 returned to *Finnlines* and placed on the Travemünde - Malmö service. In October 2011 transferred to *FinnLink*. Between January and March 2013 chartered to *Stena Line* to cover Irish Sea routes during the refit period but withdrawn from service prematurely following an accident. In April 2013 chartered to *Grimaldi Line* of Italy for five years and renamed the EUROFERRY BRINDISI. In October 2014 sold to the *Grimaldi Group* of Italy. In November sold to *Polferries* and renamed the MAZOVIA. Entered service in June 2015 on the Świnoujście - Ystad service.

NOVA STAR Built as the NORMAN LEADER by St Marine Shipyard, Singapore for *LD Lines* of France. However, delivery was not taken as she did not meet the design specification. She was registered to *Singapore Technologies Marine* and remained laid up until February 2014 when she was chartered to *Nova Star Cruises* of Canada and renamed the NOVA STAR. She operated between Portland, Maine USA and Yarmouth, Nova Scotia, Canada. In October 2015 she was arrested in Portland Arrested in Maine due to unpaid bills and the service ceased. In February 2016 she was chartered to *Inter Shipping* of Morocco and placed on their Algeciras (Spain) - Tangier Morocco service. In November 2017 chartered to *Polferries* and sub-charted to *Inter Shipping* until February 2018 when she was taken over by *Polferries*. Expected to begin operating between Gdańsk and Nynäshamn in September 2018.

WAWEL Built as the SCANDINAVIA by Kockums Varvet AB, Malmö, Sweden for *Rederi AB Nordö* of Sweden. After service in the Mediterranean for *UMEF*, she was, in 1981, sold to *SOMAT* of Bulgaria, renamed the TZAREVETZ and used on *Medlink* services between Bulgaria and the Middle East, later on other routes. In 1986 she was chartered to *Callitzis* of Greece for a service between Italy and Greece. In 1988 she was sold to *Sealink*, re-registered in The Bahamas and renamed the FIESTA. She was then chartered to *OT Africa Line*. During Autumn 1989 she was rebuilt at Bremerhaven to convert her for passenger use and in March 1990 she was renamed the FANTASIA and placed on the Dover - Calais service. Later in 1990 she was renamed the STENA FANTASIA. In 1998 transferred to *P&O Stena Line*. In 1999 she was renamed the P&OSL CANTERBURY. In 2002 renamed the PO CANTERBURY. In Spring 2003 replaced by the PRIDE OF CANTERBURY and laid up at Dunkerque. Later in the year sold to *GA Ferries* and renamed the ALKMINI A. In 2004 moved to Greece and, after a partial rebuild (including the welding up of the bow door) placed on the Igoumenitsa – Brindisi route. Later in 2004 sold to *Polferries* and renamed the WAWEL; rebuilt to increase the number of cabins. In 2005 placed on the Świnoujście – Ystad service. In May 2015 transferred to the Gdańsk - Nynäshamn route.

Under Construction

6	NEWBUILDING	33000	20	18.0k	202.4m-	400P	-	180T	BA2	-	-

NEWBUILDING Under construction by Gryfia Marine Repair Shipyard SA, Szczecin, Poland. Likely to replace the BALTIVIA on the Świnoujście - Ystad route. Dual fuel - diesel and LNG.

PRAAMID

THE COMPANY *Praamid* is the trading name of the ferry operation of the *TS Laevad*, a company owned by the Republic of Estonia. It took over the operation of services to the islands of Hiiumaa and Saaremaa in October 2016.

ADDRESS Sadama 25, Tallinn 15051, Estonia.

TELEPHONE 618 1310.

INTERNET Email info@praamid.ee **Website** www.praamid.ee *(Estonia, English)*

ROUTES OPERATED Kuivastu - Virtsu (Saaremaa) (28 mins; *PIRET*, *REGULA*, *TÕLL*; up to 25 per day), Rohuküla - Heltermaa (Hiiumaa) (1 hr 30 mins; *LEIGER*, *TIIU*; up to 11 per day).

2	LEIGER	4012t	16	10.0k	114.0m	700P	150C	-	BA	EE	9762675

3	PIRET	4012t	17	10.0k	114.0m	700P	150C	-	BA	EE	9762663
4	REGULA	3774t	71	14.5k	71.2m	580P	105C	20L	BA2	EE	7051058
5	TIIU	4012t	17	10.0k	114.0m	700P	150C	-	BA	EE	9762687
6	TÕLL	4012t	17	10.0k	114.0m	700P	150C	-	BA	EE	9762651

LEIGER, TIIU Built by Sefine Shipyard, Yalova, Turkey. LNG powered.

PIRET, TÕLL Built by Remontowa Shipyard, Gdańsk, Poland (The PIRET's hull was subcontracted to Irko, Gdańsk, Poland). LNG powered.

REGULA Built by Jos L Meyer, Papenburg, Germany for *Stockholms Rederi AB Svea* of Sweden for the service between Helsingborg and Helsingør operated by *Linjebuss International AB* (a subsidiary company). In 1980 she was sold to *Scandinavian Ferry Lines*. During Winter 1984/85 she was rebuilt to increase vehicle and passenger capacity. In 1991 ownership was transferred to *SweFerry* and operations to *ScandLines* on the Helsingborg - Helsingør service. Ownership later transferred to *Scandlines AB*. In 1997 sold to *Saaremaa Laevakompanii*. In October 2016 chartered to *Praamid*. Following delivery of new vessels, she was retained as spare vessel. However, in summer 2017 she was used on regular service and the MERCANDIA VIII of *HH Ferries* was chartered as spare vessel. In September 2017 purchased by *TS Laevad*.

SAMSØ REDERI

THE COMPANY *Samsø Rederi* is a Danish public sector company owned by the Samsø Municipality.

MANAGEMENT Managing Director Carsten Kruse.

ADDRESS Sælvig 64, 8305 Samsø, Denmark.

TELEPHONE Administration and Reservations + 45 7022 5900.

INTERNET Email tilsamsoe@samsoe.dk **Website** www.tilsamsoe.dk (Danish, German, English).

ROUTE OPERATED Sælvig (Samsø) - Hou (Jylland) (1 hr; **PRINSESSE ISABELLA**; up to 7 per day).

1	PRINSESSE ISABELLA	5478t	15	9.9k	100.0m	600P	160C	16T	BA	DK	9692806

PRINSESSE ISABELLA Built as the SAMSØ by Stocznia Remontowa, Gdańsk, Poland. Entered service in March 2015. In June 2015 renamed the PRINSESSE ISABELLA.

SCANDLINES

THE COMPANY In 2007, the owners of *Scandlines AG*, the Danish Ministry of Transport and Energy and Deutsche Bahn AG, decided to sell their shares. The new owner was a consortium of the 3i Group (UK), Allianz Capital Partners GmbH (Germany) (40% of the shares each) and *Deutsche Seereederei GmbH* (Germany) (20% of the shares). The company was subsequently transformed into a private limited company and now trades under the name Scandlines GmbH, uniting the companies *Scandlines Deutschland GmbH* and *Scandlines Danmark A/S*. With *Deutsche Seereederei GmbH* selling its shares in *Scandlines GmbH* in 2010, 3i and Allianz Capital Partners held 50% of the shares each. During 2012 *Stena Line* took over the Travemünde - Ventspils, Travemünde - Liepaja and Nynäshamn - Ventspils routes, took full control of the joint routes - Rostock - Trelleborg and Sassnitz - Trelleborg services and took over the vessels used. The freight-only route between Rostock and Hanko passed to *SOL*. In November 2013 3i Group purchased Allianz Capital Partners' share and now control 100% of the company. In March 2016 3i sold a majority share in the company to First State Investments and Hermes Investment Management.

MANAGEMENT CEO Søren Poulsgaard Jensen, **Managing Director & Chief Customer Officer** Morten Haure-Petersen.

ADDRESS Am Bahnhof 3a, 18119 Rostock, Germany.

SECTION 7 – NORTHERN EUROPE

Ferries 2019

TELEPHONE Administration & Reservations *Denmark* +45 33 15 15 15, *Germany* +49 (0)381-77 88 77 66.

INTERNET Email info@scandlines.com **Website** www.scandlines.com *(Danish, German, English)*,

ROUTES OPERATED Rødby (Lolland, Denmark) - Puttgarden (Germany) (45 mins; *DEUTSCHLAND, HOLGER DANSKE, KRONPRINS FREDERIK, PRINS RICHARD, PRINSESSE BENEDIKTE, SCHLESWIG-HOLSTEIN (HOLGER DANSKE* specially for *dangerous goods)*; half-hourly train/vehicle ferry + additional road freight-only sailings), Gedser (Falster, Denmark) - Rostock (Germany) (2 hours; *BERLIN, COPENHAGEN*; every 2 hours).

1	BERLIN	22319t	16	20.5k	169.5m	1300P	460C	96L	BA2	DE	9587855
2	COPENHAGEN	22319t	16	20.5k	169.5m	1300P	460C	96L	BA2	DK	9587867
3	DEUTSCHLAND	15187t	97	18.5k	142.0m	1200P	364C	30Lr	BA2	DE	9151541
4F	HOLGER DANSKE	2779t	76	14.9k	86.8m	12P	-	12L	BA	DK	7432202
5	KRONPRINS FREDERIK	16071t	81	20.5k	152.0m	1082P	210C	46T	BA	DE	7803205
6	PRINS RICHARD	14822t	97	18.5k	142.0m	1100P	364C	36Lr	BA2	DK	9144419
7	PRINSESSE BENEDIKTE	14822t	97	18.5k	142.0m	1100P	364C	36Lr	BA2	DK	9144421
8	SCHLESWIG-HOLSTEIN	15187t	97	18.5k	142.0m	1200P	364C	30Lr	BA2	DE	9151539

BERLIN Partly built by Volkswerft Stralsund, Stralsund, Germany for *Scandlines* to operate on the Gedser - Rostock route. The propulsion system allows for adaption to LNG. Originally due to enter service in Spring 2012, construction was seriously delayed. It was then found that she did not meet the specification and the order was cancelled. She was 90% finished and had undertaken sea trials. In March 2014, purchased by *Scandferries ApS* of Denmark (an associated company) and towed, firstly to Blohm + Voss Shipyards, Hamburg and then to Fayard Shipyard, Odense to be completed with an almost completely new superstructure. Her engines were also modified from straight diesel to diesel-electric hybrid. In May 2016 chartered to *Scandlines* and entered service on the Gedser - Rostock route,

COPENHAGEN As the BERLIN except that at the time of purchase by *Scandlines*, she had been launched but was only 50% finished. Entered service in Autumn 2016.

DEUTSCHLAND Train/vehicle ferry built by Van der Giessen-de Noord, Krimpen aan den IJssel, Rotterdam, The Netherlands for *DFO* for the Puttgarden - Rødby service. During Winter 2003/04 a new hoistable deck was added for cars by Neptun Yard Rostock, (Germany).

HOLGER DANSKE Built by Aalborg Værft A/S, Aalborg, Denmark as a train/vehicle ferry for *DSB* for the Helsingør - Helsingborg service. In 1991 transferred to the Kalundborg - Samsø route (no rail facilities). In 1997 transferred to subsidiary *SFDS A/S*. Withdrawn at the end of November 1998 when the service passed to *Samsø Linien*. In 1999 began operating between Rødby and Puttgarden as a road-freight-only vessel, carrying, among others, loads which cannot be conveyed on passenger vessels.

KRONPRINS FREDERIK Train/vehicle ferry built by Nakskov Skibsværft A/S, Nakskov, Denmark for *DSB* for the Nyborg - Korsør service. Withdrawn in 1997. After conversion to a car/lorry ferry, she was transferred to the Gedser - Rostock route (no rail facilities). In March 2017, following modifications, transferred to the Rødby - Puttgarden route to provide extra capacity for lorry traffic. Also serves as reserve vessel on Gedser - Rostock service.

PRINS RICHARD, PRINSESSE BENEDIKTE Train/vehicle ferries, built by Ørskov Christensen Staalskibsværft A/S, Frederikshavn, Denmark for *Scandlines A/S* for the Rødby - Puttgarden service. During Winter 2003/04 a new hoistable deck was added for cars by Neptun Yard Rostock, (Germany).

SCHLESWIG-HOLSTEIN Train/vehicle ferry built by Van der Giessen-de Noord, Krimpen aan den IJssel, Rotterdam, The Netherlands for *DFO* for the Puttgarden - Rødby service. During Winter 2003/04 a new hoistable deck was added for cars by Neptun Yard Rostock, (Germany).

SCANDLINES HELSINGØR - HELSINGBORG

THE COMPANY *Scandlines Helsingør - Helsingborg* is the trading name of *HH Ferries Group*, a Swedish private sector company owned by First State Investments. Previously a joint venture between *Scandlines* and *Stena Line*, it was acquired by First State Investments in January 2015. Although now a separate company, it currently operates as part of the *Scandlines* network.

ADDRESS Knutpunkten 43, S-252 78, Helsingborg, Sweden.

TELEPHONE Administration +46 (0)42 18 60 00 **Reservations** +45 33 15 15 15.

FAX Administration +46 (0)42 18 60 49.

INTERNET Email info@hhferriesgroup.com **Website** hhferriesgroup.com *(Danish, English, Swedish)* www.scandlines.com *(Danish, German, English)*

ROUTES OPERATED Helsingør (Sjælland, Denmark) - Helsingborg (Sweden) (20 mins; *AURORA AF HELSINGBORG, MERCANDIA IV, MERCANDIA VIII, HAMLET, TYCHO BRAHE*; up to every 15 mins)

1	AURORA AF HELSINGBORG	10918t	92	14.0k	111.2m	1250P	225C	25Lr	BA	SE	9007128
2	HAMLET	10067t	97	13.5k	111.2m	1000P	244C	34L	BA	DK	9150030
3	MERCANDIA IV	4296t	89	13.0k	95.0m	420P	170C	18L	BA	DK	8611685
4	MERCANDIA VIII	4296t	87	13.0k	95.0m	420P	170C	18L	BA	DK	8611623
5	TYCHO BRAHE	11148t	91	14.5k	111.2m	1250P	240C	35Lr	BA	DK	9007116

AURORA AF HELSINGBORG Train/vehicle ferry built by Langsten Verft A/S, Tomrefjord, Norway for *SweFerry* for *ScandLines* joint *DSB/SweFerry* service between Helsingør and Helsingborg.

HAMLET Road vehicle ferry built by Finnyards, Rauma, Finland for *Scandlines* (50% owned by *Scandlines AG* and 50% owned by *Scandlines AB* of Sweden) for the Helsingør - Helsingborg service. Sister vessel of the TYCHO BRAHE but without rail tracks.

MERCANDIA IV Built as the SUPERFLEX NOVEMBER by North East Shipbuilders Ltd, Sunderland, UK for *Vognmandsruten* of Denmark. In 1989 sold to *Mercandia* and renamed the MERCANDIA IV. In 1990 she began operating on their *Kattegatbroen* Juelsminde - Kalundborg service. In 1996 she was transferred to their *Sundbroen* Helsingør - Helsingborg service. In 1997 the service and vessel were leased to *HH-Ferries*. In 1999 she was purchased by *HH-Ferries*. She has been equipped to carry dangerous cargo.

MERCANDIA VIII Built as the SUPERFLEX BRAVO by North East Shipbuilders Ltd, Sunderland, UK for *Vognmandsruten* of Denmark and used on their services between Nyborg and Korsør and København (Tuborg Havn) and Landskrona (Sweden). In 1991 she was chartered to *Scarlett Line* to operate on the København and Landskrona route. In 1993 she was renamed the SVEA SCARLETT but later in the year the service ceased and she was laid up. In 1996 she was purchased by *Mercandia*, renamed the MERCANDIA VIII and placed on their *Sundbroen* Helsingør - Helsingborg service. In 1997 the service and vessel were leased to *HH-Ferries*. In 1999 she was purchased by *HH-Ferries*. Now reserve vessel. Between April and July 2015 she operated between Puttgarden and Rødby for *Scandlines*, following damage sustained by the PRINSESSE BENEDIKTE at Gdańsk during a refit. In summer 2018 chartered to *Praamid* of Estonia to act as spare vessel.

TYCHO BRAHE Train/vehicle ferry, built by Tangen Verft A/S, Tomrefjord, Norway for *DSB* for the *ScandLines* joint *DSB/SweFerry* service between Helsingør and Helsingborg.

SMYRIL LINE

THE COMPANY *Smyril Line* is a Faroe Islands company.

MANAGEMENT Adm. Director Rúni Vang Poulsen, **Accounting and Department Manager** Nina Djurhuus.

Ferries 2019

ADDRESS Yviri við Strond 1, PO Box 370, 110 Tórshavn, Faroe Islands.

TELEPHONE Administration & Reservations +298-34 59 00.

FAX +298-345901.

INTERNET Email office@smyrilline.com **Website** www.smyrilline.com (English, French, Dutch German) www.smyrilline.fo (Danish, Faroese, Icelandic, Norwegian, Swedish)

ROUTES OPERATED *Winter/Early Spring* Tórshavn (Faroes) - Hirtshals (Denmark) (36 hrs; **NORRÖNA**; 1 per week), *Spring/Early Summer/Autumn* Tórshavn - Hirtshals (36 hrs; **NORRÖNA**; 1 per week), Tórshavn - Seyðisfjördur (Iceland) (19 hrs; **NORRÖNA**; 1 per week), **Summer** Tórshavn - Hirtshals (Denmark) (30 hrs; **NORRÖNA**; 2 per week), Tórshavn - Seyðisfjördur (Iceland) (19 hrs; **NORRÖNA**; 2 per week). *Freight services* Tórshavn - Hirtshals - St Petersburg (**EYSTNES, HVITANES**), Thorlakshofn (Iceland) - Tórshavn - Rotterdam (**MYKINES**).

1F	EYSTNES	4610t	81	15.0k	102.2m	0P	-	24T	AS	F0	7922166
2F	HVITANES	4636t	80	12.0k	77.3m	0P	-	14T	AS	F0	7915541
3F	MYKINES	18979t	96	20.0k	138.5m	12P	1452C	105T	A2	F0	9121998
4	NORRÖNA	35966t	03	21.0k	164.0m	1482P	800C	134T	BA	F0	9227390

EYSTNES Con-ro vessel (only the main deck can take trailers) built as the COMETA by Fosen Mekaniske Verksteder, Rissa, Norway for *Nor-Cargo*. Until 2010 she operated for *Sea-Cargo* between Norwegian ports and Immingham; afterwards she operated on *Nor-Cargo* Norwegian domestic services. In September 2015 sold to *Smyril Line* and renamed the EYSTNES.

HVITANES Con-ro vessel (only the main deck can take trailers) built as the TANAGER by Bergen Mekaniske Verksteder, Bergen, Norway for *NorCargo* of Norway. In September 2015 sold to *Smyril Line* and renamed the EYSTNES.

MYKINES Built as the TRANSGARD by Umoe Sterkoder, Kristiansund, Norway for *Bror Husell Chartering* of Finland for long-term charter to *Transfennica* and used between Rauma and Antwerpen and Hamina and Lübeck. Later chartered to *Finncarriers*. In 2005 she underwent conversion in Poland to add a garage on top of the original weather deck and was placed on long-term charter to *UECC*. She was generally used on the Baltic or Iberian services. In 2007 renamed AUTO BALTIC. In January 2016 chartered to *Flotta Suardiaz*. In April 2017 sold to *Smyril Line* to inaugurate a new service between Thorlakshofn (Iceland), Tórshavn and Rotterdam and renamed the MYKINES.

NORRÖNA Built by Flender Werft, Lübeck, Germany for *Smyril Line*, to replace the existing NORRÖNA. Originally due to enter service in Summer 2002, start of building was delayed by financing difficulties. She was to have been built at Flensburger Schiffbau-Gesellschaft, Flensburg, Germany, but delays in arranging finance led to change of shipyard.

STENA LINE

THE COMPANY *Stena Line Scandinavia AB* is a Swedish private sector company. During 2012, the operations of subsidiary *Scandlines AB* of Sweden were absorbed and some of the Baltic operations and vessels of *Scandlines GmbH* of Germany were taken over. In *2015 Stena Line Scandinavia's* share in *Scandlines AB* where sold and the route Helsingborg - Helsingør sold to new owners.

MANAGEMENT CEO Niclas Mårtensson, **Chief Operating Officer** Peter Arvidsson.

ADDRESS Danmarksterminalen, 405 19 Göteborg, Sweden.

TELEPHONE Administration +46 (0)31-85 80 00, **Reservations** +46 (0)770 57 57 00.

INTERNET Email info@stenaline.com **Website** www.stenaline.com (Czech, Danish, Dutch, English, French, German, Latvian, Lithuanian, Norwegian, Polish, Russian, Swedish)

ROUTES OPERATED Passenger Ferries Göteborg (Sweden) - Frederikshavn (Denmark) (3 hrs 15 mins; **STENA DANICA, STENA JUTLANDICA, STENA VINGA**; up to 6 per day),

Göteborg - Kiel (Germany) (14 hrs; **STENA GERMANICA, STENA SCANDINAVICA**; 1 per day), Frederikshavn - Oslo (Norway) (8 hrs 45 mins; **STENA SAGA**; 1 per day), Varberg (Sweden) - Grenaa (Denmark) (4 hrs; **STENA NAUTICA**; 2 per day), Karlskrona (Sweden) - Gdynia (Poland) (10 hrs 30 mins; **STENA BALTICA, STENA NORDICA, STENA SPIRIT, STENA VISION**; 3/4 per day), Rostock (Germany) - Trelleborg (Sweden) (7 hrs); **MECKLENBURG-VORPOMMERN, SASSNITZ, SKÅNE**; 3/4 per day), Sassnitz (Germany) - Trelleborg (4 hrs 15 mins; **SASSNITZ**; 5 per week), Travemünde (Germany) - Liepaja (Latvia) (27 hrs; **STENA GOTHICA, URD**; 5 per week), Nynäshamn (Sweden) – Ventspils (Latvia) (12 hrs; **SCOTTISH VIKING, STENA FLAVIA**; 12 per week). **Freight Ferry**, Gdynia - Nynäshamn (18 hrs; **BORE BAY**; 3 per week).

1	BORE BAY	10572t	96	20.0k	138.8m	12P	-	105T	A2	FI	9122007
2	MECKLENBURG-VORPOMMERN	36185t	96	22.0k	199.9m	600P	445C	230Tr	A2	DE	9131797
3	SASSNITZ	21154t	89	18.5k	171.5m	875P	314C	50Tr	BA2	DE	8705383
4	SCOTTISH VIKING	26500t	09	24.0k	186.5m	800P	185C	120L	A	IT	9435454
5	SKÅNE	42705t	98	21.0k	200.2m	600P	520C	240Tr	AS2	SE	9133915
6	STENA BALTICA	22542t	07	23.0k	167.0m	160P	-	140L	BA2	UK	9364978
7»•	STENA CARISMA	8631t	97	40.0k	88.0m	900P	210C	-	A	SE	9127760
8	STENA DANICA	28727t	83	19.5k	154.9m	2274P	555C	120T	BAS2	SE	7907245
9	STENA FLAVIA	26904t	08	24.0k	186.5m	852P	185C	120L	A	DK	9417919
10	STENA GERMANICA	44372t	01	22.0k	240.1m	900P	-	250L	BA	SE	9145176
11F	STENA GOTHICA	13144t	82	18.0k	171.0m	186P	-	104T	AS	SE	7826867
12	STENA JUTLANDICA	29691t	96	21.5k	183.7m	1500P	550C	156T	BAS2	SE	9125944
13	STENA NAUTICA	19504t	86	19.4k	134.0m	700P	330C	70T	BA2	SE	8317954
14	STENA NORDICA	24206t	01	25.7k	169.8m	405P	375C	90L	BA2	UK	9215505
15	STENA SAGA	33750t	81	22.0k	166.1m	2000P	510C	76T	BA	SE	7911545
16	STENA SCANDINAVICA	55050t	03	22.0k	240.1m	900P	-	260L	BA	SE	9235517
17	STENA SPIRIT	39169t	88	20.0k	175.4m	2400P	550C	120T	BAS2	BS	7907661
18	STENA VINGA	13906t	05	18.5k	124.9m	400P	342C	106T	A	DK	9323699
19	STENA VISION	39178t	87	20.0k	175.4m	2400P	550C	120T	BAS2	SE	7907659
20	URD	13144t	81	17.5k	171.0m	186P	-	104T	AS	DK	7826855

BORE BAY Built as the HERALDEN by Umoe Sterkoder AS, Kristiansund, Norway for *Rederi AB Engship* of Finland and chartered to *Transfennica*. In 2006 *Rederi AB Engship* was taken over by *Rettig Group Bore*. In 2007 converted at COSCO Shipyard, Nantong, China to add a garage on top of the weather deck, renamed AUTO BAY and placed on long-term charter to *UECC*. Generally used on the Baltic or Iberian services. In 2017 converted back to conventional ro-ro format by Fayard, Odense, Denmark and renamed the BORE BAY. Chartered to *Grandi Navi Veloci (GNV)*.of Italy. In February 2018 chartered to *Transfennica*. In April 2018 chartered to *Stena Line* to operate between, Gdynia and Nynäshamn.

MECKLENBURG-VORPOMMERN Train/vehicle ferry built by Schichau Seebeckwerft, Bremerhaven, Germany for *DFO* for the Rostock - Trelleborg service. During Winter 2002/03 modified to increase freight capacity and reduce passenger capacity. In September 2012 sold to *Stena Line*.

SASSNITZ Train/vehicle ferry built by Danyard A/S, Frederikshavn, Denmark for *Deutsche Reichsbahn*. In 1993 ownership transferred to *DFO*. Used on the Sassnitz - Trelleborg service. In September 2012 sold to *Stena Line*. From September 2018 operates twice weekly from Trelleborg to Rostock.

SCOTTISH VIKING Built by CN Visentini, Porto Viro, Italy for *Epic Shipping* of the UK and chartered to *Norfolkline*. Operated between Zeebrugge and Rosyth until December 2010. In January 2010 chartered to *Scandlines* and placed on the Nynäshamn - Ventspils service. In September 2012 charter transferred to *Stena Line*.

SKÅNE Train/vehicle ferry built by Astilleros Españoles, Cadiz, Spain for an American trust and chartered to *Scandlines*. She is used on the Trelleborg - Rostock service.

STENA BALTICA Built as the COTENTIN by STX Finland, Helsinki, Finland for *Brittany Ferries*. Used on freight service from Poole to Cherbourg and Santander. In March 2013 replaced by

SECTION 7 – NORTHERN EUROPE

Stena Germanica *(Stena Line)*

Stena Spirit *(Stena Line)*

the BARFLEUR (operating to Cherbourg only). During summer 2013 operated twice weekly from Poole to Bilbao and Santander. In October 2013 sold to *Stena RoRo* and renamed the STENA BALTICA. In November 2013 chartered to *Stena Line* and replaced the STENA ALEGRA on the Karlskrona - Gdynia route.

STENA CARISMA Westamarin HSS 900 craft built at Kristiansand, Norway for *Stena Line* for the Göteborg - Frederikshavn service. Work on a sister vessel, approximately 30% completed, was ceased. She has not operated since 2013.

STENA DANICA Built by Chantiers du Nord et de la Méditerranée, Dunkerque, France for *Stena Line* for the Göteborg - Frederikshavn service.

STENA FLAVIA Built by CN Visentini, Porto Viro, Italy for *Epic Shipping* of the UK. Launched as the WATLING STREET. On delivery, chartered to *ISCOMAR* of Spain and renamed the PILAR DEL MAR. In 2009 laid up until February 2010 when she was chartered to *Acciona Trasmediterranea* of Spain and operated between Barcelona and Tangiers. Later that month, chartered to *T-Link* and resumed the name WATLING STREET. In May 2011 chartered to *Scandlines* and placed on the Travemünde - Ventspils service. In April 2012, sold to *Stena RoRo*; she continued to be chartered to *Scandlines*. In September 2012 charter transferred to *Stena Line*. In April 2013 renamed the STENA FLAVIA. She now operates one weekly roundtrip from Nynäshamn to Liepaja, two roundtrips to Nynäshamn to Ventspils and once weekly Ventspils - Travemünde.

STENA GERMANICA Ro-pax ferry built as the STENA HOLLANDICA by Astilleros Españoles, Cadiz, Spain for *Stena RoRo* and chartered to *Stena Line BV* to operate between Hoek van Holland and Harwich. In 2007 lengthened by 50m at Lloyd Werft, Bremerhaven and passenger capacity increased to 900. Between May and August 2010 refurbished at Gdańsk and had an 100 additional cabins added. At the end of August entered service on the Göteborg - Kiel route, renamed the STENA GERMANICA III. In September, after the previous STENA GERMANICA had been renamed the STENA VISION, she was renamed the STENA GERMANICA.

STENA GOTHICA Built as the LUCKY RIDER by Nuovi Cantieri Apuania S.P.A., Marina De Carrara, Italy, a ro-ro freight ferry, for *Delpa Maritime* of Greece. In 1985 she was acquired by *Stena Line* and renamed the STENA DRIVER. Later that year she was acquired by *Sealink British Ferries* and renamed the SEAFREIGHT FREEWAY to operate freight-only services between Dover and Dunkerque. In 1988 she was sold to *SOMAT* of Bulgaria for use on *Medlink* services in the Mediterranean and renamed the SERDICA. In 1990 she was sold and renamed the NORTHERN HUNTER. In 1991 she was sold to *Blæsbjerg* of Denmark, renamed the ARKA MARINE and chartered to *DSB*. She was then converted into a ro-pax vessel, renamed the ASK and introduced onto the Århus - Kalundborg service. Purchased by *Scandlines A/S* of Denmark in 1997. In 1999 she was, after some modification, transferred to *Scandlines Euroseabridge* and placed on the Travemünde - Klaipėda route. In 2000 she was transferred to the Rostock - Liepaja route. Lengthened by 20m in 2001 and, in late 2001, chartered to *Nordö Link* to operate between Travemünde and Malmö. In late 2002 replaced by the FINNARROW and returned to *Scandlines*. She was transferred to the Rostock - Trelleborg route whilst the MECKLENBURG-VORPOMMERN was being rebuilt. She was then transferred to the Kiel - Klaipėda route. In 2003 chartered to *Scandlines AB* to operate on the Trelleborg - Travemünde route. In April 2005 the charter ended and she returned to *Scandlines AG*. Initially she was due to replace the FELLOW on the Nynäshamn – Ventspils route during her annual refit. In Autumn 2005 moved to the Rostock - Ventspils route. In January 2009 moved to the Nynäshamn – Ventspils route. In January 2011 moved to the Travemünde - Liepaja route. In May 2011 laid up. In November introduced as second vessel. In September 2012 sold to *Stena Line*. In September 2015 moved to the Göteborg - Frederikshavn freight service and renamed the STENA GOTHICA. In September to be 2018 moved to the Travemünde - Liepaja route.

STENA JUTLANDICA Train/vehicle 'ro-pax' vessel built by Van der Giessen-de Noord, Krimpen aan den IJssel, Rotterdam, The Netherlands for *Stena Line* to operate between Göteborg and

SECTION 7 – NORTHERN EUROPE

Frederikshavn. She was launched as the STENA JUTLANDICA III and renamed on entry into service.

STENA NAUTICA Built as the NIELS KLIM by Nakskov Skibsværft A/S, Nakskov, Denmark for *DSB (Danish State Railways)* for their service between Århus (Jylland) and Kalundborg (Sjælland). In 1990 she was purchased by *Stena Rederi* of Sweden and renamed the STENA NAUTICA. In 1992 she was chartered to *B&I Line*, renamed the ISLE OF INNISFREE and introduced onto the Rosslare - Pembroke Dock service, replacing the MUNSTER (8093t, 1970). In 1993 she was transferred to the Dublin - Holyhead service. In early 1995 she was chartered to *Lion Ferry*. She was renamed the LION KING. In 1996 she was replaced by a new LION KING and renamed the STENA NAUTICA. During Summer 1996 she was chartered to *Transmediterranea* of Spain but returned to *Stena RoRo* in the autumn and remained laid up during 1997. In December 1997 she was chartered to *Stena Line* and placed on the Halmstad - Grenaa route. This route ended on 31st January 1999 and she was transferred to the Varberg - Grenaa route. During Winter 2001/02 she was rebuilt to heighten the upper vehicle deck and allow separate loading of vehicle decks; passenger capacity was reduced. On 16th February 2004 she was hit by the coaster JOANNA and holed. Returned to service at the end of May 2004 after repairs at Göteborg and Gdańsk.

STENA NORDICA Built as the EUROPEAN AMBASSADOR by Mitsubishi Heavy Industries, Shimonoseki, Japan for *P&O Irish Sea* for their Liverpool - Dublin service. Service transferred to from Liverpool to Mostyn in November 2001. Also operated between Dublin and Cherbourg once a week. In 2004 the Mostyn route closed and she was sold to *Stena RoRo*. Chartered to *Stena Line* to operate between Karlskrona and Gdynia and renamed the STENA NORDICA. In 2008 transferred to the Holyhead - Dublin service. In February 2015 replaced by the STENA SUPERFAST X and chartered to *DFDS Seaways*. She was renamed the MALO SEAWAYS and, in April 2015, placed on the Dover - Calais route. Withdrawn from traffic in February 2016 and laid up. In June 2016 charter ended. Renamed the STENA NORDICA and chartered to *GNV* of Italy to operate between Sicily and the Italian mainland. In January 2017 chartered to *Stena Line* and performed refit relief duties in the Irish Sea. In April placed on the Travemünde - Liepāja service. In October 2018 to be moved back to the Karlskrona - Gdynia route.

STENA SAGA Built as the SILVIA REGINA by Oy Wärtsilä Ab, Turku, Finland for *Stockholms Rederi AB Svea* of Sweden. She was registered with subsidiary company *Svea Line* of Turku, Finland and was used on *Silja Line* services between Stockholm and Helsinki. In 1981 she was sold to *Johnson Line* and in 1984 sold to a Finnish Bank and chartered back. In 1990 she was purchased by *Stena RoRo* of Sweden for delivery in 1991. In 1991 she was renamed the STENA BRITANNICA and took up service on the Hoek van Holland - Harwich service for Dutch subsidiary *Stena Line BV*, operating with a British crew. In 1994 she was transferred to the Oslo - Frederikshavn route and renamed the STENA SAGA. During Winter 2002/03 rebuilt to increase passenger capacity by 200.

STENA SCANDINAVICA Ro-pax vessel built by Hyundai Heavy Industries, Ulsan, South Korea, for *Stena RoRo*. Launched and delivered in January 2003 as the STENA BRITANNICA II. Chartered to *Stena Line* for use on the Hoek van Holland - Harwich service, replacing the 2000-built STENA BRITANNICA, now the FINNFELLOW of *FinnLink*. In March 2003 renamed the STENA BRITANNICA. In 2007 lengthened at Lloyd Werft, Bremerhaven. In September 2010 renamed the BRITANNICA. Between October 2010 and April 2011 refurbished and had 100 additional cabins added at Gdańsk. In April 2011 renamed the STENA SCANDINAVICA IV and entered service on the Göteborg - Kiel route. In May, after the previous STENA SCANDINAVICA had been renamed the STENA SPIRIT, she was renamed the STENA SCANDINAVICA.

STENA SPIRIT Built as the STENA SCANDINAVICA by Stocznia i Komuni Paryski, Gdynia, Poland for *Stena Line* for the Göteborg - Kiel service (launched as the STENA GERMANICA and names swapped with sister vessel before delivery). There were originally intended to be four vessels. Only two were delivered to *Stena Line*. The third (due to be called the STENA POLONICA) was sold by the builders as an unfinished hull to *Fred. Olsen Lines* of Norway and then resold to *ANEK* of Greece who had her completed at Perama and delivered as EL

Stena Danica *(John Bryant)*

Urd *(Nick Widdows)*

VENIZELOS for service between Greece and Italy. The fourth hull (due to be called the STENA BALTICA) was sold to *A Lelakis* of Greece and was to be rebuilt as a cruise ship to be called REGENT SKY; however, the project was never completed. The hull was broken up in 2004. During the summer period on some days, the vessel arriving in Göteborg overnight from Kiel operates a round trip to Frederikshavn before departing for Kiel the following evening. During Winter 1998/99 she was modified to increase freight capacity and reduce the number of cabins. In April 2011 replaced by the former STENA BRITANNICA (renamed the STENA SCANDINAVICA IV) and entered CityVarvet in Göteborg for refurbishment. In June 2011 she was renamed the STENA SPIRIT and, in July 2011, transferred to the Karlskrona - Gydnia route.

STENA VINGA Built as the HAMMERODDE by Merwede Shipyard, Hardinxveld-Giessendam, The Netherlands for *Bornholmstrafikken*. In Winter 2010 an additional vehicle deck was added for freight and some additional cabins. In November 2017 sold to *Stena RoRo* and chartered back. In September 2018 to be delivered to *Stena Line*, renamed the STENA VINGA and placed on the Göteborg - Frederikshaven service, replacing the STENA GOTHICA.

STENA VISION Built as the STENA GERMANICA by Stocznia im Lenina, Gdańsk, Poland for *Stena Line* for the Göteborg - Kiel service. During the summer period on some days, the vessel arriving in Göteborg overnight from Kiel operates a round trip to Frederikshavn before departing for Kiel the following evening. During Winter 1998/99 modified to increase freight capacity and reduce the number of cabins. In August 2010 replaced by the former STENA HOLLANDICA (renamed the STENA GERMANICA III initially) and entered CityVarvet in Göteborg for refurbishment. In September she was renamed the STENA VISION and, in November, transferred to the Karlskrona - Gydnia route.

URD Built as the EASY RIDER by Nouvi Cantieri Aquania SpA, Venice, Italy, a ro-ro freight ferry, for *Delpa Maritime* of Greece and used on Mediterranean services. In 1985 she was acquired by *Sealink British Ferries* and renamed the SEAFREIGHT HIGHWAY to operate a freight-only service between Dover and Dunkerque. In 1988 she was sold to *SOMAT* of Bulgaria for use on *Medlink* services in the Mediterranean and renamed the BOYANA. In 1990 she was sold to *Blæsbjerg* of Denmark, renamed the AKTIV MARINE and chartered to *DSB*. In 1991 she was converted into a ro-pax vessel, renamed the URD and introduced onto the Århus - Kalundborg service. Purchased by *Scandlines* in 1997. Withdrawn at the end of May 1999 and, after modification, transferred to the *Balticum Seaways* (later *Scandlines Balticum Seaways*) Århus - Aabenraa - Klaipėda route. In 2001 lengthened and moved to the Rostock - Liepaja route. In Autumn 2005 this route became Rostock - Ventspils. Withdrawn from Rostock - Ventspils in November 2009. Vessel inaugurated new service Travemünde - Ventspils in January 2010. Replaced by the WATLING STREET in May 2011 and moved to the Travemünde - Liepaja route. In October 2012 sold to *Sol Dru A/S* (a subsidiary of *Swedish Orient Line*) and chartered to *Stena Line*. In August 2013 sold to *Stena Line*.

Note The Stena 'E-flexers' under construction in Nanjing are all listed in Section 1 as the first six will all be deployed in UK waters (three for Stena Line, three on charter). A further two have been ordered but their deployment is currently unknown and they may operate in the Baltic.

STRANDFARASKIP LANDSINS

THE COMPANY *Strandfaraskip Landsins* is owned by the Faroe Islands Government.

ADDRESS Sjógøta 5, Postboks 30, 810 Tvøroyri, Faroe Islands.

TELEPHONE Administration & Reservations +298 34 30 00.

FAX Administration & Reservations +298 34 30 01.

INTERNET Email fyrisitingssl.fo **Website** www.ssl.fo *(Faroese)*

ROUTES OPERATED Passenger and Car Ferries Tórshavn (Streymoy) - Tvøroyri (Suduroy) (1 hr 50 mins; *SMYRIL*; up to 3 per day), Klaksvík - Sydradali (20 min; *SAM*; up to 6 per day), Skopun – Gamlarætt (30 min; *TEISTIN*; up to 9 per day). **Passenger-only Ferries**

Sørvágur - Mykines (1 hr 15 mins; **JÒSUP (chartered ship)**; up to 3 per day, May to August only), Hvannasund - Svínoy (40 mins) - Kirkja (20 mins) - Hattarvik (10 mins) - Svínoy (30 mins; **RITAN**; up to 4 per day), Sandur - Skúvoy (35 mins; **SILDBERIN**; up to 5 per day), Tórshavn - Nólsoy (25 mins; **TERNAN**; up to 5 per day.

1p	RITAN	81t	71	10.5k	22.1m	125P	0C	0L	-	F0	
2	SAM	217t	75	9.7k	30.2m	115P	17C	-	A	F0	7602168
3p	SILDBERIN	34t	79	7.5k	11.2m	30P	0C	0L	-	F0	
4	SMYRIL	12670t	05	21.0k	135.0m	976P	200C	32L	A	F0	9275218
5p	SÚLAN	11t	87	-	12.0m	40P	0C	0L	-	F0	
6	TEISTIN	1260t	01	11.0k	45.0m	288P	33C	2L	BA	F0	9226102
7	TERNAN	927t	80	12.0k	39.7m	319P	0C	0L	BA	F0	7947154

RITAN Built by Monnickenda, Volendam, The Netherlands. Used on the Hvannasund – Svínoy-Kirkja- Hattarvik service.

SAM Built by Blaalid Slip & Mek Verksted, Raudeberg, Norway. Used on the Klaksvik - Syòradali route and the Leirvik - Syòradali route.

SILDBERIN Built at Tvøroyri, Faroe Islands. Used on the Sandur - Skúvoy route.

SMYRIL Built by IZAR, San Fernando, Spain for *Strandfaraskip Landsins*. Operates on the Tórshavn – Tvøroyri service.

SÚLAN Built by Faaborg Værft A/S, Faaborg, Denmark. Used on the Sørvágur - Mykines service. Now conveys freight to Skúvoy.

TEISTIN Built by P/F Skipasmidjan a Skala, Skala, Faroe Islands for *Strandfaraskip Landsins*. Used on the Skopun – Gamlarætt service.

TERNAN Built by Tórshavnar Skipasmidja P/f, Tórshavn, Faroe Islands for *Strandfaraskip Landsins*. Used on the Tórshavn – Nólsoy service.

SYLTFÄHRE

THE COMPANY Syltfähre (*Syltfærge* in Danish) is the trading name of *Römö-Sylt Linie GmbH & Co. KG*, a German private sector company, a subsidiary of *FRS (Förde Reederei Seetouristik)* of Flensburg.

MANAGEMENT Managing Director RSL Birte Dettmers, **CEO Römö-Sylt Linie** Christian Baumberger, Götz Becker, Jan Kruse.

ADDRESS Germany Am Fähranleger 3, 25992 List, Germany, **Denmark** Kilebryggen, 6792 Rømø, Denmark.

TELEPHONE Administration +49 (0)461 864 0, **Reservations Germany** +49 (0)461 864 601, **Denmark** +49 461 864 601.

INTERNET Email info@rsl.de **Website** www.syltfaehre.de *(Danish, English, German)*

ROUTE OPERATED List auf Sylt (Sylt, Germany) - Havneby (Rømø, Denmark) (approx. 40 mins; **SYLTEXPRESS**; variable - approx two-hourly). **Note**: The Danish island of Rømø is linked to the Danish mainland by a toll-free road causeway; the German island of Sylt is linked to the German mainland by a rail-only causeway on which cars are conveyed on shuttle wagons.

| 1 | SYLTEXPRESS | 3650t | 05 | 16.0k | 88.2m | 600P | 80C | 10L | BA | CY | 9321823 |

SYLTEXPRESS Built by Fiskerstrand Verft A/S, Aalesund, Norway for *Römö-Sylt Linie*.

Ferries 2019

TALLINK/SILJA LINE

THE COMPANY *AS Tallink Grupp* is an Estonian private sector company. *Tallink Silja Oy* is a Finnish subsidiary, *Tallink Silja AB* is a Swedish subsidiary.

MANAGEMENT *AS Tallink Grupp:* Chairman of Management Board Janek Stalmeister, *Tallink Silja Oy* **Managing Director** Margus Schults, *Tallink Silja AB* **Managing Director** Marcus Risberg.

ADDRESSES *AS Tallink Grupp* Sadama 5/7, Tallinn 10111, Estonia, *Tallink Silja Oy* P.O. Box 100, 00181 Helsinki, Finland, *Tallink Silja AB* Box 27295, 10253 Stockholm, Sweden.

TELEPHONE *AS Tallink Grupp* +372 (0)640 9800, *Tallink Silja Oy* **Administration** +358 (0)9 18041, **Reservations** +358 (0)600 15700, *Tallink Silja AB* **Administration** +46 (0)8 6663300, **Reservations** +46 (0)8 222140, **Reservations Germany** +49 (0)40 547 541 222.

FAX *AS Tallink Grupp* Administration + 372 (0)640 9810, *Tallink Silja Oy* **Administration** +358 (0)9 180 4633, *Tallink Silja AB* **Administration** +46 (0) 8 663400.

INTERNETEmail info@tallink.ee **Websites** www.tallinksilja.com *(17 languages, see the internet page)*, www.tallink.com (corporate site) *(English)*

INTERNET Email info@tallink.ee **Websites** www.tallinksilja.com *(English, Danish, Estonian, Finnish, German, Latvia, Norwegian, Swedish, Russian)*, www.tallink.com (corporate site)

ROUTES OPERATED Tallink branded services *Passenger Ferries* Helsinki - Tallinn: **Shuttle** (2 hrs; **MEGASTAR, STAR**; up to 6 per day), **Cruise Ferries** (3 hrs 30 - 4hrs 30 mins; **SILJA EUROPA**; normally 2 per day), Stockholm - Mariehamn (Åland) - Tallinn (14 hrs; **BALTIC QUEEN, VICTORIA I**; daily), Stockholm - Riga (Latvia) (16 hrs; **ISABELLE, ROMANTIKA**; daily), *Freight-only Ferries* Kapellskär - Paldiski (9 hrs - 11 hrs; **REGAL STAR**; alternate days (round trip on Sunday)), Helsinki (Vuosaari) - Tallinn (Muuga) (3 hrs 30 mins; **SEA WIND**; 2 per day).

Silja Line branded services Helsinki (Finland) - Mariehamn (Åland) - Stockholm (Sweden) (16 hrs; **SILJA SERENADE, SILJA SYMPHONY**; 1 per day), Turku (Finland) - Mariehamn (Åland) (day)/Långnäs (Åland) (night) - Stockholm (11 hrs; **BALTIC PRINCESS, GALAXY**; 2 per day).

1	ATLANTIC VISION	30285t	02	27.9k	203.3m	728P	695C	110L	BA2	CA	9211509
2	BALTIC PRINCESS	48300t	08	24.5k	212.0m	2800P	300C	82T	BA	FI	9354284
3	BALTIC QUEEN	48300t	09	24.5k	212.0m	2800P	300C	82T	BA	EE	9443255
4	GALAXY	48915t	06	22.0k	212.0m	2800P	300C	82T	BA	SE	9333694
5	ISABELLE	35154t	89	21.5k	170.9m	2420P	364C	30T	BA	LV	8700723
6	MEGASTAR	49000t	16	27.0k	212m	2800P	-	-	BA2	EE	9773064
7F	REGAL STAR	15281t	00	17.5k	156.6m	100P	-	120T	A	EE	9087116
8	ROMANTIKA	40803t	02	22.0k	193.8m	2178P	300C	82T	BA	EE	9237589
9F	SEA WIND	15879t	72	17.5k	154.4m	260P	55C	88Tr	BAS	EE	7128332
10	SILJA EUROPA	59912t	93	21.5k	201.8m	3000P	400C	68T	BA	EE	8919805
11	SILJA SERENADE	58376t	90	21.0k	203.0m	2800P	410C	70T	BA	FI	8715259
12	SILJA SYMPHONY	58377t	91	21.0k	203.0m	2800P	410C	70T	BA	SE	8803769
13	STAR	36249t	07	27.5k	185.0m	1900P	450C	120L	BA2	EE	9364722
14	VICTORIA I	40975t	04	22.0k	193.8m	2500P	300C	823T	BA	EE	9281281

ATLANTIC VISION Built as the SUPERFAST IX by Howaldtswerke Deutsche Werft AG, Kiel, Germany for *Attica Enterprises* for use by *Superfast Ferries*. She operated between Rostock and Södertälje from January until April 2002. In May 2002 she began operating between Rosyth and Zeebrugge (with the SUPERFAST X (now the STENA SUPERFAST X)). In 2004 fitted with additional cabins and conference/seating areas. In 2005 transferred to the Rostock – Hanko (later Helsinki) route. In 2006 sold to *Tallink*. In October 2008 chartered to *Marine Atlantic* of Canada to operate on the North Sydney-Port aux Basques service and renamed the ATLANTIC VISION.

Silja Serenade *(Miles Cowsill)*

Star *(Miles Cowsill)*

Ferries 2019

BALTIC PRINCESS Built by Aker Yards, Helsinki. A large part of the hull was built at St Nazaire, France. In August 2008 replaced the GALAXY on the Tallinn - Helsinki route. In February 2013 transferred to the Stockholm - Turku service.

BALTIC QUEEN Built by STX Europe, Rauma, Finland. Currently operates between Stockholm and Tallinn.

GALAXY Built by Aker Yards, Rauma, Finland to operate as a cruise ferry on the Tallinn - Helsinki route. In July 2008 transferred to the Stockholm - Turku route and rebranded as a *Silja Line* vessel.

ISABELLE Built as the ISABELLA by Brodogradevna Industrija, Split, Yugoslavia for *SF Line*. Used on the *Viking Line* Stockholm - Naantali service until 1992 when she was switched to operating 24-hour cruises from Helsinki and in 1995 she was transferred to the Stockholm - Helsinki route. During 1996 she additionally operated day cruises to Muuga in Estonia during the 'layover' period in Helsinki. In 1997 she was transferred to the Stockholm - Turku route. in January 2013 she was replaced by the VIKING GRACE. After covering for the AMORELLA during her refit period she was laid up. In April 2013 sold to *Hansa Link Limited*, a subsidiary of *AS Tallink Grupp* and renamed the ISABELLE. In May placed on the Stockholm - Riga service, replacing the SILJA FESTIVAL.

MEGASTAR Built by Meyer Turku, Turku, Finland to operate on the Tallinn - Helsinki Shuttle. She is LNG/diesel dual powered. An option on a second vessel was allowed to lapse in March 2016.

REGAL STAR Partly built by Sudostroitelnyy Zavod Severnaya Verf, St Petersburg. Work started in 1993 (as a deep-sea ro-ro) but was never completed. In 1999 the vessel was purchased, taken to Palumba SpA, Naples and completed as a short-sea ro-ro with accommodation for 80 drivers. In 2000 she was delivered to *MCL* of Italy and placed on a route between Savona and Catania. In September of that year she was chartered to *Grimaldi Ferries* and operated on a route Salerno – Palermo – Valencia. In late 2003 she was sold to *Hansatee Shipping* of Estonia and, in 2004, placed on the Kapellskär – Paldiski route, replacing the KAPELLA. From February 2006 she was transferred to the Helsinki – Tallinn service, replacing the KAPELLA due to the hard ice conditions. She continued in this service for the summer, but the returned to the Paldiski – Kapellskär service. In June 2010 moved to the *SeaWind Line* Stockholm – Turku service for the summer seasons and returned to the Kapellskär - Paldiski route in the autumn.

ROMANTIKA Built by Aker Finnyards, Rauma, Finland for *Tallink Grupp* to operate for *Tallink* between Tallinn and Helsinki. Currently operating between Stockholm and Riga.

SEA WIND Train/vehicle ferry built as the SVEALAND by Helsingørs Skipsværft, Helsingør, Denmark for *Stockholms Rederi AB Svea* and used on the *Trave Line* Helsingborg (Sweden) - København (Tuborg Havn) - Travemünde freight service. In 1981 she was sold to *TT-Saga Line* and operated between Travemünde and Malmö. In 1984 she was rebuilt to increase capacity and renamed the SAGA WIND. In 1989 she was acquired by *Silja Line* subsidiary *SeaWind Line*, renamed the SEA WIND and inaugurated a combined rail freight, trailer and lower-priced passenger service between Stockholm and Turku. This route later became freight-only. In January 2015 transferred to the Tallinn - Helsinki freight service.

SILJA EUROPA Built by Jos L Meyer, Papenburg, Germany. Ordered by *Rederi AB Slite* of Sweden for *Viking Line* service between Stockholm and Helsinki and due to be called EUROPA. In 1993, shortly before delivery was due, *Rederi AB Slite* went into liquidation and the order was cancelled. A charter agreement with her builders was then signed by *Silja Line* and she was introduced onto the Stockholm - Helsinki route as SILJA EUROPA. In early 1995 she was transferred to the Stockholm - Turku service. In January 2013 she was transferred to the Helsinki - Tallinn route. In August 2014 chartered to an Australian company as an accommodation vessel. In March 2016 joined the BALTIC PRINCESS as second vessel on the Helsinki - Tallinn 'Cruise' service. In December 2016 resumed the role of sole cruise vessel on the route.

SILJA SERENADE, SILJA SYMPHONY Built by Masa-Yards Oy, Turku, Finland for *Silja Line* for the Stockholm - Helsinki service. In 1993, SILJA SERENADE was transferred to the Stockholm - Turku service but in early 1995 she was transferred back to the Helsinki route.

STAR Built by Aker Yards, Helsinki, Finland for *Tallink* to operate on the Tallinn - Helsinki route. In January 2017 modified at Vene Balti Shipyard, Tallinn to allow for two deck loading.

VICTORIA I Built by Aker Finnyards, Rauma, Finland for *Tallink*. Operates between Tallinn and Stockholm.

TESO

THE COMPANY *TESO (Texels Eigen Stoomboot Onderneming)* is a Dutch private company, with most shares owned by inhabitants of Texel.

MANAGEMENT Managing Director Cees de Waal.

ADDRESS Pontweg 1, 1797 SN Den Hoorn, The Netherlands.

TELEPHONE Administration +31 (0)222 36 96 00, **Reservations** Not applicable.

FAX Administration +31 (0)222 36 96 59.

INTERNET Email info@teso.nl **Website** www.teso.nl *(Dutch, English, German)*

ROUTE OPERATED Den Helder (The Netherlands) - Texel (Dutch Frisian Islands) (20 minutes; *DOKTER WAGEMAKER, TEXELSTROOM*; hourly).

1	DOKTER WAGEMAKER	13256t	05	15.6k	130.0m	1750P	320C	44L	BA2	NL	9294070
2	SCHULPENGAT	8311t	90	13.6k	110.4m	1750P	156C	25L	BA2	NL	8802313
3	TEXELSTROOM	16400t	16	15.0k	135.4m	1750P	350C	44L	BA2	NL	9741918

DOKTER WAGEMAKER Built at Galatz, Romania (hull and superstructure) and Royal Schelde, Vlissingen (fitting out) for *TESO*.

SCHULPENGAT Built by Verolme Scheepswerf Heusden BV, Heusden, The Netherlands for *TESO*. Now reserve vessel.

TEXELSTROOM Built by La Naval Shipyard, Sestao, Spain to replace the SCHULPENGAT in June 2016.

TT-LINE

THE COMPANY *TT-Line GmbH & Co KG* is a German private sector company.

MANAGEMENT Managing Directors Hanns Heinrich Conzen & Jens Aurel Scharner, **Sales Manager** Dirk Lifke.

ADDRESS Zum Hafenplatz 1, 23570, Travemünde, Germany.

TELEPHONE +49 (0)4502 801 81.

INTERNET Email info@ttline.com **Website** www.ttline.com *(English, German, Polish, Swedish)*

ROUTES OPERATED *Passenger Ferries* Travemünde (Germany) - Trelleborg (Sweden) (8 hrs 30 mins/9 hrs 30 mins; *NILS HOLGERSSON, PETER PAN*; 2 per day). *Ro-pax Ferries* Travemünde (Germany) - Trelleborg (Sweden) (7 hrs 30 mins/8 hrs 15 mins; *ROBIN HOOD*; 1 per day), Rostock (Germany) - Trelleborg (Sweden) (5 hrs 30 mins/6 hrs 30 mins/7 hrs 30 mins; *HUCKLEBERRY FINN, TOM SAWYER*; 3 per day, Świnoujście (Poland) - Trelleborg (Sweden) (7 hrs; *NILS DACKE*; 1 per day), Świnoujście (Poland) - Rønne (Bornholm, Denmark) (5 hrs (day), 6 hrs 30 mins (night); *NILS DACKE*; 1 per week) (summer only), Trelleborg - Klaipėda (Lithuania) (15 hrs; *ROBIN HOOD, TOM SAWYER*, 1 per week).

1	HUCKLEBERRY FINN	26391t	88	18.0k	177.2m	400P	280C	121T	BAS2	SE	8618358
2	NILS DACKE	26796t	95	18.5k	179.7m	300P	-	157T	BA	CY	9087465
3	NILS HOLGERSSON	36468t	01	18.0k	190.8m	744P	-	171T	BAS2	DE	9217230

Huckleberry Finn *(Richard Kirkman)*

Skania *(Matthew Punter)*

4	PETER PAN	44245t	01	18.0k	220.0m	744P	-	210T	BAS2	SE	9217242
5	ROBIN HOOD	26790t	95	18.5k	179.7m	317P	-	157T	BA	DE	9087477
6	TOM SAWYER	26478t	89	18.0k	177.2m	400P	280C	121T	BAS2	DE	8703232

HUCKLEBERRY FINN Built as the NILS DACKE by Schichau Seebeckwerft AG, Bremerhaven, Germany, as a ro-pax vessel. During Summer 1993 rebuilt to transform her into a passenger/car ferry and renamed the PETER PAN, replacing a similarly named vessel (31356t, 1986). On arrival of the new PETER PAN in Autumn 2001 she was renamed the PETER PAN IV. She was then converted back to ro-pax format, renamed the HUCKLEBERRY FINN and, in early 2002, transferred to the Rostock -Trelleborg route.

NILS DACKE, Ro-pax vessels built as the ROBIN HOOD by Finnyards, Rauma, Finland. She operated on the Travemünde - Trelleborg and Travemünde - Helsingborg routes. In December 2014 she was renamed the NILS DACKE and transferred to Cypriot registry. Moved to the Trelleborg - Świnoujście route.

NILS HOLGERSSON, PETER PAN Built by SSW Fähr und Spezialschiffbau GmbH, Bremerhaven, Germany for the Travemünde - Trelleborg route. In January and February 2018 the PETER PAN was lengthened at MWB Motorenwerke Bremerhaven AG, Germany by 30 metres.

TOM SAWYER Built as the ROBIN HOOD by Schichau Seebeckwerft AG, Bremerhaven, Germany, as a ro-pax vessel. During Winter 1992/93 rebuilt to transform her into a passenger/car ferry and renamed the NILS HOLGERSSON, replacing a similarly named vessel (31395t, 1987) which had been sold to *Brittany Ferries* and renamed the VAL DE LOIRE. In 2001 converted back to ro-pax format and renamed the TOM SAWYER. Transferred to the Rostock - Trelleborg route.

ROBIN HOOD Ro-pax vessels built as the NILS DACKE, by Finnyards, Rauma, Finland. She operated on the Travemünde - Trelleborg and Travemünde - Helsingborg routes. In January 2014, she was transferred to a new Trelleborg - Świnoujście service and changed to Polish registry. In December 2014 she was renamed the ROBIN HOOD and transferred German Registry. Moved to the Travemünde - Trelleborg route.

Under Construction

7	NEWBUILDING 1	-	21	-	-	650P	-	320T	BAS2	-	-
8	NEWBUILDING 2	-	21	-	-	650P	-	320T	BAS2	-	-

NEWBUILDING1, NEWBUILDING 2 Under construction by the Jinling Shipyard, China. It is likely that they will replace the HUCKLEBERRY FINN and TOM SAWYER.

UNITY LINE

THE COMPANY *Unity Line* is a Polish company owned by *Polish Steamship Company (Polsteam)*. The operator manages seven ferries on two routes: Świnoujście – Ystad and Świnoujście – Trelleborg. Three ships are owned by *Euroafrica Shipping* which was previously a partner in the company; the ships continue to be operationally managed by *Unity Line*.

MANAGEMENT Managing Director Jarosław Kotarski.

ADDRESS Plac Rodła 8, 70-419 Szczecin, Poland.

TELEPHONE Administration& Reservations +48 (0)91 88 02 909.

FAX Administration +48 91 35 95 885.

INTERNET Email rezerwacje@unityline.pl **Website** www.unityline.pl *(Polish, Swedish)*

ROUTES OPERATED Passenger Service Świnoujście (Poland) - Ystad (Sweden) (6 hrs 30 mins (day), 9 hrs (night); *POLONIA, SKANIA*; 2 per day). **Freight Services** Świnoujście (Poland) - Ystad (Sweden) (8 hrs (day), 9 hrs (night); *JAN ŚNIADECKI, KOPERNIK*; 2 per day), Świnoujście (Poland) - Trelleborg (Sweden) (6 hrs 30 mins (day), 9 hrs (night); *COPERNICUS, GALILEUSZ, GRYF, WOLIN*; 4 per day).

1F+	COPERNICUS	14398t	96	19.0k	150.4m	50P	-	122T	A	CY	9031703

2F+	GALILEUSZ	15848t	92	17.0k	150.4m	160P	-	115L	A		CY	9019078
3F+	GRYF	18653t	90	16.0k	158.0m	180P	-	125L	BA	BS	8818300
4F+	JAN ŚNIADECKI	14417t	88	17.0k	155.1m	57P	-	70Lr	SA2	CY	8604711
5F+	KOPERNIK	13788t	77	18.0k	160.1m	360P	-	60Lr	SA2	CY	7527887
6	POLONIA	29875t	95	17.2k	169.9m	920P	440C	145Lr	SA2	BS	9108350
7	SKANIA	23933t	95	22.5k	173.7m	1400P	430C	140L	BA	BS	9086588
8F+	WOLIN	22874t	86	17.5k	188.9m	370P	-	110Lr	SA	BS	8420842

COPERNICUS Built as the PUGLIA by Fincantieri-Cantieri Navali Italiani SpA, Ancona, Italy for *Tirrenia di Navigazione SpA*. of Italy. In 2016 rebranded as *Moby Cargo*. In December 2017 sold to *Euroafrica Shipping*, renamed the COPERNICUS and, in August 2018, placed on the Świnoujście - Trelleborg route.

GALILEUSZ Built as the VIA TIRRENO by Van der Giessen-de Noord, Krimpen aan den IJssel, The Netherlands for *Viamare di Navigazione SpA* of Italy. Initially operated between Voltri and Termini Imerese. In 1998 transferred to the Génova - Termini Imerese route and in 2001 to the Génova - Palermo route. In 2006 sold to *Euroafrica Shipping*, renamed the GALILEUSZ and in November introduced onto the *Unity Line* Świnoujście - Ystad service. In February 2007 transferred to the new Świnoujście - Trelleborg route.

GRYF Built as the KAPTAN BURHANETTIN ISIM by Fosen Mekaniske Verksteder, Fevag, Norway for *Turkish Cargo Lines* of Turkey to operate between Trieste (Italy) and Derince (Turkey). In 2002 chartered to *Latlines* to operate between Lübeck and Riga (Latvia). In 2003 chartered to *VentLines* to inaugurate a new service between Travemünde and Ventspils. In 2004 sold to *Polsteam*, managed by *Unity Line* and renamed the GRYF. Entered service in 2005. In February 2007 transferred to the new Świnoujście - Trelleborg route.

JAN ŚNIADECKI Built by Falkenbergs Varv AB, Falkenberg, Sweden for *Polish Ocean Lines* to operate between Świnoujście and Ystad. Now operates for *Unity Line* on this route.

KOPERNIK Train/vehicle ferry built as the ROSTOCK by Bergens Mekaniske Verksted A/S, Bergen, Norway for *Deutsche Reichsbahn* of Germany (DDR). Used on freight services between Trelleborg and Sassnitz. In 1992 modified to increase passenger capacity in order to run in passenger service. In 1993 ownership transferred to *DFO* and in 1994 she opened a new service from Rostock to Trelleborg. In 1997 she was used when winds precluded the use of the new MECKLENBURG-VORPOMMERN. Following modifications to this vessel in late 1997, the ROSTOCK continued to operate to provide additional capacity until the delivery of the SKÅNE of *Scandlines AB*, after which she was laid up. In 1999 she was sold to *SeaWind Line*, renamed the STAR WIND and operated in freight-only mode between Stockholm and Turku. Initial plans to bring her passenger accommodation up to the standards required for Baltic night service were dropped. In October 2002 replaced by the SKY WIND and transferred to the Helsinki - Tallinn route. She carried a limited number of ordinary passengers on some sailings. In May 2005 returned to the Stockholm - Turku service, no longer carrying ordinary passengers, but was laid up after a few weeks. In October sold to *Euro Shipping OÜ* of Estonia, a company linked to *Saaremaa Laevakompanii*, and renamed the VIRONIA. In 2006 inaugurated a new service between Sillamäe (Estonia) and Kotka (Finland). In 2007 sold to *Euroafrica Shipping*, renamed the KOPERNIK and, in April 2008, placed on the Świnoujście - Ystad route, replacing the MIKOLAJ KOPERNIK.

POLONIA Train/vehicle ferry built by Langsten Slip & Båtbyggeri A/S, Tomrefjord, Norway for *Polonia Line Ltd* and managed by *Unity Line*.

SKANIA Built as the SUPERFAST I by Schichau Seebeckwerft, Bremerhaven, Germany for *Superfast Ferries* of Greece. Operated between Patras and Ancona (Italy). In 1998 transferred to the Patras - Igoumenitsa (Greece) - Bari (Italy) route. In 2004 sold to a subsidiary of *Grimaldi Lines*, renamed the EUROSTAR ROMA and placed on the Civitavecchia (Italy) - Barcelona (Spain) service. In 2008 sold to *Polsteam* and renamed the SKANIA. After modifications, she was placed on the *Unity Line* Świnoujście - Ystad service as second passenger vessel. In during the peak summer period in 2010 operated a round trip between Ystad and Rønne for *Bornholmstrafikken*.

WOLIN Train/vehicle ferry built as the ÖRESUND by Moss Rosenberg Værft, Moss, Norway for *Statens Järnvägar* (*Swedish State Railways*) for the 'DanLink' service between Helsingborg and København. Has 817 metres of rail track. Service ceased in July 2000 and vessel laid up. In 2001 sold to *Sea Containers Ferries* and in 2002 converted at Gdańsk, Poland to a passenger ferry. She was chartered to *SeaWind Line*, renamed the SKY WIND and in Autumn 2002 replaced the STAR WIND on the Stockholm - Turku service. In 2007 sold to *Polsteam*, renamed the WOLIN and placed on the *Unity Line* Świnoujście - Trelleborg service.

VIKING LINE

THE COMPANY *Viking Line Abp* is a Finnish company Listed on the Helsinki Stock Exchange since 1995.

MANAGEMENT President & CEO Jan Hanses, **Executive Vice President/Deputy CEO and Chief Financial Officer at Viking Line Abp** Andreas Remmer.

ADDRESS Box 166, AX-22100 Mariehamn, Åland, Finland.

TELEPHONE Administration +358 (0)18 27000, **Reservations** +358 (0)600 41577.

INTERNET Email international.sales@vikingline.com **Websites** www.vikingline.com (*English*) www.vikingline.fi (*Finnish*) www.vikingline.se (*Swedish*) www.vikingline.ee (*Estonian*) www.vikingline.de (*German*)

ROUTES OPERATED Conventional Ferries - all year Stockholm (Sweden) - Mariehamn (Åland) - Helsinki (Finland) (14 hrs; **GABRIELLA**, **MARIELLA**; 1 per day), Stockholm - Mariehamn (day)/Långnäs (Åland) (night) - Turku (Finland) (9 hrs 10 mins; **AMORELLA**, **VIKING GRACE**; 2 per day), Kapellskär (Sweden) - Mariehamn (Åland) (2 hrs 15 mins; **ROSELLA**; up to 3 per day), Helsinki - Tallinn (2 hrs 30 mins; **VIKING XPRS**; 2 per day), Cruises from Stockholm to Mariehamn (21 hrs - 24 hrs round trip (most 22 hrs 30 mins); **VIKING CINDERELLA**; 1 per day),

1	AMORELLA	34384t	88	21.5k	169.4m	2450P	450C	53T	BA	FI	8601915
2	GABRIELLA	35492t	92	21.5k	171.2m	2420P	400C	50T	BA	FI	8917601
3	MARIELLA	37799t	85	22.0k	176.9m	2500P	400C	60T	BA	FI	8320573
4	ROSELLA	16850t	80	21.3k	136.0m	1700P	340C	40T	BA	AL	7901265
5	VIKING CINDERELLA	46398t	89	21.5k	191.0m	2500P	100C	-	BA	SE	8719188
6	VIKING GRACE	57000t	13	23.0k	214.0m	2800P	556C	90L	BA	FI	9606900
7	VIKING XPRS	34000t	08	25.0k	185.0m	2500P	250C	60L	BA	EE	9375654

AMORELLA Built by Brodogradevna Industrija, Split, Yugoslavia for *SF Line* for the Stockholm - Mariehamn - Turku service.

GABRIELLA Built as the FRANS SUELL by Brodogradiliste Industrija, Split, Croatia for *Sea-Link AB* of Sweden to operate for subsidiary company *Euroway AB*, who established a service between Lübeck, Travemünde and Malmö. In 1994 this service ceased and she was chartered to *Silja Line*, renamed the SILJA SCANDINAVIA and transferred to the Stockholm - Turku service. In 1997 she was sold to *Viking Line* to operate between Stockholm and Helsinki. She was renamed the GABRIELLA. In 2014, a daytime sailing during summer from Helsinki to Tallinn was introduced.

MARIELLA Built by Oy Wärtsilä Ab, Turku, Finland for *SF Line*. Used on the Stockholm - Helsinki service. During 1996 additionally operated short cruises to Muuga in Estonia during the 'layover' period in Helsinki. In 2014, a daytime sailing during summer from Helsinki to Tallinn was introduced.

ROSELLA Built by Oy Wärtsilä Ab, Turku, Finland for *SF Line*. Used mainly on the Stockholm - Turku and Kapellskär - Naantali services until 1997. From 1997 operated 21 to 24-hour cruises from Stockholm to Mariehamn under the marketing name 'The Dancing Queen', except in the peak summer period when she operated between Kapellskär and Turku. In Autumn 2003 transferred to a new twice-daily Helsinki - Tallinn ferry service. In May 2008 placed on the Mariehamn - Kapellskär route under the Swedish flag. In 2011 she was extensively rebuilt at Balti Laevaremondi Tehas in Tallinn, Estonia. Cabin capacity was lowered from 1184 to 418 and the restaurant and shop areas were increased. In January 2014 placed under the Finnish flag.

VIKING CINDERELLA Built as the CINDERELLA by Wärtsilä Marine Ab, Turku, Finland for *SF Line*. Until 1993 provided additional capacity between Stockholm and Helsinki and undertook weekend cruises from Helsinki. In 1993 she replaced the OLYMPIA (a sister vessel of the MARIELLA) as the main Stockholm - Helsinki vessel after the OLYMPIA had been chartered to *P&O European Ferries* and renamed the PRIDE OF BILBAO. In 1995 switched to operating 20-hour cruises from Helsinki to Estonia in the off peak and the Stockholm - Mariehamn - Turku service during the peak summer period (end of May to end of August). From 1997 she remained cruising throughout the year. In Autumn 2003 she was transferred to the Swedish flag, renamed the VIKING CINDERELLA and transferred to Stockholm - Mariehamn cruises. She operates these cruises all year round.

VIKING GRACE Built by STX Europe, Turku, Finland. She operates between Stockholm and Turku. She is powered by LNG. Entered service in January 2013.

VIKING XPRS Built by Aker Yards, Helsinki to operate between Helsinki and Tallinn. In January 2014 placed under the Estonian flag.

Under construction

8	NEWBUILDING	63000t	20	23.0k	218.0m	2800P	556C	90L	BA	FI

NEWBUILDING Under construction by Xiamen Shipbuilding Industry Co. Ltd, Xiamen, China. She will be LNG powered and will replace the AMORELLA on the Stockholm - Mariehamn - Turku service.

WAGENBORG

THE COMPANY *Wagenborg Passagiersdiensten BV* is a Dutch private sector company.

MANAGEMENT Managing Director Ger van Langen.

ADDRESS Reeweg 4, 9163 ZM Nes, Ameland, The Netherlands.

TELEPHONE Administration & Reservations *International* +31 88 1031000, ***Netherlands*** 0900 9238.

FAX Administration & Reservations +31 (0)519 542905.

INTERNET Email info@wpd.nl **Website** www.wpd.nl *(Dutch, English, German)*

ROUTES OPERATED *Car Ferries* Holwerd (The Netherlands) - Ameland (Frisian Islands) (45 minutes; *OERD, SIER*; up to 14 per day), Lauwersoog (The Netherlands) - Schiermonnikoog (Frisian Islands) (45 minutes; *MONNIK, ROTTUM*; up to 6 per day).

1	MONNIK	1121t	85	12.2k	58.0m	1000P	46C	9L	BA	NL	8408961
2	OERD	2286t	03	11.2k	73.2m	1200P	72C	22L	BA	NL	9269673
3	ROTTUM	1121t	85	12.2k	58.0m	1000P	46C	9L	BA	NL	8408959
4	SIER	2286t	95	11.2k	73.2m	1200P	72C	22L	BA	NL	9075761

MONNIK Built by Scheepswerf Hoogezand, Hoogezand, The Netherlands for *Wagenborg Passagiersdiensten BV* as the OERD. In 2003, on delivery of the new OERD, she was renamed the MONNIK. Used on the Lauwersoog - Schiermonnikoog route.

OERD Built by Scheepswerf Bijlsma Lemmer, Lemmer, The Netherlands for *Wagenborg Passagiersdiensten BV*. Used on the Ameland - Holwerd route.

ROTTUM Built as the SIER by Scheepswerf Hoogezand, Hoogezand, The Netherlands for *Wagenborg Passagiersdiensten BV* and used on the Holwerd - Ameland route. In 1995 renamed the ROTTUM and transferred to the Lauwersoog - Schiermonnikoog route.

SIER Built by Shipyard Bijlsma, Wartena, The Netherlands for *Wagenborg Passagiersdiensten BV*. Used on the Ameland - Holwerd route.

Amorella *(Miles Cowsill)*

Viking Cinderella *(Matthew Punter)*

WASALINE

THE COMPANY *Wasaline* is the trading name of *NLC Ferry Oy Ab*, a Finnish company, jointly owned by the cities of Vaasa and Umeå.

MANAGEMENT Managing Director Peter Ståhlberg.

ADDRESS *Finland* Skeppsredaregatan 3, 65170 Vasa, Finland *Sweden* Blå Vägen 4, 91322 Holmsund, Sweden.

TELEPHONE Administration & Reservations *Finland* +358 (0)207 716 810, *Sweden* +46 (0)90 185 200.

INTERNET *Email* info@wasaline.com *Website* www.wasaline.com *(English, Finnish, Swedish)*

ROUTE OPERATED Vaasa (Finland) - Umeå (Sweden) (4 hrs; *WASA EXPRESS*; 1/2 per day).

1	WASA EXPRESS	17053t	81	17.0k	140.8m	1100P	450C	84T	BAS2	FI	8000226

WASA EXPRESS Built by Oy Wärtsilä AB, Helsinki, Finland as the TRAVEMÜNDE for *Gedser-Travemünde Ruten* of Denmark for their service between Gedser (Denmark) and Travemünde (Germany). In 1986 the company's trading name was changed to *GT Linien* and in 1987, following the takeover by *Sea-Link AB* of Sweden, it was further changed to *GT Link*. The vessel's name was changed to the TRAVEMÜNDE LINK. In 1988 she was purchased by *Rederi AB Gotland* of Sweden, although remaining in service with *GT Link*. Later in 1988 she was chartered to *Sally Ferries* and entered service in December on the Ramsgate - Dunkerque service. She was renamed the SALLY STAR. In 1997 she was transferred to *Silja Line* to operate between Vaasa and Umeå during the summer period, under the marketing name WASA EXPRESS (although not renamed). She returned to *Rederi AB Gotland* in Autumn 1997, was renamed the THJELVAR and entered service with *Destination Gotland* in January 1998. Withdrawn and laid up in December 2003. In 2004 chartered to *Color Line* to inaugurate a new service between Larvik and Hirtshals. Renamed the COLOR TRAVELLER. Operated in reduced passenger mode on this service but in summer peak period operated between Frederikshavn and Larvik in full passenger mode. In December 2006 returned to *Rederi AB Gotland*. In 2007 renamed the THJELVAR, chartered to *Scandlines* and placed on the Gedser – Rostock route. Renamed the ROSTOCK. In Autumn 2008 withdrawn and laid up. In June 2009 sub-chartered to *Comarit* of Morocco for two months. In September she resumed the name THJELVAR. In August 2008 she was chartered to *Fred. Olsen SA* of Spain, renamed the BETANCURIA and placed on the Las Palmas - Puerto del Rosario - Arrecife service. In September 2012 laid up. In October 2012 purchased by *NLC Ferry Oy Ab* and, in November, renamed the WASA EXPRESS. Entered service in January 2013.

WYKER DAMPFSCHIFFS-REEDEREI

THE COMPANY *Wyker Dampfschiffs-Reederei* is a German company.

MANAGEMENT CEO Axel Meynköhn.

ADDRESS PO Box 1540, 25933 Wyk auf Föhr, Germany.

TELEPHONE Administration & Reservations +49 (0) 46 67 - 9 40 30.

INTERNET *Email* info@faehre.de *Website* www.faehre.de *(Danish, English, German)*

ROUTES OPERATED Dagebüll - Föhr (50min; *NORDERAUE, NORDFRIESLAND, RUNGHOLT; SCHLESWIG-HOLSTEIN, UTHLANDE*; up to 14 per day), Dagebüll - Amrun (90 min (120 min via Föhr); *NORDERAUE, NORDFRIESLAND, RUNGHOLT, SCHLESWIG-HOLSTEIN, UTHLANDE*; 7 per day), Föhr - Amrum (1 hr; *NORDERAUE, NORDFRIESLAND, RUNGHOLT; SCHLESWIG-HOLSTEIN, UTHLANDE*; up to 4 per day), Schlüttsiel - Hooge - Langeness (2 hrs; *HILLIGENLEI*; up to 2 per day).

1	HILLIGENLEI	467t	85	19.0k	38.3m	200P	22C	-	BA	DE	8411217
2	NORDERAUE	3318t	18	12.0k	75.9m	1138P	75C	16L	BA	DE	9796121
3	NORDFRIESLAND	2287t	95	12.0k	67.0m	1200P	55C	-	BA	DE	9102758

4	RUNGHOLT	2268t	92	12.5k	67.9m	975P	55C	-	BA	DE	9038660.
5	SCHLESWIG-HOLSTEIN	3202t	11	12.0k	75.9m	1200P	75C	-	BA	DE	9604378
6	UTHLANDE	1960t	10	12.0k	75.9m	1200P	75C	-	BA	DE	9548407

HILLIGENLEI Built as the PELLWORM by Husumer Schiffswerft, Husum, Germany for *Neue Pellwormer Dampfschiffahrtsgesellschaft* of Germany and operated between Pellworm and Strucklahnungshörn. In 1996 sold to Sven Paulsen, Altwarp, Germany and renamed the ADLER POLONIA. Operated between Altwarp and Novo Warpno (Poland). In 2002 sold to *Wyker Dampfschiffsreederei* and renamed the HILLIGENLEI I. In February 2010 renamed the HILLIGENLEI.

NORDERAUE Built by Neptun Werft GmbH, Rostock, Germany for *Wyker Dampfschiffsreederei*.

NORDFRIESLAND, RUNGHOLT Built by Husumer Schiffswerft, Husum, Germany for *Wyker Dampfschiffsreederei*.

SCHLESWIG-HOLSTEIN Built by Neptun Werft GmbH, Rostock, Germany for *Wyker Dampfschiffsreederei*.

UTHLANDE Built by J.J. Sietas GmbH & Co KG, Hamburg, Germany for *Wyker Dampfschiffsreederei*.

Wasa Express *(Kalle Id)*

SECTION 8 - OTHER VESSELS

The following passenger vessels are, at the time of going to print, not operating and are owned by companies which do not currently operate services or are used on freight -only services. They are therefore available for possible re-deployment, either in the area covered by this book or elsewhere. Passenger vessels operating freight-only services outside the scope of this book are also included here. Exceptionally we have included two freight-only vessels possibly to be chartered to an operator serving the UK. Withdrawn vessels not yet disposed of and owned by operating companies are shown under the appropriate company and marked '[x]'.

Conmar Shipping (Germany)

1	GRETE	5233t	10	15.0k	97.9m	600P	150C	12L	BA	DE	9474060
2	HIIUMAA	5233t	11	15.0k	97.9m	600P	150C	20L	BA2	EE	9481805
3	SAAREMAA	5900t	10	15.0k	97.9m	600P	150C	12L	BA	EE	9474072

GRETE Built as the MUHUMAA by Fiskerstrand Verft A/S, Aalesund, Norway for an Estonian bank and chartered to *Saaremaa Laevakompanii* of Estonia and operated on the Kuivastu - Virtsu service. In summer 2015 transferred to the *Elb-Link* service under the marketing name 'Grete' (but not renamed). In March 2017 laid up. Re-entered service in May 2017, October 2017 sold to *Conmar Shipping Gmbh & Co KG* of Germany renamed the GRETE, chartered to *Elb-Link* of Germany and re-registered in Germany with engines uprated to enable a crossing time of one hour. Service ceased October 2017 and laid up in Wewelsfleth, Gemany.

HIIUMAA Built by Fiskerstrand Verft A/S, Aalesund, Norway for *Saaremaa Laevakompanii*. In October 2016 charter transferred to *Praamid*. In April 2017 charter ended and laid up in Kiel, Germany. In October 2017 sold to *Conmar Shipping Gmbh & Co KG* of Germany.

SAAREMAA Built by Fiskerstrand Verft A/S, Aalesund, Norway for an Estonian bank and chartered to *Saaremaa Laevakompanii* of Estonia and operated on the Kuivastu - Virtsu service. In summer 2015 transferred to the *Elb-Link* service. In March 2017 laid up in Cuxhaven. Later laid up in Wewelsfleth, Germany. In August 2017 sold to *Conmar Shipping Gmbh & Co KG* of Germany.

Cromarty Ferry Company

| 1 | CROMARTY QUEEN | 68t | 10 | 9.0k | 17.3m | 50P | 4C | - | B | UK | |

CROMARTY QUEEN Built by Southampton Marine Services for *Cromarty Ferry Company*. Withdrawn at the end of the 2015 summer season and laid up.

Rederi AB Gotland

| 1 | GUTE | 7616t | 79 | 15.0k | 138.8m | 88P | - | 60T | BA | SE | 7802794 |

GUTE Built as the GUTE by Falkenbergs Varv AB, Falkenberg, Sweden for *Rederi AB Gotland* of Sweden. Used on service between Gotland and the Swedish mainland. In 1988 chartered to *Brambles Shipping* of Australia and used between Port Melbourne (Victoria) and Burnie (Tasmania). In 1992 she was renamed the SALLY SUN and chartered to *Sally Ferries*, operating between Ramsgate and Dunkerque. In 1994 she inaugurated a Ramsgate - Vlissingen service, which was later changed to Dartford - Vlissingen. In 1995 she was chartered to *SeaWind Line*, renamed the SEAWIND II and operated between Stockholm and Turku. In 1997 she was chartered to *Nordic Trucker Line* for the Oxelösund - St Petersburg service and in 1998 she returned to *SeaWind Line*. In 1998, after *Rederi AB Gotland*-owned *Destination Gotland* regained the franchise to operate to Gotland, she was renamed the GUTE and resumed her summer role of providing summer freight back-up to the passenger vessels, but with a number of short charters during the winter. In Autumn 2002 chartered to *Amber Lines* for the Karlshamn - Liepaja service. In February 2003 chartered to *NATO* for the Iraq crisis. Returned to *Destination Gotland* in Summer 2003. In Autumn 2003 chartered to *Scandlines Amber Lines* to operate between Karlshamn and Liepaja. In 2004 lengthened by 20.3m by Nauta Shiprepair, Gdynia, Poland. In Autumn 2004 chartered to *Riga Sea Line* to inaugurate a freight service between Riga and Nynäshamn. In Autumn 2005 the service ended and the vessel was laid up. In January 2006 chartered to *Lisco* and placed on the Klaipėda - Karlshamn route, also undertaking two trips from Klaipėda to Baltiysk. In May 2006 chartered to *SeaWind Line*. In March 2007 chartered to *Baltic Scandinavian Line*. Charter ended September 2007. Apart from a trip to Cameroon, conveying Swedish UN Troops for Chad, she remained laid up until October 2008 when she was chartered to *Baltic Scandinavian Line* to operate between Härnösand and Kaskinen. In 2009 this service closed and she was laid up. At the end of March 2015 she was chartered to *Færgen* to operate between Køge and Rønne covering for the HAMMERODDE. She returned to layup in May. In August 2017 chartered to *Stena Line* to operate as fourth ship on the Karlskrona - Gdynia route. In September 2018 to be replaced by the STENA NORDICA and the charter ended.

Humphrey O'Leary, Clare Island

1	BRUERNISH	69t	73	8.0k	24.3m	97P	6C	1L	B	IR	7310662
2	CANNA	69t	76	8.0k	24.3m	140P	6C	1L	B	UK	-
3	RAASAY	69t	76	8.0k	24.3m	75P	6C	1L-	B	UK	7340435

BRUERNISH Built by James Lamont & Co, Port Glasgow, UK. Until 1980 she served on a variety of routes. In 1980 she inaugurated ro-ro working between Tayinloan and the island of Gigha and served this route until June 1992 when she was replaced by the LOCH RANZA and became a relief vessel. In Summer 1994 she operated as secondary vessel on the Tobermory (Mull) - Kilchoan service for one season only. In December 1996 she started a vehicle ferry service between Ballycastle (on the North West coast of Northern Ireland) and Rathlin Island under charter; the route became a *Caledonian MacBrayne* operation in April 1997 and she was replaced by the CANNA. In 1997 she operated on the Tarbert - Portavadie service and in 1998 on the Oban - Lismore service. Between 1999 and 2006 she was a spare vessel. In 2006 she was sold to *Humphrey O'Leary* of Clare Island to operate freight services between Roonagh and Clare Island (County Mayo, Irish Republic). In 2008 chartered to *Arranmore Charters* and in December placed on the Burton port - Leabgarrow service. In early 2010 charter terminated and returned to *Humphrey O'Leary*. Number is Lloyds number, not IMO.

CANNA Built by James Lamont & Co Ltd, Port Glasgow, UK for *Caledonian MacBrayne*. She was the regular vessel on the Lochaline - Fishnish (Mull) service. In 1986 she was replaced by the ISLE OF CUMBRAE and until 1990 she served in a relief capacity in the north, often assisting on the Iona service. In 1990 she was placed on the Kyles Scalpay (Harris) - Scalpay service (replaced by a bridge in Autumn 1997). In Spring 1997 *Caledonian MacBrayne* was contracted to operate the Ballycastle - Rathlin Island route and she was transferred to this service. In June 2008 she was chartered by *Caledonian Maritime Assets Limited* to *Rathlin Island Ferry Ltd* who took over the operation of the service. In June 2017 replaced by the SPIRIT OF RATHLIN and withdrawn. In autumn 2018 sold to *Humphrey O'Leary, Clare Island*.

RAASAY Built by James Lamont & Co Ltd, Port Glasgow, UK for and used primarily on the Sconser (Skye) - Raasay service. In 1997 she was replaced by the LOCH STRIVEN, became a spare/relief vessel and inaugurated in October 2003 the winter service between Tobermory (Mull) and Kilchoan (Ardnamurchan). From summer 2016 operated as second vessel on Oban - Lismore route. In March 2018 withdrawn and sold to *Humphrey O'Leary*. Number is Lloyds number, not IMO.

Saaremaa Laevakompanii (Estonia)

| 1 | HARILAID | 1028t | 85 | 9.9k | 49.9m | 120P | 35C | 5L | BA | EE | 8727367 |
| 2 | KÖRGELAID | 1028t | 87 | 9.9k | 49.9m | 190P | 35C | 5L | BA | EE | 8725577 |

HARILAID, KÖRGELAID Built by Riga Shiprepair Yard, Riga, Latvia (USSR) for *ESCO* of Estonia. In 1994 transferred to *Saaremaa Laevakompanii*. In October 2016 transferred to *Praamid* until new vessels were delivered. Then laid up in Tallinn.

9 – SISTERS – A LIST OF SISTER (OR NEAR SISTER) VESSELS IN THIS BOOK

The following vessels are sisters or near sisters. This refers to 'as built' condition; some ships will subsequently have been modified and become different from their sister vessels.

ÆRØSKØBING, MARSTAL *(Ærøfærgerne)*

AMORELLA, GABRIELLA *(Viking Line)*, ISABELLE *(Tallink Silja Line)*, CROWN OF SCANDINAVIA *(DFDS Seaways)*.

ARGYLE, BUTE *(Caledonian MacBrayne)*.

ATLANTIC VISION *(Tallink)*, STENA SUPERFAST VII, STENA SUPERFAST VIII, STENA SUPERFAST X *(Stena Line)*.

AURORA AF HELSINGBORG, HAMLET, TYCHO BRAHE *(Scandlines - Helsingborg - Helsingør)*.

BALTIC QUEEN, BALTIC PRINCESS, GALAXY *(Tallink Silja Line)*.

BASTØ I, BASTØ II *(Bastø Fosen)*.

BASTØ IV, BASTØ V, BASTØ VI *(Bastø Fosen)*.

BEN-MY-CHREE *(Isle of Man Steam Packet Company)*, COMMODORE CLIPPER *(Condor Ferries)*, HAMMERODDE *(Stena Line)* (Near sisters).

BEN WOOLLACOTT, DAME VERA LYNN *(Woolwich Free Ferry)*.

BERGENSFJORD, STAVANGERFJORD *(Fjord Line)*.

BERLIN, COPENHAGEN *(Scandlines)*.

BRUERNISH, CANNA *(Humphrey O'Leary)*, CLEW BAY QUEEN *(Clare Island Ferry Company)*, COLL *(Arranmore Island Ferries)*, EIGG *(Clare Island Ferry Company)*, MORVERN *(Arranmore Fast Ferries)*, RAASAY *(Humphrey O'Leary)*, RHUM *(Arranmore Island Ferries)*.

CARRIGALOE, GLENBROOK *(Cross River Ferries)*.

CATRIONA, HALLAIG, LOCHINVAR *(Caledonian MacBrayne)*

COLOR FANTASY, COLOR MAGIC *(Color Line)*.

COLOR VIKING *(Color Line)*, STENA NAUTICA *(Stena Line)*.

CONNEMARA *(Brittany Ferries)*, EPSILON *(Irish Ferries)*, ETRETAT *(Brittany Ferries)*, SCOTTISH VIKING, STENA HORIZON, STENA LAGAN, STENA MERSEY, STENA FLAVIA *(Stena Line)*.

CÔTE D'ALBATRE, SEVEN SISTERS *(DFDS Seaways)*.

CÔTE DES DUNES, CÔTE DES FLANDRES *(DFDS Seaways)*.

DAGALIEN, DAGGRI *(Shetland Islands Council)*.

DELFT SEAWAYS, DOVER SEAWAYS, DUNKERQUE SEAWAYS *(DFDS Seaways)*.

DEUTSCHLAND, SCHLESWIG-HOLSTEIN *(Scandlines)*.

EARL SIGURD, EARL THORFINN *(Orkney Ferries)*.

ECKERÖ *(Eckerö Linjen)*, POVL ANKER *(Bornholmstrafikken)*.

ERNEST BEVIN, JAMES NEWMAN, JOHN BURNS *(Woolwich Free Ferry)*.

EUROPEAN CAUSEWAY, EUROPEAN HIGHLANDER *(P&O Ferries)*.

FENJA, MENJA *(Færgen)*.

FINNCLIPPER, FINNEAGLE, FINNFELLOW *(Finnlines)*, STENA GERMANICA *(Stena Line)*.

FINNLADY, FINNMAID, FINNSTAR, FINNSWAN *(Finnlines)*.

FINNPARTNER, FINNTRADER *(Finnlines)*.

GALICIA, SALAMANCA *(Brittany Ferries)*.

GOTLAND, VISBY *(Destination Gotland)*.

GRETE, HIIUMAA, SAAREMAA *(Conmar Shipping)*.

HJALTLAND, HROSSEY *(NorthLink Ferries).*
HUCKLEBERRY FINN, TOM SAWYER *(TT-Line).*
KING SEAWAYS, PRINCESS SEAWAYS *(DFDS Seaways).*
KONG HARALD, NORDLYS, RICHARD WITH *(Hurtigruten).*
KRONPRINS FREDERIK, PRINS JOACHIM *(Scandlines).*
LANGELAND, LOLLAND *(Færgen).*
LOCH DUNVEGAN, LOCH FYNE *(Caledonian MacBrayne).*
LOCH LINNHE, LOCH RANZA, LOCH RIDDON, LOCH STRIVEN *(Caledonian MacBrayne).*
LYNHER II, PLYM II, TAMAR II *(Torpoint Ferries).*
MARIELLA *(Viking Line),* SPL PRINCESS ANASTASIA *(Moby SPL).*
MERCANDIA IV, MERCANDIA VIII *(Scandlines - Helsingør - Helsingborg).*
MIDNATSOL, TROLLFJORD *(Hurtigruten).*
MIDSLAND, WESTFALEN *(Rederij Doeksen).*
MONNIK, ROTTUM *(Wagenborg).*
MÜNSTERLAND, OSTFRIESLAND *(AG Ems).*
NILS DACKE, ROBIN HOOD *(TT-Line).*
NILS HOLGERSSON, PETER PAN *(TT-Line).*
NORBANK, NORBAY *(P&O Ferries).*
NORDKAPP, NORDNORGE, POLARLYS *(Hurtigruten).*
OERD, SIER *(Wagenborg).*
OILEAN NA H-OIGE, SANCTA MARIA *(Bere Island Ferries).*
PRIDE OF BRUGES, PRIDE OF YORK *(P&O Ferries).*
PRIDE OF CANTERBURY, PRIDE OF KENT *(P&O Ferries).*
PRIDE OF HULL, PRIDE OF ROTTERDAM *(P&O Ferries).*
PRINS RICHARD, PRINSESSE BENEDIKTE *(Scandlines).*
RED EAGLE, RED FALCON, RED OSPREY *(Red Funnel Ferries).*
ROMANTIKA, VICTORIA I *(Tallink Silja Line).*
SILJA SERENADE, SILJA SYMPHONY *(Tallink Silja Line).*
SOUND OF SCARBA, SOUND OF SHUNA *(Western Ferries).*
SOUND OF SEIL, SOUND OF SOAY *(Western Ferries).*
SPIRIT OF BRITAIN, SPIRIT OF FRANCE *(P&O Ferries).*
ST CECILIA, ST FAITH *(Wightlink).*
STENA ADVENTURER, STENA SCANDINAVICA *(Stena Line).*
STENA BRITANNICA, STENA HOLLANDICA *(Stena Line).*
STENA GOTHICA, URD *(Stena Line).*
STENA SPIRIT, STENA VISION *(Stena Line).*
SUPERSPEED 1, SUPERSPEED 2 *(Color Line).*
WIGHT LIGHT, WIGHT SKY, WIGHT SUN *(Wightlink).*

Fast Ferries

EXPRESS 1, EXPRESS 2, EXPRESS 3 *(Mols-Linien).*
RED JET 6, RED JET 7 *(Red Funnel Ferries).*
WIGHT RYDER I, WIGHT RYDER II *(Wightlink).*

Ferries 2019

Freight Ferries

ADELINE, WILHELMINE *(CLdN/Cobelfret Ferries)*,

AEGEAN BREEZE, ARABIAN BREEZE, ASIAN BREEZE, BALTIC BREEZE *(UECC)*.

AMANDINE, OPALINE *(CLdN/Cobelfret Ferries)*.

ANVIL POINT, EDDYSTONE *(Foreland Shipping)*, FINNMERCHANT *(Finnlines)*, HARTLAND POINT, HURST POINT*(Foreland Shipping)*.

ARROW *(Isle of Man Steam Packet)*, CLIPPER RANGER *(Seatruck Ferries)*, HELLIAR, HILDASAY *(NorthLink Ferries)*.

AUTO BAY *(UECC)*, BORE BANK *(Transfennica)*, MYKINES *(Smyril Line)*

AUTO ECO, AUTO ENERGY *(UECC)*

AUTOPREMIER, AUTOPRESTIGE, AUTOPRIDE, AUTOPROGRESS *(UECC)*.

AUTOSKY, AUTOSTAR, AUTOSUN *(UECC)*.

BALTICBORG, BOTHNIABORG *(Smurfit Kappa Group)*

BEGONIA SEAWAYS, FICARIA SEAWAYS, FREESIA SEAWAYS, PRIMULA SEAWAYS *(DFDS Seaways)*.

BOTNIA SEAWAYS, FINLANDIA SEAWAYS *(DFDS Seaways)*, FINNHAWK, FINNKRAFT *(Finnlines)*.

BRITANNIA SEAWAYS, SELANDIA SEAWAYS, SUECIA SEAWAYS *(DFDS Seaways)*.

CAPUCINE, SEVERINE *(CLdN/Cobelfret Ferries)*.

CELANDINE, CELESTINE, CLEMENTINE, MELUSINE, VALENTINE, VICTORINE *(CLdN/Cobelfret Ferries)*.

CELINE, DELPHINE *(CLdN/Cobelfret Ferries)*.

CLIPPER PENNANT, CLIPPER POINT, SEATRUCK PACE, SEATRUCK PANORAMA *(Seatruck Ferries)*.

CORONA SEA *(Transfennica)*, FINNBREEZE, FINNMILL, FINNPULP, FINNSEA, FINNSKY, FINNSUN, FINNTIDE, FINNWAVE *(Finnlines)*, FIONIA SEAWAYS *DFDS Seaways)*. HAFNIA SEA *(Transfennica)*, JUTLANDIA SEAWAYS *(DFDS Seaways)*.

CYMBELINE, UNDINE *(CLdN/Cobelfret Ferries)*.

FINNCARRIER, FINNMASTER *(Finnlines)*, MN PELICAN *(Brittany Ferries)*, SC CONNECTOR *(Sea-Cargo)*.

GARDENIA SEAWAYS, TULIPA SEAWAYS *(DFDS Seaways)*.

GENCA, KRAFTCA, PLYCA, PULPCA, TIMCA, TRICA *(Transfennica)*.

MAGNOLIA SEAWAYS, PETUNIA SEAWAYS *(DFDS Seaways)*.

MAZARINE, PALATINE, PEREGRINE, VESPERTINE *(CLdN/Cobelfret Ferries)*.

MISANA, MISIDA *(Stena Line)*

MISTRAL *(Stena Line)*, SEAGARD *(Transfennica)*.

NORSKY, NORSTREAM *(P&O Ferries)*.

PAULINE, YASMINE *(CLdN/Cobelfret Ferries)*.

SCA OBBOLA, SCA ORTVIKEN, SCA ÖSTRAND *(SCA Transforest)*.

SCHIEBORG, SLINGEBORG *(SOL Continent Line)*, SOMERSET *(CLdN/Cobelfret Ferries)*.

SEATRUCK PERFORMANCE, SEATRUCK POWER, SEATRUCK PRECISION, SEATRUCK PROGRESS, *(Seatruck Ferries)*.

STENA FORERUNNER *(Stena Line)*, STENA FORETELLER *(DFDS Seaways)*.

STENA TRANSIT, STENA TRANSPORTER *(Stena Line)*.

SECTION 10 - CHANGES SINCE FERRIES 2018 - BRITISH ISLES AND NORTHERN EUROPE

DISPOSALS

The following vessels, listed in *Ferries 2018 - British Isles and Northern Europe* have been disposed of - either to other companies listed in this book or others. Company names are as used in that publication.

AUTOBAY *(UECC)* In 2017 converted back to conventional ro-ro format.in April 2018 chartered to *Stena Line* to operate between, Gdynia and Nynäshamn.

BORE SEA *(CLdN/Cobelfret Ferries)* In January 2018 chartered to *Transfennica*.

BRIXHAM EXPRESS *(Brixham Express)* Withdrawn in October 2017. Currently laid up at Killybegs, , Republic of Ireland.

CANNA *(Caledonian Martime Assets)* In Autumn 2017 sold to *Humphrey O'Leary* of Clare Island, Republic of Ireland.

CAROLINE RUSS *(Stena Line)* At the end of December 2017 moved to substitute on the Göteborg - Frederikshavn service during the refit period. In February 2017 chartered to *UPM-Kymmene* shipping of Finland (which no longer operates to the UK).

CEMIL BAYULGEN *(CLdN/Cobelfret Ferries)* In November 2017 charter ended. Returned to Mediterranean service with *U.N RO-RO*.

CORONA SEAWAYS *(DFDS Seaways)* In January 2018 redelivered, chartered to *Transfennica* and in February renamed the CORONA SEA.

BORE SEA *(CLdN/Cobelfret Ferries)* In December 2017 charter ended. In January 2018 chartered to *Transfennica*.

EIGG *(Caledonan MacBrayne)* In Spring 2018 sold *Clare Island Ferry*.

ELISABETH RUSS *(SOL Continent Line)* In October 2017 chartered to *Stena Line* to operate between Gdynia and Nynäshamn. In April 2018 charter ended.

EXPRESS *(Viking Line)* Charter ended in autumn 2017. In May 2018 chartered to *Naviera Armas* of Spain.

FADIQ *(CLdN/Cobelfret Ferries)* In December 2017 sold to *Grnf Denizcilik Ve Insaat* of Turkey.

FINNEAGLE *(Finnlines)* In October 2017 sold to *Grimaldi Line* of Italy and renamed the EUROFERRY CORFU.

FINNCLIPPER *(Finnlines)* In April 2018 chartered to *Balearia Eurolineas Maritimas SA* of Spain and renamed the ROSALIND FRANKLIN.

GRETE *(Elb-Link)* In October 2017 service ceased and laid up. Now listed unde the owner *Conmar Shipping* (Section 8).

GYLEN LADY *(Caledonian MacBrayne)* In August 2017 withdrawn and sold.

HAFNIA SEAWAYS. *(DFDS Seaways)* In January 2018 redelivered, chartered to *Transfennica* and in March renamed the HAFNIA SEA.

HIIUMAA *(Praamid)* In October 2017 charter ended and laid up. Now listed unde the owner *Conmar Shipping* (Section 8).

ISLAND PRINCESS *(Clydelink)* In May 2018 withdrawn following the transfer of the route back to Clyde Marine.

JONATHAN SWIFT *Irish Ferries* In April 2018 sold to *Balearia Eurolineas Maritimas S.A* of Spain and renamed the CECILIA PAYNE entering service on 1st June between Denia and Ibiza and Majorca.

KAROLIN *(Linda Line)* In December 2017 sold to *Golden Star Ferries* of Greece and renamed the SUPERCAT.

KAUNAS SEAWAYS *(DFDS Seaways)* In June 2018 sold to *UKR Ferry* of Ukraine.

LEONORA CHRISTINA *(Færgen)* In December 2016 sold to *Ferry Gomera*, a subsidiary of *Fred. Olsen Lines* and chartered back. Delivered at the end of August 2018.

LORELEY *(Waterford Castle Hotel)* In July 2017 sold to sold to *Arranmore Island Ferry Services*, changed back to self steering and renamed the SPIRIT OF LOUGH SWILLY.

MASSIMO MURA *(CLdN/Cobelfret Ferries)* In 2018 sold to *Moby SPA* of Italy.

MIRANDA *(Transfennica)* In January 2017 sold by owners *Godby Shipping* to *FRS* of Germany to operate for their subsidiary *FRS Iberia* between Motril (Spain) and Tanger (Morocco). Renamed the MIRAMAR EXPRESS.

MISANA *(Transfennica)* In January 2017 chartered to *Stena Line* to operate between Rotterdam and Killingholme.

MISIDA *(Transfennica)* In January 2017 chartered to *Stena Line* to operate between Rotterdam and Killingholme.

MISTRAL *(P&O Ferries)* In June 2018 sub-chartered to *Stena Line* to operate between Rotterdam and Harwich.

ML FREYJA *(SOL Continent Line)* In December 2017 sub-charter ended and she entered service for *Mann Lines*.

NORRLAND *(Sea-Cargo)* During 2017 charter ended.

POVL ANKER *(Færgen)* In July 2016 sold to *Mols-Linien A/S* and chartered back. Delivered at the end of August 2018.

QUEEN OF ARAN *(Doolin Ferry)* In 2017 sold to *Arranmore Fast Ferries* for *Tory Island Ferry*.

RAASAY *(Rathlin Island Ferry)* In Spring 2018 sold to *Humphrey O'Leary* of Clare Island, Republic of Ireland.

SAAREMAA *(Saaremaa Laevakompanii)* In August 2017 sold to *Conmar Shipping* of Germany. Continued to be laid up.

STENA FORERUNNER *(Transfennica)* In December 2017 charter ended. Chartered to *Stena Line* to operate between Rotterdam and Harwich.

STENA FORETELLER *(Mann Lines)* In December 2017 charter ended. Chartered to *DFDS Seaways*.

THE SECOND SNARK *(Clyde Cruises)* In August 2017 sold to American interests for conversion to a motor yacht.

VILNIUS SEAWAYS *(DFDS Seaways)* In June 2018 sold to *UKR Ferry* of Ukraine.

VILLUM CLAUSEN *(Færgen)* In December 2018 sold to an unknown Mediterranean buyer. Delivered at the end of August 2018.

VESSELS RENAMED

The following vessels have been renamed since the publication of *Ferries 2018 - British Isles and Northern Europe* without change of owner or operator.

FINNCLIPPER *(Finnlines)* In May 2018 chartered to *Baleària* of Spain and renamed the ROSALIND FRANKLIN.

NORDLINK *(Finnlines)* In February 2018 renamed the FINNSWAN.

OSSIAN OF STAFFA *(Blue Funnel Cruises)* In 2017 renamed the JENNY B.

WESTPAC EXPRESS *(Irish Ferries)* In March 2018 renamed the DUBLIN SWIFT.

COMPANY CHANGES

Elb-Link In October 2017 the service ceased and in November 2017 the company filed for bankruptcy.

Brixham Express In October 2017 this operator ceased trading.

Bumblebee Boat Cruises This operator has ceased trading.

Linda Line This operator has ceased trading.

FERRIES ILLUSTRATED

Ferries 2019

INDEX

FERRY DAME	155	GELLAN	122	ISLE OF CUMBRAE	59
FICARIA SEAWAYS	68	GENCA	141	ISLE OF INISHMORE	76
FILLA	94	GLEN SANNOX	66	ISLE OF LEWIS	59
FINLAGGAN	59	GLENACHULISH	121	ISLE OF MULL	59
FINLANDIA	175	GLENBROOK	114	IVAN	139
FINLANDIA SEAWAYS	68	GLÓR NA FARRAIGE	150	JACK B	150
FINNBREEZE	130	GOD MET ONS III	122	JACOB MARLEY	151
FINNCARRIER	130	GOLDEN MARIANA	83	JAMES NEWMAN	122
FINNFELLOW	177	GOOD SHEPHERD IV	94	JAN ŚNIADECKI	206
FINNHAWK	130	GOTHIA SEAWAYS	74	JENACK	122
FINNKRAFT	130	GOTLAND	168	JENNY ANN	150
FINNLADY	177	GOTLANDIA	168	JENNY BLUE	150
FINNMAID	178	GOTLANDIA II	168	JENNY R*	150
FINNMARKEN	180	GRAEMSAY	84	JOHN BURNS	122
FINNMASTER	130	GRAN CANARIA CAR	139	JOSEPHINE	155
FINNMERCHANT	130	GRANVILLE	152	JOSEPHINE II	155
FINNMILL	130	GRETE	212	JUPITER CLIPPER	152
FINNPARTNER	178	GRONINGERLAND	176	JUTLANDIA SEAWAYS	68
FINNPULP	130	GRY MARITHA	116	KALEY	122
FINNSEA	130	GRYF	206	KING HARRY FERRY	147
FINNSKY	130	GUTE	212	KING SEAWAYS	68
FINNSTAR	178	HAFNIA SEA	141	KINGSWEAR PRINCESS	150
FINNSUN	130	HALLAIG	59	KINTYRE EXPRESS V	152
FINNSWAN	178	HAMLET	191	KIRSTY M	111
FINNTIDE	130	HAMMERSHUS	184	KOEGELWIECK	174
FINNTRADER	178	HAMNAVOE	80	KONG HARALD	180
FINNWAVE	130	HAPPY HOOKER	150	KOPERNIK	206
FIONIA SEAWAYS	68	HARBOUR FERRY	151	KÖRGELAID	213
FIVLA	94	HARBOUR SPIRIT	151	KRAFTCA	141
FJORD CAT	179	HARILAID	213	KRONPRINS FREDERIK	190
FLOATING BRIDGE NO 6	147	HARTLAND POINT	144	L'AUDACE	139
FRAM	180	HEBRIDEAN ISLES	59	LA SURPRISE	139
FRAZER MARINER	115	HEBRIDES	59	LADY DI	122
FRAZER TINTERN	115	HELLIAR	80	LADY JEAN	122
FREEDOM 90	151	HENDRA	94	LANGELAND	176
FREESIA SEAWAYS	68	HERM TRIDENT V	155	LARVEN	155
FRIDTJOF NANSEN	182	HIGHER FERRY	146	LAURALINE	130
FRIESLAND	174	HIIUMAA	212	LEIGER	189
FRIGG SYDFYEN	176	HILDASAY	80	LEIRNA	94
FRISIA I	186	HILLIGENLEI	211	LINGA	94
FRISIA II	186	HJALTLAND	80	LIVERPOOL SEAWAYS	169
FRISIA III	186	HOLGER DANSKE	190	LOCH ALAINN	59
FRISIA IV	186	HONFLEUR	55	LOCH BHRUSDA	59
FRISIA VI	186	HOUTON LASS	111	LOCH BUIE	59
FRISIA VII	186	HOY HEAD	84	LOCH DUNVEGAN	59
FRISIA IX	186	HROSSEY	80	LOCH FYNE	59
FRISIA X	186	HUCKLEBERRY FINN	205	LOCH LINNHE	59
FRISIA XI	186	HURRICANE CLIPPER	152	LOCH PORTAIN	59
FYNSHAV	176	HURST POINT	144	LOCH RANZA	59
GABRIELLA	207	HVITANES	192	LOCH RIDDON	59
GALAXY	200	HYTHE SCENE	150	LOCH SEAFORTH	59
GALAXY CLIPPER	152	IKOM K	118	LOCH SHIRA	59
GALICIA (Brittany Ferries)	55	ISABELLE	200	LOCH STRIVEN	59
GALICIA (Flota Suardiaz)	139	ISLAND EXPRESS	151	LOCH TARBERT	59
GALILEUSZ	206	ISLAND FLYER	151	LOCHINVAR	59
GARDENIA SEAWAYS	68	ISLAND TRADER	150	LOCHNEVIS	59
GEIRA	94	ISLE OF ARRAN	59	LOFOTEN	180

SEATRUCK POWER	134	STENA FLAVIA	193	TRANSFIGHTER	132
SEATRUCK PRECISION	134	STENA FORERUNNER	98	TRICA	141
SEATRUCK PROGRESS	134	STENA FORETELLER	68	TRIDENT VI	155
SELANDIA SEAWAYS	68	STENA GERMANICA	193	TROLLFJORD	180
SEVEN SISTERS	68	STENA GOTHICA	193	TULIPA SEAWAYS	68
SEVERINE	126	STENA HIBERNIA	98	TUNDRALAND	137
SHANNON BREEZE	119	STENA HOLLANDICA	98	TWIN STAR	152
SHANNON DOLPHIN	119	STENA HORIZON	98	TYCHO BRAHE	191
SHAPINSAY	84	STENA JUTLANDICA	193	TYPHOON CLIPPER	152
SHIPPER	144	STENA LAGAN	98	ULYSSES	76
SIER	208	STENA MERSEY	98	UNDINE	127
SILDBERIN	199	STENA NAUTICA	193	URD	193
SILJA EUROPA	200	STENA NORDICA	193	UTHLANDE	211
SILJA SERENADE	200	STENA SAGA	193	VALENTINE	127
SILJA SYMPHONY	200	STENA SCANDINAVICA	193	VARAGEN	84
SILVER SWAN	150	STENA SCOTIA	98	VASALAND	137
SKÅNE	193	STENA SPIRIT	193	VERONA	139
SKANIA	206	STENA SUPERFAST VII	98	VESPERTINE	127
SKJOLDNÆS	165	STENA SUPERFAST VIII	98	VESTERÅLEN	180
SKY CLIPPER	152	STENA SUPERFAST X	98	VICTOR HUGO	152
SLINGEBORG	137	STENA TRANSIT	98	VICTORIA I	200
SMYRIL	199	STENA TRANSPORTER	98	VICTORIA OF WIGHT	104
SNOLDA	94	STENA VINGA	193	VICTORIA SEAWAYS	169
SNOWDROP	152	STENA VISION	193	VICTORINE	127
SOLENT FLYER	151	STORM CLIPPER	152	VIKING CINDERELLA	207
SOMERSET	127	STRANGFORD 1	115	VIKING CONSTANZA	143
SØNDERHO	177	STRANGFORD II	121	VIKING GRACE	207
SOUND OF SCARBA	103	SUAR VIGO	139	VIKING XPRS	207
SOUND OF SEIL	103	SUECIA SEAWAYS	68	VILLE DE BORDEAUX	145
SOUND OF SHUNA	103	SÚLAN	199	VISBORG	168
SOUND OF SOAY	103	SUN CLIPPER	152	VISBY	168
SPIKE ISLANDER	155	SUPERSPEED 1	166	VLIELAND	174
SPIRIT OF BRITAIN	87	SUPERSPEED 2	166	W. B. YEATS	76
SPIRIT OF FRANCE	87	SWIFT LADY	118	WAPPEN VON BORKUM	176
SPIRIT OF GOSPORT	151	SYLTEXPRESS	199	WAPPEN VON	
SPIRIT OF		TAMAR II	148	NORDENEY	186
LOUGH SWILLY	110	TAVASTLAND	137	WASA EXPRESS	210
SPIRIT OF PORTSMOUTH	151	TEISTIN	199	WAVERLEY	155
SPIRIT OF RATHLIN	119	TENERIFE CAR	139	WAWEL	187
SPIRIT OF THE TYNE	155	TERNAN	199	WESTERN ISLES	155
SPITSBERGEN	180	TEXELSTROOM	203	WESTERN LADY VI	155
SPL PRINCESS		THAMES SWIFT	151	WESTERN LADY VII	155
ANASTASIA	183	THE LISMORE	109	WESTFALEN	176
ST. CECILIA	104	THE TOM AVIS	148	WIGHT LIGHT	104
ST. CLARE	104	THE TOM CASEY	148	WIGHT RYDER I	104
ST. FAITH	104	THJELVAR	169	WIGHT RYDER II	104
STAR	200	THORSVOE	84	WIGHT SKY	104
STAR CLIPPER	152	THREE COUSINS	122	WIGHT SUN	104
STAR OF DOOLIN	150	THULELAND	137	WILHELMINE	127
STAVANGERFJORD	179	TIGER	174	WILLEM BARENTSZ	174
STENA ADVENTURER	96	TIIU	189	WILLEM DE VLAMINGH	174
STENA BALTICA	193	TIMCA	141	WOLIN	206
STENA BRITANNICA	96	TÖLL	189	WYRE ROSE	151
STENA CARISMA	193	TOM SAWYER	205	YASMINE	127
STENA CARRIER	87	TORNADO CLIPPER	152	YOKER SWAN	119
STENA DANICA	193	TRANQUILITY	151		
STENA EUROPE	98	TRANS CARRIER	132		

Other books from Ferry Publications

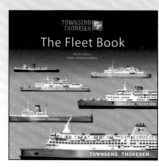